D1188035

MUTINY
On The
SPANISH MAIN

OSPREY
PUBLISHING

DEDICATION
To David Nicoll, whose support in writing this has been invaluable

ANGUS KONSTAM

MUTINY
On The
SPANISH MAIN

HMS HERMIONE AND
THE ROYAL NAVY'S REVENGE

OSPREY PUBLISHING
Bloomsbury Publishing Plc
Kemp House, Chawley Park, Cumnor Hill, Oxford OX2 9PH, UK
1385 Broadway, 5th Floor, New York, NY 10018, USA
E-mail: info@ospreypublishing.com
www.ospreypublishing.com

OSPREY is a trademark of Osprey Publishing Ltd

First published in Great Britain in 2020

A catalogue record for this book is available from the British Library.

ISBN: HB 978 1 4728 3379 2; PB 978 1 4728 3382 2; eBook 978 1 4728 3380 8;
ePDF 978 1 4728 3381 5; XML 978 1 4728 3378 5

20 21 22 23 24   10 9 8 7 6 5 4 3 2 1

Maps by Nick Buxey
Index by Zoe Ross

Typeset by Deanta Global Publishing Services, Chennai, India
Printed and bound in Great Britain by CPI (Group) UK Ltd, Croydon, CR0 4YY

Front cover: A painting by Nicholas Pocock of the cutting out of HMS *Hermione* on 24 October
1799. (© National Maritime Museum, Greenwich, London, Greenwich Hospital Collection)
Author photo on back flap by Davey Buey Photos. All other jacket images from iStock.

Frigate image on page 310 from the Stratford Archive.
Plate section image credits are given in full in the List of Illustrations (pages 6–7).

Osprey Publishing supports the Woodland Trust, the UK's leading woodland conservation charity.

To find out more about our authors and books visit www.ospreypublishing.com. Here you will
find extracts, author interviews, details of forthcoming events and the option to sign up for our
newsletter.

Contents

List of Illustrations

ILLUSTRATION CREDITS

1 Stratford Archive
2 Stratford Archive
3 Stratford Archive
4 Stratford Archive
5 Fine Art Images/Heritage Images/Hulton Archive/Getty Images
6 Map reproduction courtesy of the Norman B. Leventhal Map & Education Center at the Boston Public Library. Retrieved from https://ark.digitalcommonwealth.org/ark:/50959/x633fb00c
7 Stratford Archive
8 Historical Picture Archive/Corbis Historical/Getty Images
9 Hulton Archive/Stringer/Getty Images
10 © National Maritime Museum, Greenwich, London
11 Guildhall Library & Art Gallery/Heritage Images/Hulton Archive/Getty Images
12 Print Collector/Hulton Archive/Getty Images
13 Library of Congress, Geography and Map Division
14 Stratford Archive
15 Universal History Archive/Universal Images Group/Getty Images
16 Stratford Archive
17 Stratford Archive
18 Stratford Archive
19 Print Collector/Hulton Archive/Getty Images
20 Stratford Archive
21 The Art Institute of Chicago, Gift of Thomas F. Furness in memory of William McCallin McKee
22 The Metropolitan Museum of Art, The Elisha Whittelsey Collection, The Elisha Whittelsey Fund, 1959

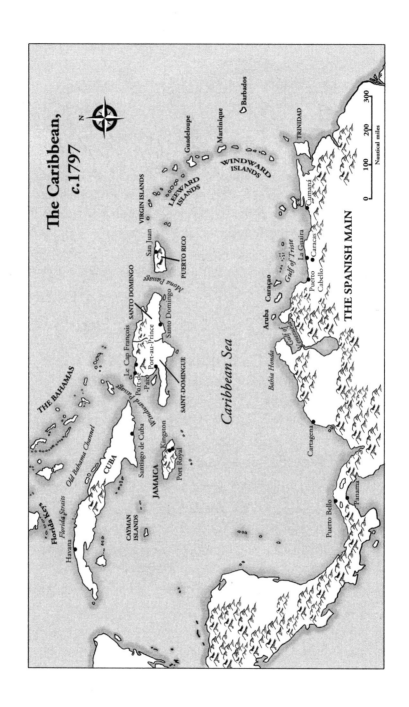

The Caribbean, *c.*1797

N

THE BAHAMAS

Florida Keys
Florida Straits

Old Bahama Channel

Havana

CUBA

Santiago de Cuba

CAYMAN ISLANDS

Windward Passage

Kingston
JAMAICA
Port Royal

Le Cap François
Port-de-Paix
SANTO DOMINGO
Port-au-Prince
SAINT-DOMINGUE
Santo Domingo

VIRGIN ISLANDS

San Juan

PUERTO RICO

Mona Passage

LEEWARD ISLANDS

Guadeloupe

Martinique

WINDWARD ISLANDS

Barbados

Caribbean Sea

Bahía Honda

Gulf of Venezuela

Aruba
Curaçao
Gulf of Triste

Cumaná
TRINIDAD

Puerto Cabello
La Guaira
Caracas

THE SPANISH MAIN

Cartagena

Puerto Bello

Panama

0   100   200   300

Nautical miles

8

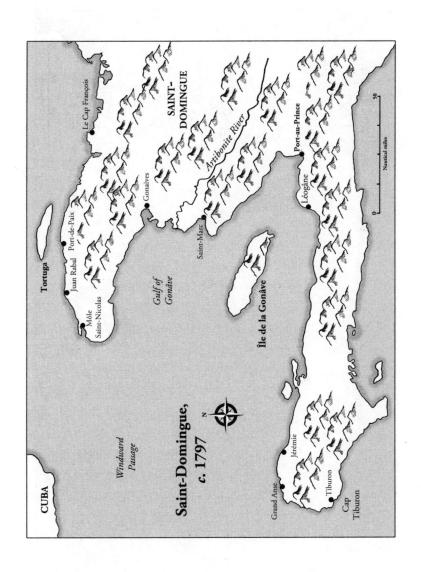

CUBA

Windward
Passage

Tortuga

Le Cap François

SAINT-
DOMINGUE

Port-de-Paix

Juan Rabal

Môle
Saint-Nicolas

Gonaïves

Artibonite River

Saint-Marc

*Gulf of
Gonâve*

Île de la Gonâve

Port-au-Prince

Léogâne

Saint-Domingue,
c. 1797

N

Grand Anse

Jérémie

Tiburon

Cap
Tiburon

0 · · · · 50

Nautical miles

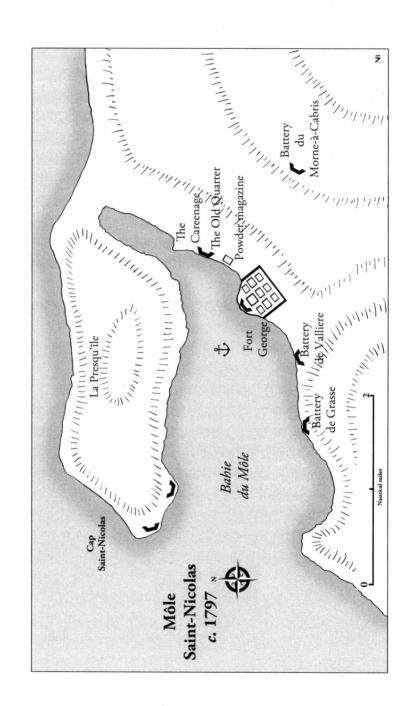

Môle
Saint-Nicolas
c. 1797

Cap
Saint-Nicolas

La Presqu'île

Babie
du Môle

The
Carenage
The Old Quarter
Powder magazine

Battery
du
Morne-à-Cabris

Fort
George

Battery
de Valliere

Battery
de Grasse

Nautical miles

0

2

N

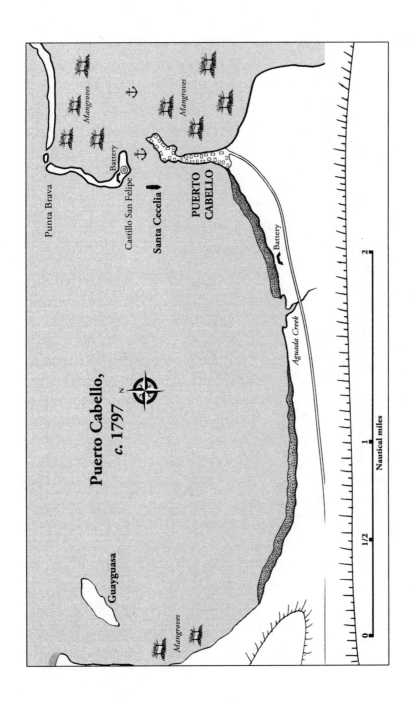

Puerto Cabello, *c.* 1797

Guayguasa

Punta Brava

Mangroves

Battery

Castillo San Felipe

Santa Cecelia

Mangroves

Mangroves

**PUERTO
CABELLO**

Mangroves

Battery

Agudua Creek

Mangroves

N

0   1/2   1   2
Nautical miles

Preface

This book was 30 years in the making. I first heard about the story it tells in the late 1980s, during a visit to the National Maritime Museum in Greenwich, on the edge of London. Most of the museum's world-class collection is displayed in the main building, a grand 18th-century structure which once housed a naval school, and was linked to the even more elegant Queen's House by a graceful colonnade. This time, though, I bypassed the museum, and entered a much less stylish Victorian building around the corner. That was where they kept the objects for forthcoming exhibits, or ones needing a bit of restoration. I worked for the Royal Armouries at the time, and I was there to discuss the loan of a few weapons for a special pirate exhibit. However, as I walked through the building I was stopped by the sight of a painting, placed there to have its frame restored.

It wasn't particularly big – the canvas was only about two feet across – but what struck me was the scene itself. It showed a sailing frigate of what looked like the Napoleonic era, her decks aglow with fire as armed men fought their way on board. Others in ship's boats were shown clambering over her bows, or rowing hard to join the fight. It was a stirring scene, and I asked a conservator what the painting was. I learned it was by Nicholas Pocock, the celebrated maritime artist whose immense, stirring paintings of Nelson's victories formed the centrepiece of the museum's displays. I was told that this much smaller painting was entitled *The cutting out of HMS Hermione, 1799*. At the time that didn't make much sense. This was a British frigate, and its 'cutting out' or capture by boarding wasn't something I expected an artist like Pocock to celebrate in such style.

Later, after I'd done my museum duty, I went round the corner to the Plume of Feathers, a lovely pub which was a favourite haunt for the museum's curators. I was there to meet two of them, David Lyon and Teddy Archibald, both friends of mine, but also experts in their respective fields of naval history and maritime art. I mentioned the painting, and asked them about the *Hermione*. They both looked pityingly at me, as if to say that this rookie should be better informed. Then, over several beers and gins, they took turns to tell me the story. It turned out this was a celebratory painting after all, featuring the recapture of a British frigate in a daring night-time boarding action. That, though, was only part of it. The tale also involved the bloodiest mutiny in Royal Naval history, treachery, intrigue, revenge, and a captain who made Bligh of the *Bounty* seem like a pussy cat. I was enthralled.

I never forgot that conversation. So, over the following years, particularly when my travels took me to Greenwich, I went to their excellent library and archives, and delved deeper into the whole affair. Before I left the pub that first day, David told me to pick up a copy of *The Black Ship* by Dudley Pope, which told the story in a style typical of that master of naval fiction. However, this was also a well-researched piece of historical enquiry. I picked up a copy from Setishia at the

Maritime Book Shop in Greenwich, and this became the starting point of my research. I later followed Pope's research trail to The National Archives in Kew, and to the Spanish Historical Archives in Madrid. Later, while working in the USA, I began unearthing further strands to the tale, which revealed a new diplomatic element to the story.

My researches eventually took me around the Caribbean, and then on to more archives as far afield as Kingston, Seville and Washington. But, during this time, I was working on other projects and the story of the *Hermione* was always 'on the back burner'. After all, I felt that Dudley Pope had told the tale so well back in 1963 that it probably didn't need retelling. However, I eventually realised that the fresh information I had found had changed the tale. It wasn't just about a bloodthirsty mutiny, a martinet of a captain, and the dashing cutting out expedition. There was now more to it – a darker thread involving international politics, and the unbending determination of the British Admiralty to bring every last mutineer to justice.

The final motivation was a re-reading of Patrick O'Brian's novels. It was David Lyon who first encouraged me to give them a go – at the time he was advising the great novelist on the nautical accuracy of his storytelling. I learned to love these Aubrey-Maturin novels, and every few years I re-read them all. In one, Captain Aubrey was entertaining his officers and guests to dinner, and one of the officers mentioned he had taken part in the cutting out of the *Hermione*. Aubrey invited him to recount the story, and then quizzed the officer afterwards. At the time, Aubrey was commanding HMS *Surprise*, the very frigate which, in real life and more than a dozen years before, had supplied the sailors and marines who recaptured the *Hermione*. I remembered that David was particularly pleased by this link between the real *Surprise* and O'Brian's one – perhaps the best-known warship in historical fiction.

So, partly as a tribute to two peerless naval curators who are no longer with us, and to the two departed authors of maritime fiction, both of whom could also turn their hand to history, I offer you this retelling of an old tale of the sea. It was last told more than half a century ago, and the new threads to the tale that have been uncovered since then make it worth recounting afresh. Above all, since I first saw that painting by Nicholas Pocock, I have been captivated by this tale, which I regard as one of the great classical sea stories – albeit one that has never been widely known. The researching and writing of this book have been an utter pleasure – almost an indulgence – as a historian is rarely given such a rich and largely untapped seam on which to work.

Angus Konstam
Herston, Orkney, 2020

I

The *Hermione*

This is the story of a sailing ship. This elegant and graceful structure of wood, rope and metal remains the central character in this tale. She was built by the hand of man, but unquestionably, in the eyes of the sailor, she took on a female form. She combined good looks with surprising power, and her pleasing lines made her as fast as she was shapely. Above all, though, she was a warship, built to fight her nation's enemies. For the 160 men and boys who formed her crew she was also home, a floating community. These sailors breathed life into her, and turned this sailing ship into what she was meant to be – a fast and powerful warship, and a credit to the nation who built her. Although she was but one of many such ships, our central character, the *Hermione*, was vividly remembered long after her passing. Unfortunately, it wasn't for the reason her owners had hoped.

———

What then, was this *Hermione*, that made her so important? The official answer sounds somewhat mundane. She was a

Hermione-class frigate of 32 guns, the namesake of her class. She carried 12-pounder guns, and at the time she was built she was an extremely useful addition to the fleet. This said, by the time this story takes place she was already over a decade old, and larger and better-armed frigates had now entered service. So, while still a useful warship, like an ageing star of the stage she was gradually being overshadowed by younger and more showy rivals. But above all, she was a frigate in His Majesty's Service – the majesty being King George III. So, HMS *Hermione* formed part of the Royal Navy. In March 1793, when she first sailed off to war, the Royal Navy was badly in need of her, and for just over four years, she would serve the navy well. Then, everything went badly wrong.

'Frigates! Were I to die at this moment, want of frigates would be found engraved upon my heart.' In 1798 Horatio Nelson, Britain's most famous admiral, wrote that in frustration, while chasing the French eastwards up the Mediterranean. In the 'Age of Nelson' full-scale naval battles were rare, and so the fleet's great ships-of-the-line didn't see much action. Instead they blockaded enemy ports, or were kept in readiness to intercept an enemy fleet at sea, and it was the frigate that was the real workhorse of the fleet. These were useful ships, used to scout ahead of a battle fleet, probe enemy harbours, protect convoys, harry enemy shipping, cruise off the enemy coast and hunt down enemy privateers. While they weren't large or well armed enough to take part in a fully fledged sea battle, they could do just about anything else.

Nelson wasn't the only admiral to complain he never had enough frigates. To a fleet commander, their most important role was reconnaissance. They were perfectly suited to finding an enemy fleet on the high seas. It was little wonder frigates were sometimes called 'the eyes of the fleet'. Without them, it was like having to fight a naval campaign while wearing a blindfold. Then, once the enemy were found, these same frigates could effectively shadow the enemy as admirals like Nelson tried to bring their fleet to battle. The *Hermione*, our main character, was just such a vessel. So, in time of war, frigates were in great demand – hence Nelson's exasperated cry. In 1793, when *Hermione* left Britain for the Caribbean, the fleet was badly overstretched; therefore, a single frigate could make all the difference in this new and rapidly escalating war with France.

The frigate first made its appearance on the naval stage in the mid-17th century. By 1780, however, the year the keel of *Hermione* was laid, *Falconer's Marine Dictionary* described a naval frigate as: 'A light nimble ship, built for the purposes of sailing swiftly.' It added that 'these vessels mounted from twenty to thirty-eight guns, and are esteemed excellent cruisers'. In fact, by the time the dictionary went to press, this definition, first penned in the 1760s, was already a little out of date. The smaller frigates were being replaced by larger ones, and by the 1790s they had become something of a rarity. In this definition, though, the term 'cruiser' was all-important. In this period that meant a fast and well-armed warship or privateer, which would cruise the sea lanes, protecting friendly commerce and hunting enemy warships. This was the important role *Hermione* had been built for.

The definition described a frigate as a 'ship'. Today, just about every surface vessel bigger than a fishing boat is described as a ship, but to the sailor of Nelson's day it had a much tighter definition. To him, a 'ship' was a seagoing vessel with three or more masts, with square-rigged sails. This meant she carried square sails, fitted to yards which were set across the masts, roughly at right angles to the axis of the ship. The opposite of this was a fore-and-aft-rigged vessel, whose sails were mounted on the same axis to the vessel. In other words, a ship was something that fits our modern idea of a 'tall ship' or a 'square-rigger' – the kind of vessel often used today as a sail training ship. Certainly, most frigates carried a few fore-and-aft-rigged sails like the driver mounted behind her mizzen mast, or the jib sails clipped to the bowsprit. But these didn't alter her status as a 'square-rigger'.

To a navy man, the other defining characteristic of a frigate was that she carried her main armament on a single gun deck. Larger ships carried their guns on more than one gun deck, but on a frigate the only guns not carried on her gun deck were a handful of lighter pieces, mounted on her forecastle or quarterdeck. Just as importantly, this gun deck wasn't really the upper deck. In most frigates of the period, it was covered over, at the bow by the forecastle and at the stern by the quarterdeck, but also, in the ship's waist which lay between them, it was partially covered by a wooden framework designed to support the ship's boats.

Wooden gangways spanned the two sides of this framework, allowing sailors to move along the upper deck from one end of the ship to the other. On larger ships, the crew slept in the gun decks. In a frigate, though, they were housed on the lower deck, one deck level below it.

In the navy, all warships carrying 20 guns or more were grouped into 'Rates'. So, a frigate like the *Hermione* was classed as a Fifth Rate. As the rating depended on the number of guns she carried this sounded some way down the scale.

However, a Fifth Rate was every bit as useful to the navy as a larger and better-armed ship-of-the-line. These were the First Rates, carrying 100 guns or more, Second Rates of 90 to 98 guns, and Third Rates – the most common type of ship-of-the-line, mounting between 64 and 80 guns. The first two rates were three-deckers – they carried their guns in three decks – while the Third Rates had two gun decks. These were the big and imposing ships which formed the heart of the battle fleet, which was usually commanded from a First Rate. At the battle of Trafalgar fought in 1805, Vice-Admiral Nelson's flagship was the First Rate *Victory*, of 100 guns.

Officially, the Fourth Rate was also considered a two-decked ship-of-the-line. In practice, though, these 50- to 60-gun ships were really considered too small to form part of a line of battle. But they did, from time to time, although their main function was to serve as convoy escorts or often as flagships on remote stations. The Fifth Rates like *Hermione* were actually divided into two groups. The first included a few old 44-gun two-deckers, but the majority of Fifth Rates fell within the second group – the frigates. These mounted anything from 30 to 44 guns, carried in a single gun deck. Smaller frigates – those with 20 to 30 guns on one deck – were classed as Sixth Rates. All 'Rated' ships were commanded by a post captain. Smaller vessels were classed as 'Unrated', and were commanded by lesser mortals such as masters and commanders – mere lieutenants, deemed 'captain' by their role rather than by their rank.

At the start of the French Revolutionary War in 1793, the Royal Navy had 47 ships-of-the-line in active service, with another 81 'in ordinary' – what today we would call 'in mothballs' or in refit. At the time, most of the active battle fleet was in home waters, but as the war developed an increasing number would be sent to the Mediterranean. Of the fleet's 55 frigates in active service, almost half were 32-gun Fifth Rates, like the *Hermione*. When the war began, she was one of a similar number being held in reserve, and which would join the fleet as soon as they could be manned and prepared for sea. Again, while most of them were in service in home waters, others were on the Newfoundland, Jamaica or Leeward Island stations, while three more were in the East Indies. It says a lot about the importance of frigates that, even with so many available, admirals were still wanting more.

Not only were frigates some of the most active warships on the navy's list, they were also the most glamorous. Usually, frigate captains were given a lot of latitude to do what they wanted during a cruise, as long as they were successful. When they captured enemy merchant ships these became prizes, and that meant prize money. Everyone benefited from prize money, apart from the foreign owners. Everyone on board got a share, divided up in proportion, with the captain getting the lion's share. If he was sailing under the orders of an admiral then he too would get a cut. It was a system designed to encourage aggression and reward success. While the crews of ships-of-the-line rarely had the chance to earn any bonus like this, a seaman on board a lucky frigate could earn a year's pay in an afternoon. So, given the choice, most naval seamen would choose to serve on board a frigate.

These sleek warships were fast and agile, and often their young captains drove them to their limits. If sailed well, they could outpace just about every other type of warship afloat. The most dashing and successful frigate captains were often feted as celebrities and so, for a young captain in command of a frigate, an independent cruise in enemy waters gave him the chance to win fame, fortune and even promotion.

Throughout the French Revolutionary and Napoleonic Wars, between 1793 and 1815, British newspapers like the *London Gazette* published official reports of successful frigate actions, written by their captains, then forwarded to the paper by the Admiralty. The public had a voracious appetite for successes. Indeed, a few frigate captains – men like Philip Broke of the *Shannon*, Lord Thomas Cochrane of the *Pallas* or Edward Hamilton of the *Surprise* – became national heroes.

For other frigate captains, though, their failures could be just as public. Throughout this period, frigates ran aground, or were damaged through accidents of seamanship or navigation. A few – a very surprising few – were lost in action with the enemy. During the ten years of the French Revolutionary Wars, the Royal Navy only lost four Fifth Rate frigates to the enemy – the *Ambuscade*, the *Castor* and the *Thames*, as well as the *Success*, a frigate which plays a part in this story. The loss of a frigate, whether through wrecking or enemy action, meant a court martial – being tried in front of a naval disciplinary board. If found wanting, an unfortunate frigate captain could find himself dismissed from the service, and exposed to a very public humiliation.

For frigate captains, then, the rewards were high, and the cost of failure was equally spectacular. None, though, paid a higher price for their failure than Captain Hugh Pigot of the *Hermione*.

———

Like many new warships, the *Hermione* was designed and built with an eye on a war that had just been, rather than one that might lie ahead. When the American War of Independence erupted in 1775, the Royal Navy found itself woefully short of modern frigates. This seemed surprising, when there were 85 in the fleet, compared to 55 in the French and 50 in the Spanish navies. However, almost two-thirds of these British frigates were Sixth Rates, which even then were considered too small to be successfully used as cruisers. In contrast, over half of the French and Spanish totals included modern frigates, armed with 32 or 34 guns. After emerging victorious from the Seven Years' War just over a decade before, the British Admiralty had rested on their laurels, and so allowed their foreign rivals to out-build them. It was clear that something had to be done, and done quickly.

The Admiralty's first priority was to reinforce its battle fleet. This was particularly important due to the rapid escalation of the war. In 1778 France entered the war as America's ally, and the following year the Spanish followed suit. In 1780 the Dutch also joined the allies. Consequently, if Britain's naval resources had been stretched in 1775, the situation had soon become much worse. So, Britain's dockyards were kept busy, as the Admiralty strengthened its wartime fleet. This proved very successful. By the time the American war ended in 1783 the British had built 43 new ships-of-the-line. These would arrive too late to help stem the tide in the Americas, but these new ships would form the backbone of the fleet when Britain and France went to war again in 1793. This, though, was only part of the solution. The navy also needed frigates – lots of them. Ideally, they also had to be designed and built as speedily as possible.

During this period, British naval architects weren't leading the pack. Home-grown designs tended to be inferior to the warships built in France and Spain. Fortunately, however, during the Seven Years' War several enemy warships were captured. Naval architects then studied the way they were designed and built. So, using them as a blueprint, they were able to improve the standard of their own designs, simply by copying the best features of their foreign rivals. But in the late 1770s there was no real time for fancy designs. With a few modifications, then, the frigate designs first produced more than a decade before would simply have to do. This programme began in earnest in 1779, with the launch of four 32-gun frigates. Eight more followed them into the water the following year, together with two slightly larger frigates. Then, in early 1780, the Admiralty commissioned the building of the *Hermione*.

She was designed by Surveyor of the Navy Edward Hunt. He first started in the royal dockyards during the Seven Years' War, when he was hired as a master boatbuilder for Portsmouth Dockyard after learning his trade in private yards. By 1762 he had become an assistant master shipwright, working in Sheerness and Woolwich. Five years later he was promoted to master shipwright – one of the navy's small circle of expert shipbuilders. In 1772 he returned to Portsmouth, where he built the first of the navy's wartime ships-of-the-line, and six years later he became the navy's surveyor. That meant he was responsible for coming up with the designs for all new warships. Having worked his way up through the shipbuilding ranks, Hunt was a man on whom the Admiralty could rely. He wasn't likely to come up with anything innovative, but he knew how to design and build a warship.

The *Hermione* was actually the first of a class of six frigates. These were based on a previous class Hunt had designed, the Active class, which in turn were modified versions of the Amazon class designed by his colleague Sir John Williams. He had been Hunt's predecessor as surveyor, and the Admiralty had asked him to stay on and share the duties with Hunt for the duration of the American war. This continuity was probably a good thing in terms of easing the workload, but it didn't encourage innovation. Essentially, the British design for the 32-gun frigate had first been developed in 1757, and at the time, largely thanks to their French influence, these proved to be good ships, and served the navy well. For the next two decades, though, this basic design barely changed. So now British frigates were being outclassed by larger and more modern French and Spanish ones.

The British way was to tweak existing designs rather than rethink them. Consequently, the Amazon-class frigates were simply an improvement of what had come before them, and in turn Hunt's first batch of Active-class frigates were virtually identical to them. The only change he made was to alter the shape of them amidships, in an attempt to make their hulls sleeker and faster. It was an experiment that didn't really work, and so, with the Hermione class, Hunt lengthened their hulls slightly, and returned to a more rounded midsection. After the first two ships in the class, *Druid* and *Hermione*, were laid down, the design was modified again, and the remaining four had slightly higher bulwarks. The real problem, though, wasn't the design itself – the ships were fine enough for what they were. It was that the British hadn't really modified their basic plans in more than 20 years.

With all this wartime shipbuilding going on, Britain's largest shipyards and the royal dockyards were already working at full capacity. So the Admiralty decided to farm out the building of its new wartime frigates to smaller shipyards. As a result, of the six ships of the Hermione class, two were built in Bristol, two in Liverpool, and one each at Bursledon in Hampshire and Rotherhithe on the Thames. The order for *Hermione* was placed in March 1780, and the contract was given to Sydenham Teast, one of Bristol's leading shipbuilders. Although a Quaker, he had made his money building ships for the slave trade. Now he and his shipwrights would turn their hand to building a frigate. Her keel was laid in Teast's shipyard in June. The shipyard is no longer there, but it once stood on the riverfront area of the city now known as Merchants Quay.

On 9 September 1782, the frigate was launched into the waters of the River Avon, then brought alongside the wharf for her fitting out. A month before, Captain Thomas Lloyd had arrived in Bristol to supervise the launch and completion of the navy's new frigate. He would also become her first captain. This initial fitting out was finally completed in January 1783. By then, though, the American war was all but over, and a preliminary peace treaty had already been agreed in Paris. As a result, the navy wasn't really in any hurry to send their new frigate to sea. So, assisted by a skeleton crew, Captain Lloyd brought the frigate round to Sheerness, where she spent the spring being fully fitted out with all her guns and naval stores. In April, Lloyd was succeeded by Captain John Stone, who was ordered to prepare the new frigate for active service.

Although an experienced officer, until then Stone's only commands had been a small fireship, and then the armed storeship *Dromedary*, but now he had command of a brand-new 700-ton frigate. On 17 October 1783, he took her to sea, where he joined the Fifth Rate two-decker *Assistance*, of 50 guns. She flew the broad pennant of Commodore Sir Charles Douglas, a man whose previous job had been the flag captain of Admiral Hugh Pigot. The two warships then headed round the Kentish coast and through the English Channel, before heading west across the Atlantic. Douglas was on his way to take command of the North American station, a much-diminished posting now that the American war was almost over. The weather, however, was atrocious, and a succession of westerly gales kept them from their destination, the port of Halifax. Instead they headed for New York.

In late 1783 the British had already evacuated the city, but still held on to a couple of nearby outposts. One of these was Sandy Hook, a fortified spit in New Jersey, guarding the approaches to New York harbour. It was a useful anchorage for the British as they prepared for their final evacuation of their American colonies. It was also the site of a tragedy, when the flagship's first lieutenant and a party of 14 men, including ten midshipmen, froze to death when they were caught in a blizzard while out hunting for deserters. This incident helped encourage Commodore Douglas to move south for the rest of the winter, and so his two ships headed for the warmer waters of the Caribbean. He only reached Halifax the following spring, and the *Hermione* remained there, patrolling American waters, until she was finally recalled home in August 1785.

On reaching the Thames, the *Hermione* was paid off in Chatham, and Captain Stone retired on half pay. He died the following year, in his house in Covent Garden. Meanwhile the *Hermione* was all but forgotten – part of the 'mothballed' fleet moored on the River Medway. She remained in limbo for another five years, until the Admiralty decided they might need her again. In October 1790 she was towed the 12 miles up the Thames to Northfleet, where she began a major 'half-life' refit in Samuel Todd's shipyard. The shipyard has gone, but today a pub called 'The Shipwright's Arms' stands near the site. This extensive refit would last the best part of two years. It involved a complete overhaul and the replacement of any rotting timbers. By the time the *Hermione* re-emerged, she would be almost as good as new, and fully ready to play her part in a new war.

Essentially, a sailing frigate was a large piece of machinery – a complex assemblage of hull, masts, rigging, guns and sails. What really made her, though – what turned her into a real warship – was her crew. The crew of the *Hermione* hauled on her sails and ropes, manned her guns and took her wherever the navy ordered her to go. She was a warship, but she was also a home to these men and boys, many of whom would remain on board for several years, often without the chance to set foot ashore. The *Hermione* was a floating community, and these sailors worked, ate, drank and slept on board. Of course, this wasn't a community of equals. In Nelson's day the navy was a rigidly hierarchical organisation, and the way the frigate was manned was a perfect reflection of this. From her captain down to the youngest ship's boy, everyone in the *Hermione* had his place.

At the apex of this hierarchical pyramid was the captain. On a sailing frigate privacy was almost impossible, but the captain lived in splendid isolation. He had his own suite of cabins – a large great cabin, dominated by windows which spanned the whole width of the ship; a night cabin where he slept; and a third cabin which was often used as a pantry. The captain had his own cook, steward and clerk, as well as his coxswain, who commanded his official boat, or 'captain's barge'. He dined alone, attended by his steward and sometimes a servant, unless he decided to invite one or more of his officers to eat with him. Similarly, when he stepped onto the frigate's quarterdeck, the other officers and men would stay clear of the windward side of the deck, as this was his preserve too.

His quarters were at the after end of the gun deck, where the frigate's 12-pounders were housed, and four of these guns intruded into his suite of cabins. When the frigate went into action the wooden partitions which separated his domain from the rest of the ship were taken down, and his furniture stored in the hold. Effectively, this created one long, open gun deck. After all, the *Hermione* was a warship, and even the captain's needs played second fiddle to her role. In action, the captain commanded his ship from the quarterdeck. On deck, nobody would address him without permission, and there would be absolutely no questioning of his orders. His authority was backed up by the navy's Articles of War, its regulations governing discipline and punishment. In the *Hermione*, the captain's word was law, and just how he coped with this absolute power could make all the difference between a happy ship and a dangerously discontented one.

Next in the hierarchy were the officers. The *Hermione* carried three naval lieutenants, with the first lieutenant being the most senior, and the captain's deputy. The frigate also usually carried a lieutenant of marines, who commanded his own Royal Marine detachment of up to 33 men. Officially, they were there to act as sharpshooters in a naval battle, or to spearhead landing parties ashore. Mostly, though, they were there to enforce the captain's will, and to protect the officers. Their sleeping arrangements, situated between the officers and the men, reflected this key role. In addition, the frigate carried a surgeon, a purser and a master, all of whom were officially rated as warrant officers. The first two posts are self-explanatory, but the master was usually a highly experienced seaman, who was in charge of navigation.

These officers berthed in the gunroom – only larger ships had wardrooms – where each had their own cabin. This was another temporary structure, a six-foot cube which opened out on to the gunroom proper, where they ate their meals. It lay at the after end of the lower deck, just below the captain's quarters. Also housed there, usually forward of the others, were the midshipmen – the 'young gentlemen', who effectively were officers in training. Officially a 32-gun frigate could carry six of them on board, but in 1797 the *Hermione* only had three. The other principal warrant officers were the boatswain, the gunner and the carpenter. They berthed forward of the others, as did the captain's clerk. The boatswain was in charge of the sails and rigging of the ship, and so was a key figure on board the frigate.

All of these warrant officers had one or two assistants, or 'mates'. They were deemed petty officers, and so they assisted the warrant officers, although the boatswain's mates had the additional job of enforcing discipline on board. They were the ones who wielded the cat-o'-nine-tails during a flogging, or who 'started' – beat – men with a rope's end when they were slow to do their duty. The *Hermione* also carried a master-at-arms, whose sole job was to maintain discipline on board, assisted by a pair of corporals. The cook was also a petty officer, a man who was usually an experienced seaman, but one whose age or infirmity stopped him from going aloft. Additionally, the frigate carried an armourer and a quartermaster and his mates who manned the wheel, and looked after stowage on board.

As in most warships, the warrant officers and petty officers were crucial to the smooth running of the frigate. These were men who were seen as thorough professionals, and where their job called for it, they were highly experienced seamen. In a well-run ship, they would be able to anticipate the orders of the captain or the officer-of-the-watch, and would make sure the evolution was carried out smoothly, whether it was the reefing of sails, coming to anchor or lowering boats off the side. As befitted their position, these men were berthed midway between the officers and the rest of the ship's company. What is particularly noticeable in the *Hermione* is that, when discipline began to fall apart, it was the petty officers who seemed to bear the greatest grudge against their superiors.

The rest of the ship's company berthed on the lower deck, forward of the mainmast. While a few of these men had volunteered for a naval life, most of them had been conscripted by the press gang, taken from merchant ships or fishing boats, or in some cases had elected to join the navy rather than serve their time in prison. While most were born in Britain or Ireland, the muster books of the *Hermione* show how many others had been pressed into service. The frigate carried several Americans on board, as well as seamen from Denmark, France, Hanover, the Italian states, Norway, Portugal, Prussia, Spain and Sweden. Most of the men pressed into service were already trained seamen, but a few were landsmen, with no previous seagoing experience. In 1797, though, at least in the *Hermione*, the frigate had been in commission so long that most of the crew could 'hand, reef and steer'.

After a year at sea, a man was rated as an ordinary seaman. Those who showed a little more ability than their shipmates were trained and tested, until they were deemed worthy of becoming able seamen. These were all prime seamen, men who could be relied upon to carry out even the most complex tasks of seamanship with a minimum of supervision. These, too, were the kinds of men a naval boarding party preferred to press from a merchant ship, if they could. A few hopeless landsmen were given less-demanding roles, such as serving as gunroom servants or stewards, captain of the head – cleaning the area around the toilets, or heads, forward of the forecastle – or looking after any livestock carried on board. There were a few ship's boys too, who effectively were learning their trade as sailors, and who often performed the role of officers' servants.

Life was hard before the mast. Still, so too was life for most working people in late 18th-century Britain. While the men slept in hammocks, crowded together in the often-fetid atmosphere of the lower deck, at least they were well-enough fed with three meals a day, and received their rum ration. The food might have been monotonous but at least it was reasonably healthy, as long as the ship hadn't run out of fresh supplies. The food was issued to each mess and would then be cooked under the supervision of the ship's cook before being taken away and eaten in the lower deck, the men grouped together with their messmates – usually the crew of the gun they served. Rum watered down into grog was issued twice a day, at noon and again in the early evening. The captain and officers, though, had their own supplies, cooks to prepare their meals, and stewards to serve it out.

The ship's company were divided into two divisions – larboard (port) and starboard, which worked on alternate shifts. Each was separated into different 'parts of ship', usually divided by the three masts – fore, main and mizzen. The youngest, smartest and most agile seamen were 'topmen' – the men who went aloft to man the upper yards, while the 'forecastlemen' were usually just as experienced, but a little older and less agile. They worked the anchor. The 'waisters', working amidships, tended the ropes and braces of the mainmast, while the 'afterguard' did the same for the mizzenmast. Officially, the naval day began at noon, and was divided into watches, each of four hours. The exception were the dog watches, between 4pm and 8pm, which were split into two. The two divisions stood alternate watches, and so by dividing the day into seven segments rather than six, this meant there was some rotation in the watches each division stood.

Hands were roused at 4am, the start of the morning watch, and lights out was usually at 8pm, at the start of the first watch. The time was called by the ringing of the ship's bell every half hour. So in most cases eight bells marked the end of a watch. During the hours of daylight, the off-duty watch still had tasks to perform – swabbing the decks, cleaning the ship or servicing the guns. The other key time of the naval day was 11am – six bells in the forenoon watch. That was when the hands were usually called so they could be inspected, or to witness punishment. On Sundays, it might be when a church service was held. On the *Hermione*, however, this time was often the moment when one of the men would be flogged. Under two successive captains, this became a depressingly regular ritual. Eventually, it would act as the catalyst for the most bloody mutiny the Royal Navy has ever experienced.

2

Crisis in the Caribbean

The bloody mutiny on board the *Hermione* was the climax to dramatic events which spanned four years. The first link in this chain was the killing of a king. At 10am on 25 January 1793, a green carriage entered the Place de la Révolution, escorted by a troop of cavalry. It pulled up in front of a large wooden scaffold erected in the middle of the huge square. The carriage door was opened by a soldier, and King Louis XVI clambered down, accompanied by his Irish priest and confessor. Dressed in shirt and breeches, the French king stood for a few moments, as if to compose himself. His eyes would have swept over the large crowd, kept at bay by a double rank of militiamen from the National Guard. In front of them stood a corps of drummers. Then he mounted the steps and stood in front of 'Madame Guillotine'. A large wicker casket lay beside it, where two men waited to bundle the king's decapitated body into it. The king glared at the drummers, forcing them to stop their beating, and as silence fell on the great crowded square, he began to speak.

Louis declared himself innocent of any crime, and then he magnanimously pardoned his executioners. Finally, he prayed that the shedding of his royal blood would prevent further bloodshed among the French people. Then, as the drums began rolling, the executioner's father, Charles Sanson, tied the king's hands together with a handkerchief. Next, his son Henri's two assistants trimmed the king's hair, and cut away the collar of his shirt. Without ceremony the king was strapped down to a board, and the razor-sharp blade of the guillotine was hoisted. Then, as the drummers reached a frenzied crescendo, the blade fell. Henri picked up the king's severed head by the hair, and showed it to the madly cheering crowd. Apparently, it wasn't a clean cut – the blade passed through the back of the king's skull and through his jaw. Still, the deed was done, and France, already a Republic, had literally severed its last ties with the *Ancien Régime*.

This very public regicide caused outrage in the courts of Europe. Revolutionary France was already at war with the Austrian Empire and the kingdoms of Prussia and Sardinia. Britain had been preparing for war since the arrest of King Louis the previous autumn, and in the aftermath of the execution Prime Minister William Pitt the Younger expelled Monsieur Chauvelin, the French ambassador. On 1 February 1793 the French National Convention responded by declaring war on Britain. For good measure they did the same to Spain and the Dutch Republic. In fact the first shots had already been fired – on 2 January the coastal batteries guarding Brest had opened fire on a British brig, HMS *Childers*. So, by the time King Louis's severed head was being shown to the crowd, the Admiralty in

Whitehall was already a hive of activity, as the Royal Navy prepared itself for war.

At this time the Royal Navy was in pretty good shape. Normally in peacetime much of the fleet was 'in ordinary'. Ships were moored off the major ports, with their topmasts and running rigging removed, all guns and stores put ashore, and the crew dismissed, apart from a skeleton crew to maintain the vessel. However, there had been a war scare with Holland in 1787, and another, the Nootka Sound Incident, with Spain three years later. So, part of the fleet had been taken 'out of ordinary', and the warships re-rigged, manned and re-commissioned. New ships had been ordered, too, including First Rate ships-of-the-line. Therefore, at the start of 1793 there were 26 ships-of-the-line in commission, with another 86 still 'in ordinary', or laid up for repair. That didn't include the ships-of-the-line deemed too small to stand in a line of battle, or the dozens of frigates and smaller warships which were already fully manned and armed, and at sea.

When the war began, the frigate *Hermione* was lying off Chatham on the River Medway, taking on men and stores, and preparing for active service. She had been there since September, 'fitting out' in the royal dockyard there, after completing a major refit some 10 miles away at Northfleet on the River Thames, just upriver from Gravesend and Tilbury. This refit, or 'grand repair' as it was called at the time, was a major operation, and one that usually took place roughly halfway through a ship's life. She went in to the shipyard owned by Joseph Todd in October 1790, during the Nootka Sound Incident, after spending five years 'in ordinary' at Chatham. In Todd's yard the frigate's masts were removed, and her timbers were inspected, and many were replaced. She was re-sheathed in copper below the waterline, new iron fittings were added, and her decks were re-laid. Then, in September 1792 she was towed round to Chatham for her fitting out.

This process usually took place after a ship was launched, and involved adding her masts and rigging, all her internal compartments, and all the fixtures and fittings she would need as a seagoing vessel. In the case of the *Hermione* this involved hoisting her masts into place, and the re-rigging of the ship. This was a busy period for the royal dockyard, as *Hermione* wasn't the only warship going through the same process. So, to speed things along, the Admiralty used this time to man the ship, so there was enough manpower available to do all the hard work. Manning was often a problem for the Royal Navy, despite Britain having the biggest pool of seamen in Europe. Sensibly, most preferred to sail on merchant ships, where pay and conditions were better. The solution, then, at least in wartime, was to resort to the press gang. The first wave of men, though, were the ship's officers, senior non-commissioned officers, and a handful of volunteers, mostly reliable veteran seamen.

These thoroughgoing professionals helped turn the *Hermione* from a floating hulk into a real ship. Drafts of men began to join them, and in December 1792 Captain John Hills arrived to take command of the frigate and to supervise her re-commissioning. Once the masts and rigging were in place, and after new drafts of seamen arrived, the guns and their fittings were hoisted on board. By now the *Hermione* was looking like a proper warship again. Officially, the ship's fitting out ended in late January 1793, when the dockyard handed over control of the ship to Captain Hills. He warped the frigate out into the River Medway, and for the next six weeks the *Hermione*'s captain and crew busied themselves taking on men and stores. In February, a port embargo prevented all British merchant ships from sailing until the manpower needs of the navy were met. This led to an influx of fresh hands, either as reluctant volunteers, or supplied by the press gang.

In late February Captain Hills was given his orders. After finishing the taking on of water and stores, and with provisions on board for six months, he would put to sea, and set sail for Jamaica. The *Hermione* would be joining the Jamaica Station. So, just before dawn on 10 March, Hills ordered the *Hermione* to raise her anchor, and once it was free of the mud and ooze of the Medway, the frigate slipped down the river, and into the lower reaches of the Thames. By nightfall she was lying off Deal, on the east coast of Kent. The following day, after taking on mail and the Admiralty's dispatches, the *Hermione* entered the English Channel, and set a course towards the Atlantic. A few miles off her larboard beam lay the enemy coast. Accordingly, the frigate made the passage with her hands called to action, in case they encountered a French privateer putting out from Boulogne or Le Havre, or an enemy frigate that might slip through the British squadrons blockading Cherbourg or Brest.

The passage itself was uneventful. After passing Ushant, the *Hermione* headed south. Then, after taking on water in the Azores, she sailed westwards across the Atlantic. The ship's log shows the voyage was fairly speedy for that time of year, and landfall was eventually made in Barbados. In late April *Hermione* dropped anchor off Port Royal, Jamaica, and Captain Hills's bargemen rowed him over to the Fourth Rate *Europa* of 50 guns. She flew the broad pennant of Commodore John Ford, Commander-in-Chief of the Jamaica Station. This was a key appointment, especially in wartime, as the station encompassed much of the Caribbean – a key battleground in any new war with France. Ford himself had only been in the job a few weeks. An experienced post captain who had seen action in the American war, he had been appointed as a wartime stopgap, until a more senior commander could be sent out. In fact, he would stay in the post for two turbulent years.

Commodore Ford welcomed Captain Hills warmly, as he needed every frigate he could get. When news of the declaration of war reached him, Ford had been told that it was unlikely he would be reinforced for several months. The strategic situation was fluid, as the French Revolution had caused turmoil in the country's colonies in the West Indies. French revolutionaries were now locked in a regional civil war with French Royalists, while on several islands slave insurrections had also broken out, inspired by revolutionary promises of liberty and egality. Vice-Admiral Laforey, commanding a small British squadron based at Barbados, had successfully captured Tobago, but a similar assault on Martinique had been repulsed. Now, Ford was getting pleas for help from the French Royalists on Saint-Domingue (now Haiti). These pro-Royalist planters were facing a large-scale slave insurrection, incited by local revolutionaries. So it looked like *Hermione* and her crew would see action soon enough.

The political situation in Saint-Domingue was complex, and it seemed to change by the day. Of all of France's colonies it was Saint-Domingue that suffered the most from the turmoil of the French Revolution. Before 1789, the colony's economy was booming, and her largest port, Le Cap François (now Cap-Haitien), was busier than any other harbour in the Caribbean. This booming trade, however, was built on the miseries of slavery. While the white French plantation owners, the *Grands Blancs*, were at the top of the social pyramid, the freed slaves of mixed race (known then as 'mulattos') and white Creoles born in the colony formed a resentful underclass. Right at the bottom of the pyramid though were the black slaves – some half a million of them, whose labour supported everyone else.

News of the revolution and the declaration of the rights of man reached the colony in September 1789. While this caused widespread unrest, at first this was confined to the 'mulattos' and the Creoles. They pressed for equal rights with the white colonists, and in April 1792 they got it. By then the colony had been reinforced by troops from France, whose revolutionary fervour ignited more tension between the pro-Royalist plantation owners and the largely pro-Republican lower orders. However, this political unrest was nothing compared to what happened next. In August 1791, amid a raging thunderstorm and buoyed up by voodoo rituals, the slaves of Saint-Domingue rose up in bloody revolt. Violence erupted through the colony, as 200 plantations were razed to the ground and most of their resident *Grands Blancs* butchered. It was said that the raging fires from the burning plantations could be seen from Jamaica and the Bahamas.

By then the colony's new governor general, freshly sent out from France, was General François Thomas Galbaud. Although he served France's Republican government, as an absentee plantation owner himself his sympathies lay with the established order. He soon realised, though, that there wasn't much he could do. There was just too much distrust between the pro-Royalist and pro-Republican factions in the colony. In Saint-Domingue the *Grands Blancs* were supported by most of the regular troops, while the National Volunteers sent out from France were Republicans to a man. So too were the local militia, which had rebranded itself as the National Guard. For the most part their ranks were filled by 'mulattos', who distrusted the white ruling elite. Galbaud managed to protect Le Cap François and a few other major towns like Port-au-Prince, but he was hampered by the Republicans, many of whom openly sympathised with the slaves.

This volatile situation erupted into civil war in June 1793, when the Republican National Volunteers and National Guard turned on the Royalists. The pro-Royalist regular troops, backed by sailors, tried to hold their ground, but the game was up when the Republicans called on the slaves to help them. At that point thousands of Royalist refugees fled the colony, accompanied by Galbaud and many of his men. Behind them, Le Cap François, the city once described as the Paris of the Antilles, was burned to ashes. So, Saint-Domingue became a Republican colony. One of the first acts of its new Republican commissioner was to emancipate the slaves. The slave revolt also threw up another heroic figure. Toussaint L'Ouverture was born into slavery, but he was a natural leader, and during the slave revolt he formed his own armed band, which soon grew into a highly motivated slave army. In the process, L'Ouverture became the real power broker in the ravaged colony.

This was the volatile situation which faced Commander Ford that summer. Jamaica was less than a hundred miles from the south-western tip of Saint-Domingue. Unlike the islands of the West Indies, which were closer to Britain's naval base on Barbados, the French colony lay firmly within Ford's area of operations. So when the French Royalists begged for his support, he felt he needed to help stem the tide of both French Republicanism and the slave insurrection. He was promised the support of pro-Royalist factions within the French colony, if he would only intervene on their behalf. His real problem, though, was that he didn't have enough military muscle to tackle the Republicans head-on. Therefore, Ford needed to find a way to intervene in Saint-Domingue without his small force being overwhelmed. With the benefit of hindsight, he'd probably have been better leaving the blood-soaked French colony well alone, and letting its warring factions tear themselves apart.

Actually, Ford's naval force was just powerful enough now that *Hermione* had joined him. His 50-gun flagship *Europa* gave Ford all the firepower he needed, unless a more powerful French squadron arrived in the Antilles. She was also roomy enough to serve as a makeshift troop transport. The *Powerful*, a Third Rate of 74 guns, was still being overhauled in the dockyard, while the *Intrepid* of 64 guns was on its way out from Plymouth. Apart from the *Hermione*, the 32-gun frigates *Iphigenia* and *Penelope* were also at Port Royal, along with the 16-gun sloop *Hound* and the 14-gun sloop *Goelan*, recently captured from the French. He also had two small schooners of six to ten guns apiece, the *Flying Fish* and the *Spitfire*, both captured French privateers, and now turned against their former owners. This small but potent force would have to do the job until reinforcements arrived.

However, Ford was pitifully short of troops. Only one regiment was available, the 13th Foot, plus a detachment from the 49th Foot, some light dragoons and a three-gun battery of field artillery. That came to just 600 men. According to the *Grands Blancs*, there were around 3,500 French Republican troops on Saint-Domingue – a mixture of National Guard, National Volunteers and some regular troops. But these were backed up by Toussaint L'Ouverture's slave army. So not only did he have to capture a port to use as a base, but he also had to hold it against a much larger enemy. Fortunately for Ford, Saint-Domingue was a sprawling colony covering over 8,000 square miles. Its shape, like a back-to-front letter 'C', coupled with its hilly jungle-clad interior and poor roads, would make it difficult for the enemy to concentrate their forces. So, if he could seize a suitable base, and with the promise of reinforcements, he might be able to achieve something on Saint-Domingue.

Ford decided that Môle Saint-Nicolas would be a near-perfect base. It was a small port on the western tip of the long peninsula which made up the north-eastern portion of Saint-Domingue. It lay just 75 miles west of Le Cap François, but the peninsula in between was arid and mountainous, so the only way in or out of the port was by a rutted coastal track. Ford's experienced military adviser, Lieutenant Colonel John Whitelocke assured him that, if they could capture the port, then the western end of the peninsula could be defended until reinforcements arrived. The main problem was that Môle Saint-Nicolas was protected by three powerful and well-fortified coastal batteries. The Royalists weren't sure if these would be manned or not, but the likelihood was that the Republicans hadn't garrisoned them properly. Ford therefore planned to seize the batteries in a surprise attack, and then leave it to Whitelocke to protect his newly won harbour.

In the end the operation went without a hitch. First, on 20 September, the troops landed unopposed at Jérémie on the colony's southern peninsula, and captured the gun battery there. When he met the local Royalist sympathisers, Whitelocke told them that this was merely a testing of the waters, to gauge the French colonists' goodwill. Whether they believed him or not wasn't recorded. Then, leaving behind a small garrison, the troops re-embarked, and Ford's squadron headed off again towards the north. Just before dawn on 22 September Ford dropped anchor off Môle Saint-Nicolas. Landing parties of sailors and marines were quickly sent ashore to seize the batteries. This was done with hardly a shot being fired. The few militiamen on duty there quickly fled into the hills. So, Ford had his base. Next, Whitelocke's troops were ferried ashore to protect it.

Whitelocke set up fortified positions astride the coastal track running around the peninsula. Now, Ford was able to transfer stores from Jamaica, and began turning Môle Saint-Nicolas into a forward base for his squadron. Luckily enough, the port was already well-stocked with French stores, having served as a small naval base before the revolution. Therefore, Ford now had a fine sheltered harbour to operate from, a secure fortified base, and a foothold on Saint-Domingue. Captain Hills and the *Hermione* played their part in all this, covering the landing with the *Hermione*'s guns, and then patrolling in the Windward Passage, to deter any French naval counter-attack.

The situation gradually improved. Regular French troops – men of an Irish infantry regiment in French service – began to defect, and formed the nucleus of a Royalist force. Further inland, word reached the British that Toussaint L'Ouverture had fallen out with the Republicans. Apparently, this was due to a reluctance in Paris to grant freedom to all of the colony's black slaves. So, L'Ouverture sided with the Spanish. They were sending a military force of their own to Saint-Domingue, to invade the colony from the east. It seemed that the Republican Commissioner Léger-Félicité Sonthonax was going to be too busy to deal with what for now was a minor British threat. So, Commodore Ford wrote letters begging for help, while his ships spent the winter patrolling the waters of the Windward Passage, and bottling up the French privateers off Le Cap François, Port-de-Paix and Port-au-Prince.

Meanwhile, news of the capture of Môle Saint-Nicolas reached Britain. Instead of sending out a few reinforcements, Pitt's government took advantage of the chaos by sending a full-scale expedition to the Caribbean. Meanwhile, Ford decided that with his base secure, he could begin launching pinprick raids against Republican-held ports, without getting entangled in a major battle. Môle Saint-Nicolas was certainly well placed for this. A short way down the north coast of Saint-Domingue lay Port-de-Paix and then La Cap François beyond it. To the south, on the far corner of the Gulf of Gonâve was Port-au-Prince, the colony's capital. Just to its west, near the base of the colony's southern peninsula, lay another port,

Léogâne (now Miragoâne). Further on was Jérémie, which was already in British hands. There was certainly no shortage of suitable targets for Ford's seaborne raids.

In October Whitelocke led a 50-man detachment in a raid on Saint-Marc, a fishing village on the Gulf of Gonâve, midway between the two peninsulas. He soon found it was occupied by a company of French troops, but thanks to *Hermione* and another frigate offshore, he was able to convince the defenders they faced overwhelming numbers. The French surrendered, but it could have gone very badly wrong. Other probes followed, but it wasn't enough to even threaten the Republican hold on the colony. The *Grands Blancs* began to think they'd been duped into supporting an enemy power who wouldn't even send troops to help them. Even the Spanish did more, invading the French colony with 14,000 men. However, even they made little headway, due in part to their realisation that Saint-Domingue was a colony at war with itself, with blacks, 'mulattos', Creoles and whites seemingly hell-bent on slaughtering each other.

Fortunately for Commodore Ford, things were about to change. Back in Britain a force of 7,000 soldiers were being embarked onto transport ships – a total of six infantry regiments, plus the elite companies of several more, supported by artillery. These veteran troops were placed under the command of Lieutenant General Sir Charles 'No Flint' Grey, a 64-year-old veteran of wars against the Spanish, French and Americans. His nickname was earned in 1777, when he ordered his men to unload their muskets before launching a surprise attack on an American camp. These transports were escorted across the Atlantic by a powerful naval squadron of five ships-of-the-line and eight frigates commanded by Vice-Admiral Sir John Jervis, Admiral of the Blue, who flew his flag in the *Boyne*, a Second Rate of 98 guns. The expedition sailed from Portsmouth on 26 November 1793, and six weeks later it reached Barbados. By then, though, Grey and Jervis had changed the plan. Rather than heading straight for Saint-Domingue, they would begin their campaign in Martinique.

It was late March 1794 before the French there were subdued, and buoyed up by this success the expedition went on to capture nearby Guadeloupe and Saint Lucia. A portion of this tardy expedition finally reached Môle Saint-Nicolas on 19 May. By then, thanks to disease, campaign losses and the need to garrison those newly won islands, only 1,600 fit soldiers were left. These troops were commanded by Major General John Whyte, who also took command of Whitelocke's men. Even so, he now had barely 2,400 troops under his command. The French had 6,000 regulars on the island, backed up by 14,000 militiamen, largely 'mulattos', of the National Volunteers. Then there was the slave army, of at least 25,000 men. True, the loyalty of the French regulars was divided. While most were solidly Republican, some were pro-Royalist. Still, even if that tipped the scales slightly, the balance of forces in Saint-Domingue was firmly weighted in favour of the French.

Before these troops arrived, Ford and Whitelocke had been busy. In early 1794 Whitelocke had sent two messages to Port-au-Prince, the capital of the French colony. They both demanded the surrender of the town and garrison. Inevitably, Commissioner Sonthonax rejected them. Meanwhile, on the northern coast, Whitelocke even tried to bribe the garrison of Port-de-Paix to surrender. This incensed the local commander so much that he challenged the British colonel to a duel. It was never fought. Now, though, with reinforcements, the British could do more than just posture. Reinforced by three more ships-of-the-line, and with Whyte's sickly troops embarked, Ford headed south to Port-au-Prince. There they found the harbour filled with over 40 French merchant ships laden with cargo – a rich plum indeed if they could be captured. First, however, they had to overcome the defences of the port.

Hermione played her part. She duelled with a shore battery at Carrefour, to the west of the city, exchanging fire for more than two hours. *Hermione* was hit several times in the duel. Then one of the 6-pounder guns on the larboard side of her forecastle blew up. This was probably caused by the poorly cast barrel overheating. The explosion killed or wounded most of the gun crew, and set off another explosion in an open cartridge case of ammunition. In all, five men were killed, and another seven severely wounded. As a ship's officer later put it: 'We suffer'd very severely.' Nevertheless, the frigate remained in action throughout that day, and those which followed. On 31 May the first of the forts guarding the town were captured, and two days later Fort Brissoton was taken by storm. It was the key to the defences, and so, on 4 June, Port-au-Prince was surrendered to the British.

During the surrender, Sonthonax, his governing council and his leading Republican supporters were allowed to march out of the town. In return, the merchant ships were left behind. This turned a real success into a hollow victory. Whyte had had the chance to cut the head off the Republican cause in Saint-Domingue. Instead the campaign dragged on.

Worse, Toussaint L'Ouverture chose that moment to switch sides again, declaring his support for the Republicans. That effectively ended the Spanish drive on the French colony. It also gave the Republicans a much-needed reprieve. All the British had to show for their efforts was an unhealthy and fever-wracked port, which now needed to be garrisoned. The only real gain was the capture of those 40 merchant ships. They were worth a small fortune once they were evaluated and sold in Jamaica. The officers and men of the *Hermione* would eventually get their due share of the prize money.

The defection of L'Ouverture allowed the Republicans to regain the initiative. The Spanish expedition had recently reached Gonâve, and so cut Saint-Domingue in two. Now, though, the slave army began pushing them eastwards towards the colony's border with Spanish-owned Santo Domingo. The Republicans under General Laveaux still held Le Cap François, and it was there that Sonthonax established a new seat of power. Meanwhile, in the south of the colony, André Rigaud, a 'mulatto' leader of the National Volunteers, caused the British further headaches. Grey had recently occupied Léogâne, midway along the southern peninsula between Port-au-Prince and Jérémie. Now, Rigaud's largely 'mulatto' force stormed and captured the port. Many of the survivors of the small British and Royalist garrison were rescued by the *Hermione* as they fled down the coast towards Port-au-Prince.

On Christmas Day, Rigaud struck again. This time his target was Tiburton, another small harbour near the western tip of the colony's southern peninsula. In this attack, Rigaud was helped by his own makeshift squadron of French privateers, operating out of Aux Cayes, on the peninsula's southern coast. After a brisk fight the heavily outnumbered British and Royalist garrison fled. Most were hunted down before they reached the safety of Jérémie, some 25 miles away across the hills. Later, Jérémie itself would be evacuated as Rigaud's men closed in. All in all, it had been a bleak campaigning season for the British, whose only gain had been Port-au-Prince. Worse, though, the expedition itself was falling apart as malaria, fever and dysentery swept through the ranks. Even Sir Charles Grey fell ill during a brief visit to the colony. He quickly left for Britain, accompanied by his entourage.

They were the lucky ones. Of Grey's garrison in Port-au-Prince – one of the most unhealthy towns in Saint-Domingue – 600 men had died from yellow fever within two months of capturing the place. Of the 7,000 troops who sailed from Britain with him, more than two-thirds had perished before the end of the year. Many fell sick on board their troop transports, which themselves had become floating charnel houses. Over a thousand of the transport ships' crews were now dead. It was later estimated that the final toll for the year was as high as 12,000. Unfortunately, the British government didn't learn from this. Their solution was to double down and send out an even larger expedition. The campaign in this unhealthy place would continue, and thousands more British soldiers would succumb to fever before it drew to a whimpering end in 1799, when Môle Saint-Nicolas was finally evacuated.

The sailors of Ford's squadron fared a little better than Grey's soldiers. At least their ships could put out to sea and escape the fetid atmosphere of the coast. However, this wasn't always enough. The crews of the ships-of-the-line anchored off Port-au-Prince suffered the most, and while Môle Saint-Nicolas was a healthier anchorage, the losses continued. On board *Hermione*, which had spent much of the year in the Gulf of Gonâve, many of her crew had contracted yellow fever or malaria during the course of 1794. Of these, some 40 had died. In late August, Captain Hills himself fell ill, laid low first by dysentery and then yellow fever. He died on 4 September. This hardy naval veteran had been a well-liked captain, and while he maintained a taut ship, he did so with a light hand. As he was buried at sea off Port-au-Prince, the crew of the *Hermione* couldn't help wondering if his successor would be cut from the same cloth.

3

The Seeds of Mutiny

A mutiny doesn't just happen out of the blue. It's usually the explosive climax of a long-running problem – a festering feeling of resentment, injustice or discord that has been seething away unchecked for weeks, months or even years. Then, one dark night, it erupts in a frenzy of violence and bloodshed. To some, the warning signs were there to see – the sullen looks, the insubordination, the shirking of duty by men who were once eager to play their part. The ship's log begins to record a growing catalogue of punishments for things like drunkenness, talking back to superiors, or refusing a direct order. Every ship has its share of troublemakers, but when these punishments are meted out to men who were once sober, diligent and industrious, then the rot has already set in. What happened on board the *Hermione* in 1797 was no exception. For those who cared to look, trouble had been brewing for years before the murderous eruption.

It probably began on 5 September 1794, as *Hermione* lay at anchor off Port-au-Prince. Like the rest of the crew, John

Harris, the frigate's first lieutenant, was dressed in his best uniform, and stood waiting on the frigate's spotless deck. Not a speck of sun-melted tar dropping from the rigging was allowed to blemish the woodwork that hot and humid morning. He watched the ship's boat from the *Europa* pull alongside, and once it hooked on a figure sprang onto the steps on the ship's side. As his gold-brimmed bicorn appeared over the gunwale Harris nodded, the waiting file of marines presented arms, and the boatswain's mate piped the frigate's new captain on board. He knew little about his new commanding officer save his name, and the fact that he had just been rated a post captain.

Hours before, Philip Wilkinson had been a lieutenant. Now, thanks to Commodore Ford, he was a post captain. After he 'read himself in' by reciting his commission to the assembled ship's company, he became the unquestioned ruler of all he surveyed. In fact, Wilkinson had done extremely well to reach that point in his career. Now, if he kept his nose clean, he could expect to rise by seniority, and eventually, if he lived long enough, he would become an admiral. There was no doubt about it – Philip Wilkinson had come a long way.

His father, Thomas Wilkinson, owned a profitable barber's shop in Harwich, but his son had no wish to run the family business. Instead, encouraged by the sights and smells of the bustling Essex port, he hankered after a career at sea. Fortunately for him, his father had family connections. His uncle was Sir Philip Stephens, the son of a rector, who became the secretary of Rear-Admiral Anson – the future Lord Anson. From there, he moved to the Admiralty and became the secretary of the navy in 1763. He held the post for over 30 years, during which time he also became a Member of Parliament, representing Sandwich in Kent. With his help, in March 1782, Philip Wilkinson became a midshipman in the Royal Navy. He passed his Lieutenant's Exam in October 1790. Less than four years later, in March 1794, he was given his first command, the sloop *Actif* of ten guns.

She began her career as the British privateering brig *Active* of 16 guns, built in Liverpool. She was sent to cruise in the West Indies, but in May 1793 she was captured by the French frigate *La Semillante*. She duly became the French privateer *L'Actif*, which operated from ports in Saint-Domingue. This ended in mid-March 1794, when she and another smaller privateer were captured off Léogâne by the British frigate *Iphigenia*. Captain Patrick Sinclair, who commanded the frigate, decided to take the *Actif* into naval service, and appointed one of his lieutenants to command her. Four months before, when the *Iphigenia* and the *Penelope* captured the French frigate *L'Inconstante* off Saint-Domingue, one of his senior lieutenants, Philip Wilkinson, had displayed considerable dash and bravery. So, he was rewarded with the command of a brig. Wilkinson's appointment as master and commander was duly ratified in July by former Commodore Ford, now a rear-admiral.

The *Actif*, her armament reduced to improve her sailing qualities, was re-designated a sloop of war, armed with ten 4-pounders. She didn't have a particularly distinguished career, spending much of her time escorting convoys to and from Port-au-Prince. However, Commander Wilkinson's professionalism impressed Commodore Ford, particularly after he helped fight off two attacks by French privateers based in Léogâne. Consequently, when Captain Hills of the *Hermione* died of yellow fever, Ford decided to promote Wilkinson, and gave him that all-important elevation to the rank of post captain. In his place, Lieutenant John Harvey of the *Europa* was given command of the *Actif*. However, five weeks later the *Actif* foundered in a storm somewhere off Bermuda, while she was carrying dispatches to Britain. All of her crew were lost. Wilkinson had taken several of the *Actif*'s crew with him when he took command of *Hermione*, so they at least were spared their shipmates' fate.

Nobody could doubt Wilkinson's professionalism, or his courage. He had amply demonstrated his skill and bravery. His family connections helped overcome his poor social roots, and may have eased him along the ladder of promotion. However, he had needed more than that to have got where he had. His service in *Iphigenia* had stood him in good stead, and Rear-Admiral Ford was satisfied with his handling of the *Actif*. Ford might well have seen Wilkinson as the best available man to fill Captain Hills's shoes. Ford, though, also knew that he would soon return to Britain. So, promoting the nephew of the current secretary of the navy would almost certainly help his own prospects. Whatever the real reason behind it, *Hermione* now had a new captain. It is unfortunate that *Actif*'s ship's log and master's log were lost when the sloop foundered. If he'd read them, they might have given Ford pause to reflect on the wisdom of his decision.

We can learn something of Wilkinson from an account written a few years later, when he commanded the 38-gun frigate *Hussar*. One of her crew, John Wetherell, described Wilkinson as a brutal man, and gave examples of his harshness. While the *Hussar* lay at anchor off Plymouth, the port admiral, Sir Robert Calder, had to go on board to investigate a serious incident which could well have lead to a man being hanged. A fight had broken out between a seaman and a young officer – a midshipman. This was such a grave breach of naval discipline that Calder decided to visit the *Hussar* and see things for himself. He ended up censuring Captain Wilkinson for creating such a bad atmosphere on board. He even told him to 'look back on the unfortunate *Hermione*'. It seemed that Wilkinson hadn't learned anything from what happened on board his old command.

Moreover, Wilkinson's discipline problem was already well known, as Calder added that he had been told of the poor state of morale in the *Hussar* by Admiral Cornwallis, Commander-in-Chief of the Channel Fleet. In fact, shortly before, *Hussar*'s crew had petitioned Cornwallis to save them from their captain's cruelty. The admiral, though, did nothing about it, apart from telling Wilkinson about the complaint. Clearly Wilkinson was a problem captain. In naval terms, the sailors often described such a man as 'a right tartar' – a captain who ruled by harshness and discipline. In the end the problem sorted itself, as in February 1804 the *Hussar* ran aground off Brest. Wilkinson and his crew survived, but while the captain reached the safety of a British ship, most of his crew became prisoners of war.

However, that wasn't the end of Captain Wilkinson's naval career. Although he had lost his frigate, the Admiralty offered him another chance. He was given command of the floating battery *Gorgon*, anchored off the mouth of the River Shannon. Then, in 1809, Wilkinson's mentor died. Sir Philip Stephens left his fortune to his nephew, on condition that he assume his patron's surname, therefore Captain Wilkinson became Captain Stephens. In late 1811 he was given command of the 74-gun *Courageux*. She spent two years serving in the Baltic, and from the look of her book it seems her captain had finally learned his lesson. The cat-o'-nine-tails was rarely used. Stephens's ill luck with grounding continued, though, as he ran her aground twice. Despite this, in 1813, when *Courageux* returned home, Stephens finally became a rear-admiral. He retired the following year.

During the last months of 1794 *Hermione* was based at Port-au-Prince. Her main task was to escort coastal convoys through the Gulf of Gonâve, protecting them from French privateers based at Léogâne. It was monotonous work, but at least it kept them away from the fever-ridden port. The only break in the routine was the monthly run up to Saint-Marc Bay, 40 miles to the north, where the ship would take on wood and water. This was the crew's only chance to go ashore, but even here they were guarded by armed marines. Then, at the end of November, Captain Wilkinson was given welcome orders. The *Hermione* was to carry dispatches to Port Royal, and then undergo a short refit. That meant the chance to go ashore in a port whose taverns and brothels were well used to the needs of 'Jack ashore'. So it was a cheerful crew that raised *Hermione*'s anchor, and set course for Jamaica.

The *Hermione* reached Port Royal on 6 December. It turned out, though, that the refit would take several weeks, so the men were occasionally given shore leave. Port Royal was, after all, a secure naval base. Marines guarded the narrow spit of land leading to the mainland of Jamaica, meaning that there was no real chance to desert. However, it was here that the punishments began – or rather the ones we know about. On 25 January 1795, two seamen, Joseph Cadell and

John Evans, were both sentenced to a dozen lashes, one for neglect of duty, the other for fighting and quarrelling. This punishment would have been carried out while the frigate lay alongside in the small shipyard, her upper deck screened by an awning, and the whole ship's company gathered beneath it. On 1 February 1795 the *Hermione* finally left Port Royal and headed back to Saint-Domingue, and resumed her monotonous routine.

Occasionally – if she was lucky – the frigate put in to Môle Saint-Nicolas, where there was mail and fresh supplies to be had and men from other ships to speak to. Meanwhile the floggings continued. In late February a man was given two dozen lashes for 'drunkenness, fighting and quarrelling', while two weeks later another, Thomas Page, was sentenced to another two dozen lashes for 'contempt to superior officers'. Then, in April, there were two major incidents. On 19 April two men were each given a dozen lashes for 'rioting' while the frigate was lying off Saint-Marc. Then, eight days later, three of the crew were flogged – two were given 24 lashes for drunkenness and quarrelling, while a third was flogged for 'insubordination to a superior officer'. The drunkenness is understandable, especially in the heat of the tropics. Still, these punishments were severe, and taken together they suggest a steady deterioration of discipline on board the *Hermione*.

A flogging could break a man's spirit. A ship's captain had immense latitude when it came to issuing punishments. Officially, he couldn't sentence a man to more than a dozen lashes without consulting his superiors, but this rule was never properly enforced. In practice, captains frequently ordered punishments of up to three dozen lashes. More serious crimes, which warranted the death penalty or imprisonment, were dealt with by court martial, made up of several captains sitting in judgement on the accused. The same court martial system was used to deal with officers facing dismissal or reduction in rank. However, all more minor offences were dealt with by the ship's captain. So, Wilkinson had complete authority to dole out whatever punishment he saw as appropriate, as long as it lay within the limits set by naval precedence. Normally, an officer or petty officer would report a man to the captain for some breach of discipline, and then they as well as the man would be brought before the captain for judgement. In these cases, the decision of the captain was final.

Sometimes, these summary trials were held in public, on the upper deck. In most cases, though, the proceedings took place in the captain's great cabin. There was no right of appeal. Judgement given, the flogging would usually take place a day or two later, when the routine of the ship allowed. A captain could order other punishments, too – a man could be disrated, he could have his rum ration stopped, while for theft a man could be made to run the gauntlet, where the crew themselves would perform the beating. In Captain Wilkinson's case, however, flogging was his preferred form of punishment. On the day of punishment all hands would be called on deck to witness it. The offender would usually be lashed to a grating, generally set up in the waist of the ship, just below the quarterdeck. In the *Hermione*, though, he was lashed to the spars of the capstan, just forward of the ship's wheel.

Armed marines guarded the prisoner, and separated the ship's company from the captain and his officers. The flogging was carried out by one or more boatswain's mates. The boatswain himself would stand behind his mates with a starter or cane, ready to strike them if he felt they weren't whipping hard enough. The man would be led forward, stripped to the waist, and his hands and feet would be bound to the top and bottom corners of the grating. When the captain or first lieutenant ordered the punishment to begin, a boatswain's mate would take his cat-o'-nine-tails from its red baize bag, shake its nine rope tails out, position himself carefully, and then draw his arm back to deliver the first stroke. The blows were delivered with full force, and the two-foot-long tails of the whip, made from quarter-inch-thick knotted rope, were hard enough to crack an inch-thick plank of wood.

One witness of a shipboard flogging recounted what he witnessed – a very different scene from the more stoic versions recounted in naval fiction. 'When a poor fellow is being punished, his agonised cries pierce you to the soul. The scene is awful! Hot boiling lead poured onto a criminal's back would be but nothing in comparison to the suffering of those who came under the lash of the unrelenting boatswain's mates.' The blows tended to fall around the man's shoulders, where they would dig bloody grooves into his back, or flay his tendons. Accounts from people being flogged claim they felt the pain in their lungs was even more severe than on their backs, and they felt their internal organs were about to burst. Most men would have been unable to retain their composure after the first few strokes.

After anything from six to 12 lashes the boatswain's mate would be relieved by another one, who would run his fingers through the cat to rid it of bits of blood or tissue, and then continue the punishment. In many cases, by the time the offender had taken a dozen blows to his back, he was often semi-conscious. In some cases a captain could intervene and stop the punishment, or order the ship's doctor to examine the offender, to see if he could handle more strokes. In other cases he merely ordered the man be revived by throwing water over him, and the brutal punishment would continue. By its end, particularly after two dozen lashes, the man's back would be covered in blood, and sometimes the lash marks would be so deep that they would expose bone or organs. The deck too would be splattered. Then, the punishment completed, the man would be cut down, and led forward, into the care of his messmates.

On occasion, if an offender was well liked, his shipmates would give him tots of rum before the punishment began, so he wouldn't feel the pain so much. Others simply had to suffer. It would have been a horrendous experience, and a very public one. The humiliation of being stripped and flogged in front of the entire ship's company would have been bad enough. It would have been worse – much worse – if they didn't even try to face their punishment with as much dignity and stoicism as they could muster. By the end, though, the resilience of most offenders would be broken by the experience. But the flogging wasn't the end of it. The ship's doctor would treat a man's wounds as best he could, and in time the physical damage would heal. However, physical scars would remain on the man's back, and in most cases the mental damage the flogging inflicted could run very deeply indeed. For many, this experience could change a man's character, and rarely for the better.

The log of the *Hermione* suggests that from late April until mid-August 1795, there were no more floggings on board the frigate. However, this didn't mean that the men weren't regularly 'started' – beaten with a rope's end by the boatswain's mates. It may be that during the summer of 1795 Wilkinson's crew were simply too busy to quarrel, fight or display insolence. The *Hermione* was employed escorting convoys between Port-au-Prince and Môle Saint-Nicolas, or through the Gulf of Gonâve into the Windward Passage. There, off Punta de Maisí, the easternmost tip of Cuba, or Navassa Island, 30 miles west off Saint-Domingue's south-western tip, they would hand her charges over to other escorts, and return to Port-au-Prince, either to pick up a new convoy or else merely to take on stores before putting to sea again. It was a dreary routine, but at least it kept everyone occupied.

One thing that might have helped buoy up their spirits was that they might fall in with a French privateer. So, that summer, as their convoys passed close to Léogâne, the crew of the *Hermione* would have been on the lookout for trouble. Unfortunately for them, nobody attacked their convoys, and so there was no glory-filled fight, no capture of an enemy ship, and even more importantly, no share of any prize money. The only break from the routine came when they were left swinging at anchor for weeks on end off Port-au-Prince, or occasionally, running 50 miles up the coast to Saint-Marc Bay, to take on firewood for the galley, as well as fresh water. Captain Wilkinson, for all his faults, knew better than to water his ship in Port-au-Prince, where yellow fever was rampant, and the local water far from clean and fresh.

A change in the routine came in early July, when *Hermione* was ordered to Jérémie, 120 miles to the west of Port-au-Prince.

The small port was a gathering place for neutral ships, waiting for a convoy. Most of the two dozen merchant ships in the crowded anchorage flew the American flag. Early on Saturday 4 July the *Hermione* glided in among them and dropped anchor. She then lowered her boats and sent a boarding party over to the nearest ship. This ship was searched from stem to stern, the British looking for prime seamen to replace those who had recently died of yellow fever. Ideally, they would be born in Britain rather than the United States, but frankly the boarders weren't too fussy – anyone who didn't have the right paperwork was likely to be seized. By the late afternoon the *Hermione*'s searchers had boarded 20 American ships, and taken 67 pressed seamen back with them to the frigate.

The Americans were outraged. The day of the raid was deliberately chosen to offend them, and this, together with the high-handed attitude of the *Hermione*'s crew meant that the incident would cause a furore in the United States. The pressed men were held prisoner for two days, and were deliberately denied food and sleep, to wear them down. Wilkinson wanted them to 'volunteer' for British service. However, all of them refused to give in, and stood on their rights as American citizens to avoid serving a foreign power. During the long war with France, over 10,000 American seamen were press-ganged like this, but rarely had it been done so methodically, and on Independence Day. Nevertheless, most would end up in British warships. As a result, *Hermione* was a name that Americans were unlikely to forget.

By August the *Hermione* was back in Port-au-Prince and, with no convoys to escort, the old tensions resurfaced. Two hands tried to desert, but were soon recaptured by the garrison, and flogged for their temerity. At the same time Walter St John was also given 16 lashes for neglect of duty. The inference in the records is that he helped his two shipmates slip over the side. Back in April, St John had been given 24 lashes for drunkenness and quarrelling. If this was meant to be a deterrent then it didn't work. On 4 October, St John was flogged again, receiving 24 lashes for neglect of duty and insolence. So too did his friend James Pollard, of the same mess. Just over a week later the ship's clerk, Simon Marcus, was flogged for desertion, after making a break for it while ashore in the town. Given the atmosphere on board, it was understandable that these men wanted to jump ship.

The failure of morale on board was largely due to Captain Wilkinson's regime. It compared poorly to Captain Hills's days in command, when the cat was rarely taken out of its bag. The only things that might have eased the tension were a break in the routine, and the chance of an independent cruise and a pocket-full of prize money. Recently several frigates on the station had captured prizes, and their crews had enjoyed the windfall. For two years, though, the *Hermione* didn't catch a whiff of prize money. Wilkinson of the *Hermione* never got the chance to spread his wings. This wasn't necessarily down to Captain Wilkinson's ability. It was more a matter of favouritism. In late 1795, Wilkinson's mentor Commodore Ford was made a rear-admiral, and returned home. His replacement as commander-in-chief of the Jamaica Station had his own favourites, and Wilkinson clearly wasn't one of them.

This new commander was Vice-Admiral Sir Hyde Parker, a veteran of the American war. He was also a protégé of Admiral Lord Howe. So, when Parker arrived in Saint-Domingue in early 1796, it was his turn to dish out plum assignments to his favourite captains. These were post captains who already enjoyed his patronage, or who had friends or family with strong links to the admiral. These men could therefore expect preferential treatment. As a result, the best jobs went to his favoured young frigate captains, William Ricketts of the *Magicienne*, Henry Warre and his successor Robert Otway of the *Mermaid* and Hugh Pigot of the *Success*. All three of these 32-gun frigates were given independent cruises, or sent on raids against French shipping in the West Indies. That all but guaranteed lucrative prizes. While their crews got their share of prize money, there was no windfall for the *Hermione*'s.

Instead, there were just more convoys to escort, and throughout 1796 this dull routine continued. The only respite from the tedium came in February, spurred by the arrival of 1,600 British regulars at Port-au-Prince. These reinforcements were used to drive back the French outposts on the heights overlooking the town. Then, when Major General Williamson left for home in March, command of the British troops was passed on to Major General Gordon Forbes. He decided to use these fresh troops to launch an attack on Léogâne. As a major base for French privateers, the port was a real thorn in the British side. So, with the help and support of Vice-Admiral Parker, Forbes made his move. *Hermione* took part in the attack on Léogâne, escorting the transport ships on the short voyage from Port-au-Prince, and then waited offshore, for fresh orders that never came.

The attack itself didn't go well. In a letter to a friend, Parker summed up what followed: 'On the 21st [March] the army was landed in two divisions, to the eastward and westward of the fort and town, covered to the westward by *Ceres* and *Lark*, and to the eastward by the *Iphigenia*, the *Cormorant* and *Serin* sloops.' Like *Hermione*, *Ceres* and *Iphigenia* were 32-gun frigates, while *Lark* and *Cormorant* were 16-gun sloops and *Serin* a ten-gun brig. The real firepower was provided by the 74-gun *Leviathan* and the 64-gun *Africa*. They sailed close inshore to engage the fort, while the 74-gun *Swiftsure* bombarded the town. Parker wrote: 'The fire of the latter [*Swiftsure*] was interrupted in the course of half an hour from the situation of the army on shore, but the two former [*Leviathan* and *Africa*] kept up an unremitting carronade for nearly four hours against the fort'.

The bombardment lasted until nightfall. Meanwhile, the army spent the day consolidating their beachhead and probing the port's defences. Then, as Parker politely put it: 'The next day, from what they had observed, the enemy were found so exceedingly numerous that it was resolved best for His Majesty's Service to re-embark the army, and postpone the operations for the present.' In other words, Léogâne was much stronger than anyone had expected and, without artillery, the 700 British troops had no hope of storming the port's defences. At one point, Forbes even demanded that Parker land the heavy guns from his ships-of-the-line, to bolster the troops' firepower. Sensibly, Parker refused. After all, both *Leviathan* and *Africa* had been damaged during their duel with Léogâne's fort, and he also had no faith in the army's ability to protect his guns if they had to evacuate the beachheads.

So, by the evening of Saturday 23 April the whole expedition was back in Port-au-Prince, with nothing to show for their efforts but wounded men and damaged ships. This time the *Hemione*'s crew were the lucky ones. After the debacle of Léogâne they returned to their convoy work, which at least spared them the horrors of Port-au-Prince. That spring the yellow fever took hold with a vengeance, and the town's cemetery was filled with the dead. All but 300 of the reinforcements died there before the end of the year, leaving the British garrison struggling to man the defences of the port. The military situation was changing, too. The previous summer Spain had made peace with France, which eased the pressure on Toussaint L'Ouverture. Then, on 7 October 1796, Spain actively sided with France by declaring war on Britain. That strategic sea change led indirectly to the *Hermione*'s first real taste of action.

Until then, the British and their French Royalist allies had been fighting a guerrilla war against L'Ouverture's men in the valley of the Arbonite River. It flowed east to west across Saint-Domingue, and divided the colony in two. The river finally entered the sea just north of Saint-Marc. Now, though, with Spanish support, the slave army were gradually gaining the upper hand. Coincidentally, in late November the frigate put in to Saint-Marc to carry out a refurbishment of the rigging. While this was hard work, it did mean a break from the usual routine. The refit was scheduled to take a month. Just as it was completed, and two days after Christmas, Wilkinson was given fresh orders. He was to take the *Hermione* up the coast to the river mouth, and raid a coastal village which was used by L'Ouverture as a supply base. Now, finally, the crew had a chance to play a more active part in the campaign.

However, the operation turned out to be disappointingly mundane. Daybreak on Thursday 29 December saw them approaching the coast close to the enemy supply base at Grande-Saline. The ship's log records what happened: 'At 8am run inshore and fired a broadside at Cordians salt pans.

1/2 past 9 a lieutenant and two master's mates with the boats manned and armed went on shore and set fire to the village.' The small French garrison fled into the jungle. So, with the village ablaze and its stores destroyed, the *Hermione's* boats cruised off the Arbonite river mouth, and captured two boats. By then the enemy troops had returned with reinforcements, and were massing just out of range of the frigate's guns. Wilkinson recalled his ship's boats, then headed back to Saint-Marc, towing his captured fishing boats behind him. In the scale of the campaign it was nothing exciting, but it was, at least, a start.

Some of the *Hermione's* crew would have hoped this little operation marked a change in their fortunes. They were right. Change was in the offing, but it was of a kind that most of them wouldn't welcome. For some, it would cost them their lives. The first word of it came on Saturday 14 January 1797, when a cutter arrived with orders from Vice-Admiral Parker. Wilkinson would wait to take on stores, then sail the *Hermione* north to Môle Saint-Nicolas, where he would report immediately to the admiral. The storeship finally arrived at the end of the month, so, on Saturday 4 February, the *Hermione* dropped anchor close to the admiral's flagship. As Captain Wilkinson changed into his best uniform, he must have wondered what Parker had in store for him. The frigate was awash with rumours, but nobody really knew what to expect. To their eternal cost, they would soon find out.

4

The Fortunate Son

Captain Wilkinson of the *Hermione* didn't know it yet, but he'd been ordered to Môle Saint-Nicolas to take part in a cover-up. One of Vice-Admiral Parker's favourite frigate captains had become embroiled in a major diplomatic incident, and the admiral needed Wilkinson to help make the problem go away. It was all down to an unfortunate encounter Captain Hugh Pigot of the frigate *Success* had had the previous summer. The flames of diplomatic outrage were still burning brightly in mid-January 1797, when a formal court of inquiry was held into the incident. The board was made up of captains loyal to the admiral, so the final verdict was never in doubt. What the admiral feared now, though, was any more backlash from the Admiralty in London, fanned by bad publicity in the press. Wilkinson, a captain who didn't enjoy the admiral's protection, was now expected to help bail out Captain Pigot, who was one of the vice-admiral's protégés.

It had all started on the night of 30 June 1796, some 30 miles to the north-east of Léogâne. A convoy was at sea, heading southwards from Saint-Marc Bay to Port-au-Prince. There were a dozen merchant ships in it – a combination of British-flagged ships and neutral ones. Their escort was the 32-gun frigate *Success*, commanded by Captain Hugh Pigot. At just 26, Pigot was one of the youngest frigate captains in the navy, an honour that reflected his background and connections more than his merits. That said, he was a perfectly good seaman, and a man capable of making quick decisions. His main problem was his mercurial temper. That evening, it would get him into some serious trouble. To a young naval captain, escorting convoys was frustrating work. Merchant crews were unused to sailing in formation, and were often slow to obey orders. However, that evening Captain Pigot was feeling especially exasperated.

The worst offender was a neutral merchantman, the brig *Mercury* of New York. Earlier in the short voyage, her jib-boom had almost rammed into the frigate's stern, just above the stern davits. She had been unable to hold her place in the convoy, and was often off station, or tacking the wrong way. That evening, Captain Pigot retired to his cabin at 10pm, halfway through the evening watch. He expected to reach port the following morning, and needed to catch up on his paperwork. Then, at 1am, he was roused by shouting from the quarterdeck above his head. It was the officer-of-the-watch, who was yelling at another ship in the darkness. Pigot tried to get back to sleep, but was startled by a splintering crash. He ran up on deck to find the ship in utter confusion. The jib-boom of another ship was lying across the frigate's waist and was entangled in her mainmast rigging.

Inevitably, the problem was the *Mercury*. She had struck the *Success* amidships, despite being yelled at to alter course.

The result was a shambolic mess of spars, canvas and rigging. Still, seamen were already leaping forwards, as the officer-of-the-watch directed them to cut the frigate free. Captain Pigot took charge, and within a quarter of an hour the two vessels had been disentangled and were lying beside each other, rolling gently. By now Captain Pigot was furious. The collision couldn't have happened in a more dangerous place – practically within sight of the largest French privateering base in Saint-Domingue. Surely that wasn't a coincidence. He didn't particularly like 'Jonathans' – the popular nickname for Americans – and so Pigot began to think that the collision was deliberate. That meant the *Mercury*'s skipper was probably in league with the French.

Pigot was convinced that the American captain was either a fool or a villain. That clouded his judgement, making what followed all the more inevitable. Of course, there are two versions of the incident – one told from the British side, and the other by the Americans. According to William Jessup, the master of the *Mercury*, the harsh words began when the British sailors were trying to separate the two vessels. Jessup called over, begging Pigot's men not to cut away more rigging than they had to. He later claimed that Pigot ordered his men to cut away everything they could, and to take the *Mercury*'s jib-boom and sheets too, as they would do for making trousers. When Jessup complained, Pigot ordered his men to 'bring the damned rascal that spoke on board the frigate'. In his report, Pigot stated that he said no such thing, and it was Jessup who was yelling out profanities at the British crew.

However it happened, Jessup came on board the *Success*, and watched the separation of the two vessels. Then, according to his petition, Pigot ordered his boatswain's mates 'to give the damned rascal a good flogging'. When he told Pigot he was the commander of the *Mercury*, Pigot was unimpressed, and ordered his men to flog him anyway. As Jessup claimed in his petition of complaint: 'These orders were instantly obeyed in so severe and cruel a manner that your petitioner was nearly bereft of his senses.' He added that during this he begged for compassion, but instead of mercy, he was 'brutally beaten and ill-treated'. Naturally enough, Pigot remembered things differently. He claimed that the American captain was only 'started' a few times with a rope's end, and then let go. Clearly someone wasn't telling the truth. Whatever happened though, Jessup was beaten to some degree on board the *Success*, and the punishment was carried out on Pigot's orders.

During the night the convoy got under way again, and late that morning it reached Port-au-Prince. Pigot considered himself lucky that no privateers had put out from Léogâne that night and attacked the convoy while the *Success* was powerless to protect it. Therefore, all the ships reached port safely – even the *Mercury*, which limped in under the watchful eye of the frigate. The first thing Jessup did was to go ashore and seek out the American consul, Mr Lewis MacNeal. He told him what had happened. Three days later Jessup and MacNeal lodged a petition with the British military authorities in Port-au-Prince. It demanded justice and redress. It stressed that Jessup had made no move to antagonise Pigot, and hadn't even used offensive language. In fact the petition went even further and declared that it was the *Success* that had collided with the *Mercury*, rather than the other way round! This defied the evidence of *Mercury*'s jib-boom, now neatly stowed on board the frigate.

To add more spice to the petition, and at MacNeal's suggestion, it was backed up by a statement by 37 of the town's 'most respectable' inhabitants, testifying that they had personally seen 'the marks and lashing inflicted' on Jessup's back. The petition landed up on the desk of Port-au-Prince's military governor, Major General Forbes and languished there, unread. Had he even read it, he would probably have deemed it irrelevant, and set it aside. However, MacNeal had foreseen this, and sent copies to his contacts in the American press. By the end of the month these had been published in several leading American newspapers, together with even more lurid accounts of the incident supplied by Captain Jessup and Consul MacNeal. The result was that what should have been a fairly minor naval disciplinary affair soon turned into a major diplomatic incident.

British diplomats in the United States were keenly aware of the furore, and of the high passions the Jessup affair created. As ever, the press exaggerated the story. After reading an account in a Boston newspaper, a local doctor recorded in his diary that 'Captain Jessup, flogged on board Pigot's frigate 'til he fainted, then vomited blood, and just escaped with his life'. The general feeling was that it was an outrage that a respectable American sea captain had been, as one editorial put it, 'stripped and whipped like a thief'. At the time there wasn't much love lost between Britain and the United States, so it didn't take much to fan the flames of righteous indignation. Inevitably, news of this reached Britain. The Lords of the Admiralty learned of the furore in late September when a copy of the *New York Diary* reached Whitehall, decrying 'the very extraordinary behaviour of Captain Pigot'.

Although this only told one side of the story, the picture it painted was a black one. Acting on instructions from the Board of the Admiralty, the board's secretary, Evan Nepean, wrote to Vice-Admiral Parker, demanding a 'full and circumstantial account' of the incident. This had only just been sent when Britain's foreign secretary, William Wyndham, the Lord Grenville, received an urgent letter from Robert Liston, Britain's minister plenipotentiary (ambassador) to the United States. Liston had borne the full brunt of America's outrage, and his letter to Grenville held nothing back. He mentioned the 'complaints of acts of injustice and insult committed by our officers against American citizens', before being more specific. He added: 'A deep impression has in particular been made by persons of all ranks in the enclosed statement of an outrage offered to Mr. William Jessup.'

So, Nepean sent off another even more strongly worded missive to Parker. It even referred to 'the outrageous and cruel behaviour of Captain Pigot', demanding a full enquiry be held without delay, and that Parker should pass on the findings to the Admiralty. Then they could take whatever disciplinary steps were necessary. In other words, they would decide if Pigot was guilty or not. In the end, both letters went out in the same fast packet – a dispatch vessel – sailing from Falmouth to Barbados. The packet finally reached Môle Saint-Nicolas in mid-November, where Parker read the letters with alarm. He already knew of the incident from Major General Forbes, and from the American papers. So far he had managed to keep a lid on the affair. Now, though, he had no option. No option but to hold an official enquiry, and let the dice fall as they may.

As the commander-in-chief of the Royal Navy's Jamaica Station, Vice-Admiral Sir Hyde Parker wielded a lot of power.

He had absolute authority over his ships and men, and could make or break the careers of officers under his command. What he couldn't do, though, was defy the Admiralty. So, their strongly worded demand to hold an enquiry couldn't be ignored. However, he did have some leeway in the way the enquiry would be run. Tradition demanded that the board consist of three experienced officers, chosen by Parker. He selected his deputy, Commodore John Duckworth, who commanded the *Leviathan*, to preside over the board – an experienced and intelligent officer. He would be assisted by Captain James Bowen of the *Thunderer* and Man Dobson, Parker's flag captain on board the *Queen*. This done, Parker ordered that the court of inquiry be convened on board the *Success* on 19 January 1797.

It was held in Pigot's great cabin. The three senior officers sat behind Pigot's dining table, with the cabin's huge stern window behind them letting in the sunlight through its meticulously scrubbed panes. More light poured in from the skylight above Duckworth's head, diffused by the awning stretched over the quarterdeck. In front of the table, a pair of 12-pounder guns sat on their carriages, imparting a suitably martial air over the place. Two clerks sat at the right-hand side of the table, one to serve as Duckworth's mouthpiece, and the other to record the proceedings. Outside the cabin's door, and wearing his best uniform, Captain Pigot waited for his summons. Clutched in his hand was his own report of the incident.

At 10am precisely, Commodore Duckworth ordered Captain Pigot to be called in. There, he bade the clerk read out the admiral's orders to hold the enquiry, and explain its remit. Next, the petition of complaint lodged with Major

General Forbes was read out, together with all its supporting paperwork. That done, Duckworth asked Pigot to give his side of the story. This was when he presented his prepared statement. Duckworth had the clerk enter it as evidence, then read it out. In it, Pigot stated that he had been asleep in his cabin, and that the sailing master had the watch. At 1am he was woken by the master shouting from the quarterdeck above his head. He'd cried out: 'Put your helm to starboard, or you'll be aboard of us.' Pigot heard the master repeat it several times, followed by a more urgent cry to throw all aback – take the speed off the approaching ship. Moments later the other ship slammed into the starboard side of the *Success*.

When Pigot came on deck he found that the *Mercury* had rammed the *Success* amidships, and that the American brig's bowsprit was stuck through the frigate's main shrouds. Then, according to him, 'our people were immediately employed endeavouring to clear the two ships'. He claimed they didn't cut away more of the *Mercury*'s rigging than they had to, and that they repeatedly hailed the American brig, demanding they take steps to help. However, as Pigot put it: 'Not a soul belonging to the *Mercury* made the smallest effort ... to clear the ships of each other.' In other words, it was the Americans who caused the collision, and who then refused to untangle the two ships. All of this helped Pigot decide that 'the *Mercury*'s running aboard the *Success* was not accident but design'. That, in his opinion, was done to leave the convoy undefended, and at the mercy of the enemy privateers based in Léogâne. That thought coloured what happened next.

Pigot stated: 'So firmly was I impressed with this idea ... that passion overcame my reason, and I am sorry to acknowledge, the master of the *Mercury* coming on board the *Success*, I immediately ordered him to be punished by the boatswain's mate with the end of a rope.' In his statement, Pigot then apologised that his passion had led him to exceed 'the bounds of propriety' by ordering the punishment. Clearly Pigot had sought advice. He knew that he needed to issue a very public apology, to avoid a full court martial. However, he stuck to his guns with everything else, insisting it was the American ship which had done the ramming, and that apart from the summary punishment, he and his men had acted with patience and restraint. With that, Pigot was allowed to leave the cabin. His fate was now in the hands of others.

Four of these, though, were the witnesses whom Pigot had selected from his crew. The master, who had been on watch that night, was languishing in the naval hospital in Jamaica. However, the frigate's first lieutenant, William Hill, was able to testify, as was the ship's surgeon, John Crawford. After their accounts had been given, two petty officers were called: Master's Mate John Forbes and Boatswain's Mate Thomas Jay. Lieutenant Hill went first. He confirmed it was the *Mercury* that had been the problem, and added that her master had 'murmured greatly at our people when on board, assisting him to get clear of us'. By 'murmuring' he meant cursing. When Pigot called the American master on board the frigate 'the American [was] still murmuring and abusing our people'. At that, 'Captain Pigot directed me to send two boatswain's mates aft, and ordered them to thrash him'.

Hill reckoned that the American had received 'about twenty strokes with a rope's end on his back'. The cursing continued as the American was put into the frigate's boat and rowed over to his brig. When Crawford was called, the board asked him if, in his medical opinion, Jessup had been beaten as severely as it had been claimed. The surgeon replied he didn't think it 'could injure him materially'. With that, the court adjourned for the day. The next morning it was the turn of Forbes, who had been on deck during the collision. He confirmed the *Mercury* was the culprit, that Jessup 'had received from twenty to twenty-four strokes', and that when the American went into the boat he vowed to give his own mate a similar punishment. Finally Jay, who administered the beating using a length of handy rope cut from a severed ratline, claimed that in his view the punishment wasn't severe at all.

With that, Commodore Duckworth and his two deputies began their deliberations. Having heard Jessup's version read out, and then listened to the British crew's account, they were now convinced that the American captain had been lying. The *Mercury* rather than the *Success* had caused the collision. They decided to believe Pigot rather than Jessup. The only bit of Pigot's story they didn't support was his notion that the ramming had been deliberate. All of the four other witnesses were asked about that, and all of them said they felt it was accidental. This was duly recorded in Duckworth's official findings. He also praised the master of the *Success* in trying to avoid the collision, and Captain Pigot and his crew for extricating the two vessels, with none of the wanton destruction claimed by the American captain. Essentially, then, the findings of the court of inquiry had exonerated Pigot.

The only black mark against Pigot was the fairly reserved comment: 'We must lament that the agitation and torment produced in his mind by this act of negligence and inattention, or wantonness or design had so put him off his guard, as an officer and gentleman, that he did improperly … direct the said Mr. William Jessup to be punished with some stripes with a rope's end across his shoulders.' It wasn't much of a censure, and it even repeated the fact that Pigot had apologised for his actions. The main thing for both Parker and the Admiralty, however, was that these findings showed there was no anti-American malice on Pigot's part. He took action against an individual, not an entire country. Sir Hyde was delighted, and forwarded the report, along with a wish that their lordships and the foreign secretary could now see the truth, and so should be pleased by the outcome.

Parker, though, was left with a problem. According to Admiralry orders the *Success* had to return to Britain with the next homeward-bound convoy. After four years in the Caribbean, the frigate was in dire need of a refit. However, while the frigate had to head home, there was no reason her captain had to go too. The admiral knew that if Pigot returned home while the Jessup affair was still unresolved then there was a chance he could still be thrown to the wolves, just to appease the Foreign Office. Therefore, it was better if he stayed in the Caribbean, under Parker's protection. That, of course, meant that someone else had to command the *Success* – ideally the captain of a frigate which was staying put. Parker's covering letter to the Admiralty was written on 24 February, four days after the court of inquiry finished its work. The next day, Parker issued his order to Captain Wilkinson.

So, when the *Hermione* dropped anchor, Wilkinson was rowed over to the *Queen* and ushered into the admiral's great cabin. Parker couldn't force Wilkinson to change places with Pigot, but he would have made his wishes clear, and offered him his future support and patronage. So Wilkinson agreed.

In any case, after several years in the Caribbean he was keen to go home. As the convoy was due to set sail for Britain on 14 February, the exchange would have to take place within the next week – just long enough for both captains to put their affairs in order. Both of them, for instance, had to deal with a mountain of paperwork, and select any officers and men they wanted to take with them. This was customary in the service, and both captains took advantage of the arrangement. In the end, 21 men accompanied Pigot when he moved from the *Success* to the *Hermione*.

The exchange took place on Friday 10 February 1797. Early that morning, Pigot bade farewell to his remaining officers and men, and left the *Success* for the *Queen*. There he was given his orders by the admiral's secretary. Meanwhile, Captain Wilkinson left the *Hermione* and rowed directly to the *Success*. He was piped on board, met his new officers and 'read himself in' – reading out his commission. With that done, he became the frigate's new captain. A few minutes later, Pigot came on board the *Hermione*. There the same ceremony was repeated. Having read his commission to the assembled ship's company, Hugh Pigot became the new commanding officer of HMS *Hermione*. Many of the men assembled in the frigate's waist would have hoped their new commander would be more benevolent than his predecessor. Their hopes, though, would soon be dashed.

Hugh Pigot was just 28 years old when he took command if the *Hermione*, his second frigate. He had taken command of the *Success* in early September 1794, when he was just 25 – one of the youngest post captains in the navy. In fact, from the first time he stepped on board a warship, he was on the fast track to promotion. That first step couldn't have taken place in more auspicious circumstances. It occurred in early May 1782, as the 12-year-old boy followed in the coat tails of his father, Admiral Hugh Pigot, as he boarded his flagship the *Jupiter*, a Fourth Rate of 50 guns. She was lying at anchor off Plymouth at the time, and about to carry the admiral to the Caribbean to take command of the Leeward Islands Station. Young Pigot was enrolled on the ship's books as the admiral's servant, and so this voyage would mark the start of his training in the navy.

The admiral, born in 1722, was the youngest of three brothers. He was 13 when he first went to sea, and he gained his first command ten years later. He became a post captain the following year, and in 1737 he was given command of the *Ludlow Castle* of 50 guns. He distinguished himself during the Seven Years' War, commanding the ship-of-the-line *York* off Louisbourg, and ending the war commanding the First Rate *Royal William*. However, when peace came he was sidelined and spent several years ashore. He was a widower by then, with two children, but he remarried in 1768, and dabbled in politics, becoming a Whig (Liberal) Member of Parliament. In 1769 his second wife, Frances, gave birth to a son, whom they named Hugh. As the daughter of a baronet and the sister-in-law of the prime minister, Lord Grafton, Frances had impeccable family connections.

Hugh's two older brothers had useful connections, too. George, the eldest, joined the East India Company, and rose to become the governor of Madras. He amassed considerable wealth, and in 1765 he bought Patshull Hall in Shropshire, where he lived after relinquishing his office. He too became a Whig Member of Parliament, and a baronet. However, he returned to India in 1775, and resumed his position as governor. There, he antagonised his ruling council, was duly arrested by them and, in 1777, he died while under house arrest in Madras, before he could stand trail. As he was unmarried, his estate went to his oldest surviving brother, Sir Robert, an officer in the British Army. At the time he was a newly promoted major general, having fought with distinction at Bunker Hill (1775). He ended the American war as a lieutenant general.

While Robert was serving abroad, Hugh ran the Patshull estate on his behalf and, apart from a brief foray as captain of the Third Rate *Triumph* in 1771, he remained on shore. As a prominent Whig, Hugh was out of favour with the ruling Tory (Conservative) government, and so he was denied any important commands. However, his seniority on the captain's list ensured his promotion, and he duly became a rear-admiral in 1775, and a vice-admiral the following year. Then, when the Whigs returned to power in 1782, Pigot joined the Board of the Admiralty as a full admiral. Due to his political loyalty he was given command of the prestigious Leeward Islands Station, despite not having been at sea for a decade. However, the coming of peace in 1783 brought an end to the admiral's brief return to active service, and he retired soon after his return home.

His son Hugh, though, was now firmly established on the lowest rung of the naval officer's ladder. He remained in the Caribbean, and was rated as a midshipman in 1784, serving on board the Fourth Rate *Assistance*, and then the Fourth Rate *Trusty*. He finally passed his Lieutenant's Examination in 1790, becoming the fifth lieutenant on board the Third Rate *Colossus*, commanded by a family friend. He had risen to third lieutenant by 1791, but the following year he returned to the *Assistance*, this time as her fourth lieutenant, which represented a surprising demotion. The details surrounding this are unclear. Still, he regained his old position as third lieutenant in early 1793, shortly before the outbreak of the war with France. The coming of war meant an expansion of the fleet and new opportunities.

He returned to Britain in late 1793 to serve on board the Second Rate *London*, fitting out in Portsmouth. By January 1794, though, he was named the first lieutenant of the frigate *Latona*. Less than a month later he became the acting commander of the eight-gun fireship *Incendiary*. This, however, was merely a vehicle for a more substantial promotion. In late February, Pigot was given command of the 18-gun sloop *Swan*, then serving on the Jamaica Station. So, he re-crossed the Atlantic, and took charge of his first real command in April 1794. Strangely, by then Pigot was 24 years old, but despite having spent more than a decade at sea, he had no real experience of authority, having spent most of his career as a relatively junior officer on board ships-of-the-line. Now, though, he was a master and commander, responsible for a small but powerful warship, with a crew of 80 men.

The *Swan*, however, was just a stepping stone. Just six months later, Commodore Ford gave Pigot command of the *Success*. Her commander, Captain Francis Roberts, had just died of the 'yellow jack'. Pigot was available, and he had the kind of connections that could help Ford as well. The *Success*, though, was over twice the size of the *Swan*, with twice the armament, and a complement of 215 men and boys. She was a 32-gun frigate, first commissioned in 1781. More importantly for Pigot, she was a post ship. For Hugh Pigot that meant a promotion to post captain. This all-important step-up came just days after his 25th birthday. Wearing his new epaulettes, Pigot 'read himself in' on 4 September 1794. Now this young captain, with only five months of experience of command behind him, was the unquestioned master of a powerful frigate, and her crew.

For the first few weeks, *Success* remained in Port Royal in Jamaica, completing a refit. She then sailed for Môle Saint-Nicolas, where she would be based for the next two years. So began an otherwise tedious routine of convoy work, interspersed with the occasional independent mission. Her service during this period was unremarkable, save for her capture of a French privateering brig in late September 1795. What was more noteworthy was that the ship's records show her inexperienced young captain was inordinately fond of using the whip. For his first four months in command the cat-o'-nine-tails stayed in its red baize bag. However, that ended on Wednesday 22 October 1794. Five men were flogged that day, for drunkenness and showing contempt to a superior officer. And now began a regime of brutality which lasted for more than two years – until Pigot was transferred to the *Hermione*.

Just over a month later, three more received a dozen lashes for neglect of duty, while a fourth seaman was given two dozen lashes for theft. On 8 December, William Morrison was given two dozen lashes for disobeying orders, followed by another two dozen just two days later. Morrison had already been given a dozen in late October, for drunkenness. Five more men would be flogged before the end of the month – one of them being flogged twice in five days. The pattern continued throughout 1795. The charges rarely varied – contempt, drunkenness, disbediance and neglect of duty were the most common charges, but a few men were flogged for other reasons, such as theft, gambling or lack of cleanliness. In Pigot's first year in command of *Success*, no fewer than 43 of his crew were flogged, or almost a fifth of the *Success's* complement. That was only part of it. This list included several men who had been flogged over and over again.

A clear pattern emerged. In late October 1794, William Morrison received a dozen lashes for drunkenness. Just over six weeks later he got another four dozen lashes, spread over two days. This time his charge was disobedience and contempt. He was whipped again in April 1795, and again in May, for gambling and disorderly behaviour. In all, the man received 84 lashes in the space of just seven months. But he wasn't even the crewman who suffered the most. During 1795 John Bowen was given a total of 108 lashes, most of which were received over the space of a month. The last four dozen were for attempting to escape, after the previous punishment. The record, however, was Martin Steady. In all he was flogged eight times in the space of a year, on charges ranging from neglect or drunkenness to mutinous behaviour. In the process he was struck 120 times – enough to scar his back for life.

This reveals a ship where the whip was used with brutal abandon. It also suggests the ship's company were divided. On the one hand were the men whom Pigot evidently favoured – those given promotion, or who escaped punishment. Then there were the others, symbolised by the fifth of the ship who were flogged under Pigot's orders. The worst were the dozen men who were punished repeatedly, one of whom actually died a few weeks after his last flogging. Some were whipped so many times, and with so little time between punishments, that their backs never had a chance to heal. So, their raw backs would have been cut up all over again. If Captain Wilkinson of the *Hermione* was seen as 'a right tartar', and a 'flogging captain', Captain Pigot of the *Success* made him look like a soft-hearted libertarian. Now, on the *Hermione*, Pigot's brutal regime would continue unchecked.

The Caribbean Honeymoon

When a new captain assumes command of a ship, his new crew usually watch him closely, to see what kind of officer he is. Many of the *Hermione*'s crew would have heard of Pigot's brutal reputation in the *Success*. Life under Captain Wilkinson hadn't been particularly enjoyable, and while few expected a greatly improved atmosphere, nobody suspected the situation would become much worse. So, the men gave Captain Pigot a period of grace – a honeymoon period if you like – when the crew tried to gauge their new captain. For his part, Pigot had almost certainly been taken to task by Vice-Admiral Parker over his penchant for flogging. So he too was trying to improve his image. For a few brief months this honeymoon would continue. That said, during this time seeds of discord were being sown on board the frigate. They would soon bear fruit.

———

Normally, when a captain moves from one ship to another, he is allowed to take a number of his crew with him. For a start, there's what amounts to his personal entourage – his cook, his steward, his clerk and his coxswain. He could also take a number of prime seamen with him – men he knew well, and could rely upon in his new ship. The official number for a frigate was 14 of them, but Wilkinson had already agreed to let Pigot take a few more with him out of the *Success*. After all, Wilkinson was taking the frigate back to Britain to be paid off before going into refit so he wouldn't need his full complement. Pigot would, though, as *Hermione* was staying on in the fever-ridden Caribbean. So Pigot drew up a list of the men he wanted. The *Success* was a divided and unhappy ship, but these two dozen men and boys were the captain's favourites – the men who had always been spared the lash.

Until their summons, these men had been expecting to return home. Now, though, they had a choice to make. Once they arrived they stood in a nervous huddle in front of Pigot's desk. Their captain then stood up and greeted them. According to one of the men, Pigot was unusually friendly when he spoke to them: 'My men – I am going to inform you of my leaving this ship. I should be glad to go home as well as you, but I dare say you know the reason.' The men knew perfectly well he was speaking about the Jessup Incident. Then he dropped his bombshell: 'I would wish to carry you along with me, if you are agreeable … not that I can force you against your inclination.' He offered them a day or two to think it over. In fact they didn't need to. All but two of them agreed on the spot to transfer to the *Hermione* with him.

This might seem strange, as all of them knew perfectly well how brutal a captain Pigot was. Yet these men had all been favoured by Pigot, and so had enjoyed his protection. Even that, though, wasn't enough. The real draw was prize money.

Over the past few months the *Success* had captured several French prizes off the coast of Saint-Domingue. If the men stayed on board the *Success*, the chances of them receiving their prize money were greatly reduced, especially if the ship's company was to be split up during the frigate's refit. At least by staying with Pigot they could make sure that they'd get their share. One of the men, Richard Redman, said later: 'He behaved to me very kindly in several respects ... he would endeavour to get whatever prize money be due to us.' So, money – the equivalent of a year's wages for a seaman – was what really bound these men to their old captain.

This meant that when Pigot took command of the *Hermione* on Monday 10 February he was accompanied by a number of former *Successes*. These included his quiet and well-mannered cook, John Holford, a 44-year-old from Surrey, and his 13-year-old son, also called John, who acted as the captain's servant. Then there was Pigot's coxswain, Patrick Foster, a 30-year-old from Galway. A coxswain was a key figure on board – an expert seaman, and in charge of the captain's barge and its crew. In a boarding action he always served as the captain's shield or 'covering man', and in most ships he acted as a conduit of information between the captain and his crew. In the case of Pigot and Foster, however, on board the *Hermione*, this back channel didn't work. Also in the group was Thomas Jay, the 33-year-old boatswain's mate who hailed from Plymouth, a man we'll hear much more of later.

Pigot didn't have a clerk – his last one had died of the 'yellow flux'. That would be a problem, as he needed help dealing with the paperwork involved in running a frigate. Another key person was the captain's steward, who ran his cabin and quarters, a bit like a combination of butler, housekeeper and batman. However, Pigot didn't like his steward and so he didn't make the list. In all then, a total of 21 men and two boys would accompany Pigot to the *Hermione*. In most frigates it would take time for them to be absorbed into the ship's company. In this case, though, it took a mutiny to weld them together. On their last ship, these men had formed a clique. Now they would do the same on board the *Hermione*. Despite these men being the captain's favourites, this didn't necessarily guarantee their loyalty. When the crisis came, many of them would turn on their old captain.

Captain Pigot also needed officers. On board the *Hermione* he already had a first lieutenant, John Harris, but the second lieutenant had transferred to the *Success* with Captain Wilkinson. Pigot filled the post by transferring another favourite from the *Success* – Third Lieutenant Samuel Reed. He was accompanied by a midshipman, John Wiltshire, whose father was a friend of the Pigots, and by John Forbes, a master's mate. When Pigot assumed command he met the *Hermione*'s warrant officers: the sailing master, William Ewing, and the surgeon, Hugh Sansom. Of these, Ewing was due to leave the *Hermione* in a few weeks, while Sansom was a relative newcomer to the ship. These were all men Pigot needed to rely on if he was to weld the *Hermione* into an efficient ship. Unfortunately, Pigot lacked the skills to make the most of these all-important officers.

A few days later Pigot and his crew were given their first mission. The homeward-bound convoy was due to sail from Môle Saint-Nicolas on Wednesday 15 February, 1797.

Commodore Duckworth was in charge of it, flying his flag in the *Leviathan*. The Third Rate was returning to Britain too, so she and the *Success* under Captain Wilkinson made up the convoy's escort. This, though, would be part of a larger operation. Vice-Admiral Parker also planned to take a squadron of six warships to sea, led by his flagship the *Queen*. Their job was to bolster the convoy's escort on its way through the Windward Passage. Once it was safely on course for the Bahamas Channel away to the north-west, the admiral's squadron would leave the convoy. While most of the squadron would eventually return to Môle Saint-Nicolas, a couple of frigates would set off on a cruise of their own, along the northern coast of Saint-Domingue.

The *Hermione* was to join Parker's squadron, which meant Pigot had just five days to prepare her for the operation. His officers and men were kept busy, so it was a relief when on Saturday 11 February a boat arrived with a young lieutenant, Archibald Douglas. The 26-year-old Scot had been serving on Parker's flagship as fifth lieutenant so this move to become the *Hermione*'s third lieutenant represented an advancement. By then Pigot had solved another of his problems. After reading himself in, he retired to his cabin to read through a pile of muster books, ledgers and forms. Tucked among them was a note written by William Johnson, one of the frigate's crew. Just 15 years old, he had previously been employed as a merchant's clerk in Port-au-Prince. However, he had been captured by a French privateer and, on his release, had been press-ganged by Captain Wilkinson of the *Hermione*.

In the note, the teenager begged his new captain to let him go, as he wasn't used to a life at sea. Instead, Pigot summoned him to his cabin. Given the youth's experience, Pigot had decided to employ him as his writer. He also promised the boy a fast-track promotion to the important post of captain's clerk. Consequently, his request to be put ashore was denied, and the unhappy teenager duly became Pigot's writer – his de facto clerk in training. At noon on Monday 13 February, a boat carrying several new sailors arrived, as well as a new addition to the midshipman's berth. David Casey, a 19-year-old from County Cork, was being transferred from the *Ambuscade*. Despite his youth he had a fair degree of experience, having already served as an acting lieutenant until a recent demotion. Casey later wrote that Pigot received him in the kindest manner, but was unable to rate him as anything other than a midshipman.

So when the convoy sailed from Môle Saint-Nicolas on the morning of Wednesday 15 February 1797, *Hermione* was almost up to her full complement. She had all of her officers, save for the lieutenant of marines, but for the moment Sergeant John Plaice was competent enough to fill the gap. Pigot was still short of a few warrant officers and hands, but he had enough crew to carry out his orders. *Hermione* accompanied Parker's flagship the *Queen*, the Third Rate *Valiant*, and the frigate *Quebec* as they followed the convoy out to sea. The weather soon deteriorated, and for the next few days they were barely able to see the convoy through the rain. Parker had intended that his squadron would keep to windward of the convoy and snap up any French ships pursuing them. Now, though, the bad weather meant that the chances of finding any French ships at sea were remote.

Then, on Sunday evening, *Hermione* lost contact with the rest of the squadron. The frigate had been out of sight of her consorts when Parker gave the order to tack. As the *Queen* steadied on a new course the *Valiant* and *Quebec* followed her, as did a new addition, the frigate *Mermaid*. A rain squall had hidden this from the *Hermione*, and so she stayed on her old course. By the time the officer-of-the-watch realised what had happened, the rest of the squadron was nowhere to be seen. Pigot must have roundly cursed his new first lieutenant, who held the watch that night. In fact, due to the squall, it couldn't have been helped. They spent two full days looking for the rest of the squadron, and it wasn't until 4.30am on Wednesday 22 February that they finally spotted Parker's flagship. As soon as they came within hailing range, Parker ordered Pigot to come on board. There he gave Pigot fresh orders.

The previous day, Parker had sent Captain Otway of the *Mermaid* off to cruise in the Mona Passage, which lay between the Spanish island of Puerto Rico to the east and Hispaniola (the combined land mass of Saint-Domingue and the Spanish colony of Santo Domingo) to the west. The passage itself was around 70 miles wide and 40 miles long. It was a popular route for merchant shipping of all nationalities, but in time of war it was also a haven for privateers. Now that Spain had sided with France, the channel was especially dangerous. The new instructions were for Pigot in the *Hermione* to join Otway in the *Mermaid*, and together the two ships would 'cruise on that station as long as they have provisions and water, then to return to the Mole'. As the senior officer, Captain Pigot would command the two-ship force. The two British frigates would search for enemy ships, and either capture or destroy them.

Although Pigot was in charge, Otway was the more experienced captain, having fought in a major sea battle, and just a year later he captured a larger French warship in a small-ship action. He was also an old hand when it came to hunting privateers. It was Friday 24 February when the two frigates rendezvoused off Punta Borinquen, the north-west tip of Puerto Rico. They then began their patrol, keeping just within sight of each other, about 16–20 miles apart. That way the two ships could cover a large swathe of up to 60 miles of sea. If they encountered an enemy ship then they were still just within signalling distance of each other, and so could come to each other's aid. With hostile shores on either side of the channel, and the coasts littered with reefs and shoals, the two ships were sailing in dangerous waters. Out there, so far from a friendly base, they were very much on their own.

In fact the patrol proved uneventful. They spent almost three weeks there, but they had nothing to show for their efforts. So, in mid-March, Pigot decided to change tactics. Clearly the enemy were keeping away from the main channel. It was decided that the frigates would cruise much closer to the Puerto Rican shore, where Otway thought privateers might be hiding. The two frigates parted company to hunt independently. On Wednesday 22 March, *Hermione* was patrolling off Punta Jiguero, Puerto Rico's most westerly tip. Having found nothing in the Bahía de Aguadilla to the north of the point, they sailed south and rounded the headland. Then, the *Hermione's* lookouts spotted something. A cluster of masts could be seen, which meant several vessels were anchored close inshore. Pigot decided to bring his frigate in for a closer look.

As the drums beat to quarters, Pigot led his officers into his cabin, where he unfurled a chart of the coast. He had a plan. He intended to cut out the enemy vessels, and destroy those he couldn't capture. The Royal Navy excelled at 'cutting out' expeditions, which involved sending small boats in to capture enemy vessels in their own harbour. The raiders would cut the anchor cables of their prizes and sail off in them. Pigot planned to use all six of his ship's boats in the operation. His first lieutenant, John Harris, would remain in charge of the *Hermione*, while Lieutenant Samuel Reed would lead the boat attack. Pigot would direct operations from the frigate. By then the ship was ready for action. They were still drawing closer to the coast, and soon the frigate would be within gun range of the shore. The danger was that the enemy would have hidden gun batteries there, to protect the anchorage.

As the *Hermione* crept inshore, leadsmen in the bow heaved their weighted lines and called out the depth as they went. By the time they came within half a mile of the beach the seabed was just 9 fathoms below them – 54 feet. That meant there was roughly 39 feet of water under their keel. At that moment three white puffs erupted from the tree-lined shore. It was the enemy battery. These opening shots fell short. Undeterred, Pigot swung the frigate round, so she was gliding along parallel to the shore. He ordered his gun crews to open fire when their guns bore on the battery. Soon, one by one, *Hermione*'s port-side guns opened up, and case-shot began scything through the trees around the enemy battery. That was enough for the French gunners, who had just missed with their second round. They hurriedly abandoned their guns and fled into the jungle. That meant that now, with the frigate's guns covering the shore, the ship's boats could make their way in to the anchorage.

Lieutenant Reed's 60 men looked more like pirates than British sailors. On Pigot's orders, they were well armed with cutlasses, boarding axes and pistols – the larger firearms were left behind on board the *Hermione*. An operation like this was more about seamanship than firepower. In the end they found the anchored ships had been abandoned by their crews. On seeing the boats' approach, the French sailors rowed or swam for the shore. Soon Reed and his men were in charge of the anchorage and all the vessels in it. There were 16 vessels in all. The largest was a two-masted brig from Bremen. Pigot described her as being valuable and well-laden. She was towed out to sea and was brought alongside the *Hermione*.

All of these vessels, though, appeared to have been prizes captured by privateers, rather than privateering ships themselves. However, it was still a spectacular haul. Most of the 15 smaller craft had been scuttled by their crew, but Reed managed to refloat 13 of them. However, none of them carried any sails – these had been removed. The two remaining ones had been driven aground, so Reed's men staved in their planking with axes. The others weren't much use either, so Pigot ordered them to be set on fire. Soon all 13 vessels were ablaze. For good measure, Pigot also ordered Reed to destroy the guns in the French battery. So, that afternoon, as *Hermione* headed back out to sea with her prize towed behind her, the anchorage was wreathed in flame. A successful little action like that should have gone a long way to unifying the *Hermione*'s crew. Instead, as the frigate returned to Môle Saint-Nicolas, the general sense of resentment against the favoured *Successes* hadn't changed. The frigate's crew were just as divided as ever.

After the *Hermione*'s return, Vice-Admiral Parker ordered Pigot to escort his prize to Jamaica. Once in Port Royal, the brig would be handed over to the prize courts, and the frigate would undergo a short refit. When the courts had made their valuation, the *Hermione*'s crew could expect a pocketful of prize money. Then, the same courts also presented Pigot and the former *Successes* with another windfall – the prize money that had been owed to them from their time in the *Success*. For most of these men, this represented the equivalent of a year's worth of wages. While this didn't necessarily antagonise their new shipmates, as all sailors welcomed these payouts, Pigot's reward caused considerable resentment on board. Most of the crew of the *Hermione* hadn't set foot ashore for years, but Pigot gave his old crew a six-hour 'run ashore' in Port Royal, from noon to sunset.

The ship began her week-long refit in the port's small naval yard. There, Pigot received some unwelcome news. For over a year, Silas Talbot, the American consul in Kingston, had been corresponding with Vice-Admiral Parker, demanding the release of American seamen impressed into the Royal Navy. Parker eventually agreed, and with the *Hermione* conveniently close by, Talbot demand that Pigot hand over eight of his crew. Pigot had no other option. After all, Parker had agreed to the arrangement. So, much to the envy of their shipmates, the eight Americans finally stepped ashore as free men. That reduced the *Hermione*'s ship's company to just 172 officers and men, not counting her six marines, and three ship's boys. Incidentally, there were still four American citizens on board, as well as almost three dozen from other foreign countries.

By early April the *Hermione* was back at Môle Saint-Nicolas, where Pigot picked up fresh orders, along with a trained captain's clerk, John Manning. William Johnson, the unhappy teenage writer, was duly returned to the seaman's messdeck. The orders were even more welcome: Pigot was to lead a raid on a French-held port. While *Hermione* was in Port Royal, Parker heard that a 38-gun French frigate – also called the *Hermione* – had arrived in Le Cap François and was operating off Saint-Domingue's north coast. Built in Rochefort in 1778–79, *Hermione* achieved fame in 1780 when she transported the French General La Fayette to the United States. So it was with particular delight that, when Parker put to sea with three ships, he managed to corner her and drive her onto the rocks to the east of Port-de-Paix. From a prisoner, the British admiral then learned what the French frigate had been doing there.

Over recent months French privateers based on Saint-Domingue's north-western coast had captured several merchant vessels bound for British-held ports. The prizes were held in Port-de-Paix and the smaller harbour of Juan Rabal, 30 miles to the west. So, the French *Hermione* had been ordered to gather up these prizes and convoy them to Le Cap François. Pigot had missed hunting down his ship's namesake, but his new orders made up for that. Parker ordered him to put to sea in the *Hermione*, accompanied by the frigates *Mermaid* and *Quebec*, the brig *Drake* and the sloop *Penelope*. Port-de-Paix was too well defended to attack, but according to the admiral, Juan Rabal was only protected by a single three-gun battery. Pigot's mission was to go there and 'cut out' the prizes from under the noses of the French.

By the evening of Wednesday 19 April Pigot's small squadron was lying 12 miles to the north of Juan Rabal. Pigot instructed his four captains to gather in his cabin. These were

Captains Robert Otway of the *Mermaid* and John Cook of the *Quebec*, and Lieutenants John Perkins of the *Drake* and Daniel Burdwood of the *Penelope*. There, after serving them wine, Pigot outlined his plan. It was simplicity itself. They would wait until the following night and then approach the anchorage from the east, under cover of darkness. Two miles from the port, they would launch all of their ship's boats and fill them with armed men. Then, while the warships sailed in to distract the French gunners, the boats would make straight for the anchorage, and 'cut out' the ships. The plan approved, the captains returned to their ships. Then the waiting began.

The following evening they closed with the coast again, and by the early hours of Friday 21st they caught sight of the shoreline. It was a good landfall, within sight of the low rocky headland that lay to the north-east of the small port. Behind it, a high hill hid them from sight. They heaved-to a mile from the rocky shore, and Pigot gave the signal to lower the boats. The men clambered on board, and the small flotilla set off, with Lieutenant Reed of the *Hermione* leading the way in the frigate's longboat. Once again, Pigot had chosen Reed over his first lieutenant. Once the boats came within 100 yards of the coast they turned and crept along it to the west, rowing with muffled oars. Pigot then ordered his squadron to keep pace with them under greatly reduced sail. It took almost half an hour for the boats to reach the eastern approaches to the anchorage. So far everything had gone well, and Pigot began to hope the boats would make it in without being detected.

Then, lookouts on the *Hermione* saw sparks and flashes on the shore, a mile to the south-west. It was the French gunners preparing their guns. A brief fusillade of musketry erupted from the shore, a sure sign that the approaching boats had been spotted. Moments later the battery opened fire, and three large columns of water erupted halfway between the British ships and the shore. The guns – almost certainly 32-pounders – were firing short. In reply, Pigot gave the order to open fire. Their broadsides lit up the bay, and while the British guns probably couldn't silence the battery, they certainly acted as a good distraction. In fact, Pigot soon discovered that the boats had already made it – the French musket fusillade was fired in response to seeing the attackers board the prizes. Soon a small flotilla of prize vessels was heading out to sea, towing the British boats behind them. By 4am they were all safely out of range of the French guns.

The mission had been a resounding success. The prizes had all been recaptured, and by mid-afternoon this convoy entered Môle Saint-Nicolas, escorted by Pigot's squadron. The total haul was nine vessels – a ship, three brigs, three schooners and two sloops. All but one of these vessels were American. Most of them were laden with provisions destined for Port-au-Prince. Now, thanks to Pigot, they would reach their destination, instead of their cargos replenishing the storehouses of Le Cap François. Vice-Admiral Parker was delighted, particularly as the whole operation had been carried out without a single British casualty. Best of all, the heroes of the hour were his two most favoured captains – Hugh Pigot and Robert Otway.

A few weeks later, Parker rewarded his favourite captains with another plum mission. After taking on stores, Pigot and Otway would put to sea again. This time they would cruise the waters of the Spanish Main – the Caribbean coast of South America – to hunt for Spanish prizes. By then, Robert Otway had changed ships. The *Mermaid* was due to head back to Britain for a major refit, and was therefore ordered home with the next homebound convoy. As the admiral was unwilling to part with his protégé, he arranged for Otway to exchange commands with Captain Newman of the 32-gun frigate *Ceres*, which had recently joined the Jamaica Station. Unfortunately for Otway, he found the *Ceres* a drunken, ill-disciplined lot. Clearly Captain Newman had been no flogging captain. Still, Otway hoped that during the cruise he could knock his poor-quality crew into shape.

The two frigates sailed from Môle Saint-Nicolas in mid-May, and by the end of the month they had picked up the coast of the Spanish Main near Cabo Codera, to the west of Caracas. Before leaving Saint-Domingue, a new master had joined *Hermione*. Edward Southcott was an experienced navigator, and he knew these waters well. So, armed with Southcott and the latest charts, Pigot expected no difficulty working his way along the coast. Once they could see the mountainous coast of Caracas province they headed east, with the two frigates just within sight of each other. They found nothing off La Guaira, or Puerto Cabello, 60 miles to the west. Hiding his disappointment from his crew, Pigot gave orders to veer off and head towards the Dutch island of Curaçao, 100 miles to the north-west. Pigot hoped to find better pickings in the bottleneck between the island and the mainland.

They never got there. Instead, some 25 miles to the north-west of Puerto Cabello lay Punta Tucacas. This headland marked the mouth of the small Gulf of Triste, near the modern beach resort town of Chichiriviche. Pigot planned to keep

about 12 miles to seaward of the point, which he expected
to pass during the morning of Wednesday 24 May. The only
hazard in these waters was the fringe of low-lying cays, or
mangrove-covered islands fringing the seaward entrance to
the gulf. On Tuesday night, Pigot made sure *Ceres* was on
station a quarter of a mile away to larboard, and then he
went to bed. At midnight the *Hermione*'s first lieutenant took
the watch. Everything was quiet, and Harris stood on the
quarterdeck, with two men on the wheel. Six lookouts were
posted about, either in the bows or the mastheads. It was a
pitch-dark night, and there was nothing out there to see.

The frigate was making 5 knots, with a light wind blowing
over her larboard quarter. Suddenly, just after 2am, Harris
thought he saw a darker line off the port bow. Could it be
land? He asked both quartermasters what they thought, and
one of them agreed with him. Harris decided to take no
chances. He sent someone to rouse the master, then ordered
the ship to be turned to starboard – towards the open sea.
As the frigate turned, the topmen of the watch sprang aloft
to haul the yards round. Slowly, the *Hermione* began to turn
away from the black line in front of them. Then, thinking
of the *Ceres* to port – hidden in the darkness – he ordered a
gun to be fired. It would warn her crew of the danger that lay
ahead. That done, Harris ordered 'All hands on deck!', and
went below to rouse the captain.

When Southcott, the master, came on deck he thought he
could see land too. Then Captain Pigot appeared, followed
by the frigate's other officers. The frigate was now heading
towards the north, and leadsmen in the bows reported that
the depth had been much less than anyone had expected.
Now, though, they were heading back into deeper water and

almost everyone could see three small cays off their larboard beam. It was now clear that Harris's quick thinking had spared the ship from disaster. With the frigate safe, Pigot began worrying about the *Ceres*. She was somewhere to larboard of them in the darkness, and much closer to the line of cays than they were. When they reached the 12-fathom line (72 feet of water), Pigot ordered the frigate to drop anchor. There they would wait out the night, hoping that Captain Otway had been able to keep his ship out of harm's way.

In fact, the crew of the *Ceres* hadn't seen the danger until it was too late. Captain Otway had been asleep, and his first lieutenant had the watch. The first he or his lookouts knew of the danger was a loud thud. Then the frigate stopped dead in the water. Before the watch on deck could spill the wind from the sails there were more grinding thuds from beneath them. It was clear they had hit a reef, and the ship was being driven further onto it. Otway raced on deck, along with most of the crew. He was confronted by a scene of pandemonium. All discipline seemed to have gone. Gradually, though, he and his officers began bringing things under control. Still, as Otway reported later, 'Little or no attention was paid to my orders.'

He ordered a boat to be lowered, ready to lay out a stern anchor to help drag them off the reef. However, a group of sailors commandeered it, and made off into the darkness. Others broke into the spirit locker, and were soon roaring drunk. All this time the waves kept pushing the ship further onto the reef. The carpenter was sent below to assess the damage, and reported the frigate was taking on water fast. The situation was quickly becoming desperate. Eventually, Otway found enough sober, willing men to man the pumps.

By this time the frigate was hard aground, so there was no immediate danger of sinking. The plan now was to pump out the water, plug the leaks and then try to float the *Ceres* off. For the moment, though, and with such an ill-disciplined crew, all Otway could really do was to wait for help from the *Hermione*.

When dawn broke, Pigot and his men finally saw the *Ceres* about 6 miles away. She was lying motionless, as if she was stuck on a reef. Pigot had already launched all of his boats, and began leading them towards the *Ceres*, sounding the depth as they went. He planned to bring the *Hermione* as close as he could to his consort. In the end, thanks to a reef, the *Hermione* couldn't get any closer than within 3 miles of her. Whatever help Pigot and his men could give would have to be done using the boats. When Pigot eventually came on board, Otway told him his frigate was still taking on water, and the pumps were barely coping. Otway's men were building a raft large enough to carry their heaviest anchor as their largest boat had already been stolen. The situation still looked bleak, but at least with the *Hermione*'s arrival, the men at the pumps could have a brief rest, some rum and a bite to eat.

More pumps were rigged, which in turn allowed the two ships' carpenters to get at the leaks. With these plugged and the water pumped out, they set about getting the *Ceres* off the reef. Clearly this involved lightening the ship. They could pump out the ship's water, dump her stores, or, if all else failed, jettison her guns and carriages, or even her masts and rigging. Whatever the material cost, they had to free the ship. In the end, Otway managed to refloat her by ditching most of his stores and water, her foremast and several of her guns. After a week of hard work, Pigot was satisfied that the *Ceres* was out of danger. So, he left Otway to it, and returned to Saint-Domingue to break the news to Vice-Admiral Parker. He also began hatching a plot to absolve himself of any blame for what had just happened. His subsequent actions would play a large part in what happened just a few months later.

6

The Floating Powderkeg

As the *Hermione* sailed back into Môle Saint-Nicolas, Captain Pigot began his calculations. He knew perfectly well that he was responsible for what had happened off the Gulf of Triste. As the commander of the two-frigate force, he was the one who had decided what course to steer that night. The *Hermione*'s master, Edward Southcott, had told him that in those waters off the coast of the gulf the local currents circled in a clockwise direction, which meant they would have pushed the ships towards the north-west. Pigot had ignored the advice, or forgotten it when he gave his orders. So, imperceptibly, *Hermione* and *Ceres* would have been pushed crabwise to larboard – towards the reef-lined entrance to the Gulf of Triste. However, Pigot had no intention of shouldering any blame for what had happened. He needed a scapegoat. As his frigate neared Saint-Domingue, he came up with a scheme which would pin the blame firmly on someone else. This ploy, though, would have dire consequences.

When Pigot reported to Vice-Admiral Parker on Friday 9 June he made sure to avoid mentioning his own shortcomings. He was also smart enough to avoid criticising Parker's other protégé, Captain Otway. Instead he hatched his plot with a lot more subtlety. First, he handed over three documents. The first was a description of the incident, while the second two were requests for a pair of court martials. The first was for the trial of the *Hermione*'s boatswain, Thomas Harrington, while the second was to try a deserter, Thomas Leech. So far Pigot hadn't revealed his full hand. He also passed on a similar report of the grounding from Otway, along with copies of the *Ceres*'s log entries for that night. In his report, Pigot went out of his way to praise the actions of Captain Otway, before speaking of his own culpability in his report's closing paragraph. He wrote: 'I feel great satisfaction in meeting any public investigation you might think proper to direct.'

Pigot clearly knew his mentor well. Parker immediately brushed off any suggestion that Pigot had been at fault. In fact, he was happy to absolve both of his favoured captains of any blame. Instead, Parker listened to Pigot when he offered up his scapegoat. In his report, Pigot had said he thought there had been some impropriety in setting the lookouts on board the *Hermione* that night, as the frigate had passed 'within pistol shot' of the mangrove-covered cays in the darkness. He blamed the officer-of-the-watch for this, and added that the grounding of *Ceres* 'is in great measure to be imputed to neglect'. In other words, he was pinning the whole thing on his own first lieutenant, John Harris. He, of course, was the very man who had saved the *Hermione* that night. Pigot even recommended that there should be a full inquiry. Effectively, this meant a court martial. Parker, eager to spare his two protégés, was more than happy to oblige.

According to the Admiralty's rules, the commander-in-chief of a fleet stationed overseas couldn't preside over a court martial. Instead, that task would fall to his deputy, Rear-Admiral Sir Richard Rodney Bligh. Normally the rear-admiral was stationed in Port Royal, as the two admirals didn't get on, but since Commodore Duckworth's departure, Bligh was at Môle Saint-Nicolas, on board his 74-gun flagship *Brunswick*. Sir Richard was duly ordered to try Lieutenant Harris of the *Hermione*, as well as the two others – the boatswain and the deserter. The hearing was set for the following week – Friday 16 June. None of the three men had any real chance to prepare themselves for what lay ahead. For Harris and Harrington, their careers lay on the line. For the deserter, the stakes were much higher.

On that Friday morning, a gun booming from the *Brunswick* as she swung at anchor off Môle Saint-Nicolas signalled the start of the trial. Four post captains sat with Bligh at the table in his great cabin, two on either side of him. The fleet's judge advocate sat at the end of the table on the admiral's right. He would act as the clerk for the court martial. A chair for witnesses stood in front of the table to the right of it, while another was placed on its left side for the accused. The court martial of Lieutenant Harris began with him being summoned, together with several witnesses. Sir Richard read the order from Vice-Admiral Parker to convene the court martial, and then ushered the accused and all but one of the witnesses from the cabin. He would begin by examining the first witness – the captain of the *Hermione*. After being sworn in, Pigot gave his own account of the incident – a version of the story which was designed to incriminate his first lieutenant.

He told how the *Hermione* had passed the cays without them being seen. He mentioned the current in the area, but insisted the course he had set hadn't placed the *Hermione* in danger. Sir Richard, though, wasn't easily deflected, and he quizzed Pigot extensively about the current, and whether he had left the watch officers with specific instructions. Pigot had to admit he hadn't. With that, the frigate's captain was dismissed from the court, and the *Hermione*'s master was called. He couldn't say how far away the cays were when they were sighted, nor could the master's mate, John Forbes. Both men confirmed, however, that their captain hadn't issued any particular orders that evening. It was all starting to look like negligence after all – but not on the part of Harris. This trend continued when the two quartermasters were questioned – the men on the wheel that night. Both of them revealed it had been Harris who had first spotted the cays, rather than the lookouts.

All through this, the accused was allowed to quiz the witnesses himself. It soon became clear that the charge of not keeping a good lookout was nonsense. So, with no more witnesses, Harris spoke in his own defence. His main declaration, though, was that if his counterpart on the *Ceres* had been as vigilant, then the grounding wouldn't have happened. That done, Harris was sent out of the cabin to await the court's decision. Pigot was already pacing the quarterdeck of the *Brunswick*, so it would have been an awkward time for both men. However, they didn't have to wait long for the court to consider their verdict. Within half an hour Harris was called back in, together with most of the witnesses, including Pigot. There, the judge advocate read out the verdict. He said: 'The court is of the opinion that the charge has not been proven against the prisoner.' Harris was in the clear. In fact, the court went on to praise Harris for his vigilance, and the part he had played in saving his ship.

So, Pigot's attempt to set Harris up as a scapegoat had failed. Worse, Lieutenant Harris had actually been praised for his actions, despite Pigot's testimony against him. Naturally, there was no chance of Harris remaining in his post. He was moved temporarily to the *Brunswick*, until another posting could be found. Meanwhile, on the *Hermione*, Pigot named his young protégé Samuel Reed as his new first lieutenant, while Archibald Douglas became the second lieutenant. The third lieutenant post was filled by Henry Foreshaw, a newly promoted midshipman sent over from Parker's flagship. At the same time, Parker also sent Pigot a new lieutenant of marines, Robert McIntosh. Therefore, for the first time since Pigot assumed command, the *Hermione* had her full complement of officers. But thanks to the court martial, the frigate had lost a highly competent first lieutenant. In his place was a very inexperienced one, a young man who owed his rank to patronage rather than to merit. The ship's company of the *Hermione* had already been divided before the *Ceres* ran aground. The two groups – the *Hermiones* and the *Successes* – had grown further apart during the court martial.

As one of the *Successes* put it later: 'There was a continual murmuring among the *Hermione*'s ship's company concerning his [Pigot's] followers'. The bad feeling was markedly increased by Pigot's persecution of his first lieutenant. Harris had been a popular officer, and had repeatedly spoken up for the men during Captain Wilkinson's time on board. To the *Hermiones* he had been one of their own, an officer who was seen as strict but fair, and who looked out for their welfare. Captain Pigot's charges against him were seen as grossly unjust, especially after the lieutenant's exemplary performance on the night of the grounding. By contrast, most of the *Hermiones* had little respect for Reed. What happened later that summer might well have been avoided if Harris had still been on board.

Harris's court martial wasn't the only one that Rear-Admiral Bligh presided over. The following day, the same court tried Pigot's boatswain, Thomas Harrington. He was a *Hermione* man, and it seems Pigot had taken an instant dislike to him. Harrison was probably a competent boatswain as, before he left, Captain Wilkinson had issued him with a certificate of good conduct. Under Pigot's command, however, Harrington had become a problem, and the charges against him ranged from sleeping on watch to insolence, drunkenness and insubordination. Even Lieutenant Harris had testified against him. So, the outcome was inevitable, and the court ruled that Harrington be dismissed from the ship. Many of the *Hermiones*, though, saw this as another example of victimisation against their shipmates. The real reason for his poor conduct was Harrington's disillusionment at serving a captain who loathed him.

The final court martial hearing was also a cut-and-dried affair. Thomas Leech had deserted from the *Success* in 1794, and had been recaptured the following year. Amazingly, Pigot had taken him back on board, after Leech promised not to desert again. He seems to have become one of Pigot's favourites. Then, in August 1796, he deserted once more, only to give himself up while on the run. He was taken back to Môle Saint-Nicolas and sent to the *Hermione*, where his old captain could deal with him. Strangely, in front of Bligh's court, Pigot testified to Leech's character. Leech's guilt was never in doubt, but now, thanks to Pigot's reference, he was sentenced to just three dozen lashes. Without his old captain's character reference, the outcome might have been very different. Leech might well have been hanged from the *Brunswick's* yardarm. This, of course, was seen by some of the *Hermiones* as yet another example of one of the old *Successes* getting preferential treatment.

After the trial, the *Hermione* was sent to Jamaica as the escort to a convoy. While lying off Port Royal, Pigot was delighted to see the *Ceres* being towed in and taken to the dockyard for repairs. When the two captains met, they must have both expressed relief at escaping censure. In fact, Otway was so grateful to Pigot that he presented his colleague with a silver teapot, a memento of the support he had given to Otway after the grounding.

For the trip back to Môle Saint-Nicolas, *Hermione* escorted the packet *Westmoreland*. They arrived back at their old anchorage in the afternoon of Tuesday 18 July. There, while Pigot and his men waited for their next mission, and the mail from the packet was distributed around the ships, Vice-Admiral Parker busied himself reading his bulky package of letters from the Admiralty. They brought word of a major mutiny at Spithead – the fleet anchorage off Portsmouth – but this had been 'happily terminated'.

In fact, the dispatches, dated 3 May 1797, were written prematurely. What the Admiralty's letter didn't say was that, shortly after it was sent, the mutiny spread to the Nore in the Thames Estuary. Altogether, over 16 ships-of-the-line at Spithead and 30 at the Nore were taken over by the mutineers. The fear was that these were inspired by French Revolutionary fervour, and that the rebellion would spread elsewhere. However, this wasn't the case at all. The mutineers were always careful to declare their loyalty. What they wanted wasn't liberty as the French saw it, but justice. Their demands were simple – improved pay and conditions, better-quality food, leave when in port and decent medical care. Even by the standards of the day these were fair demands. When the government acceded to some of them, the mutiny lost its momentum. In the end it petered out, and the crews returned to their duties. Only the mutiny's most radical ringleaders were punished.

In its letter, the Admiralty urged Parker to keep an eye out for any signs that this mutinous behaviour might spread to the Jamaica Station. In fact, it already had. On 19 April, the day after the Admiralty letters reached him, Parker drafted his own report to them. He said: 'A report prevails which I am very apprehensive is founded upon truth, that the crew of HM schooner *Maria Antoinette* mutinied, threw the lieutenant and another officer overboard, and have carried the schooner into Gonaives [Gonâve].' The schooner had been captured from the French in September 1793, when Commodore Ford's squadron arrived off Môle Saint-Nicolas. In French service she had been known as the *Convention Nationale*, but the British took her into service, and gave the schooner her old pre-revolutionary name. In early 1797 Lieutenant John McInerheny took command of her, and his brutish behaviour made life for his 36-strong crew a living hell.

Fed up with their young Irish officer's brutal regime, with its weekly floggings and random victimisation, a number of the crew took to mutiny. The sloop was in the Gulf of Gonâve at the time, on its way from Port Royal to Môle. During the night of 6/7 July, and led by the schooner's quartermaster, Robert Jackson, the mutineers broke open the schooner's armoury, then burst into their captain's cabin. McInerheny was dragged on deck at knifepoint, stabbed, then thrown overboard, to let the sharks finish him off. His second, a midshipman who tried to stop Jackson, was also bundled over the side. The remaining warrant officer and the five crew who remained loyal were thrown into the forepeak and held there under guard. After a brief debate, the mutineers decided to turn themselves over to the French. So, they headed for the nearby French-held port of Gonâve, on the coast of Saint-Domingue midway between Môle Saint-Nicolas and Saint-Marc.

What set the *Maria Antoinette* mutiny apart from those at Spithead and the Nore was its brutality. This was murder plain and simple, followed by an act of treason. The schooner's crew had been pushed so far that they felt they had had no alternative apart from bloody insurrection. Mutiny wasn't usually something that happened on a whim. It meant that if the rising was successful, then the mutineers could never return home to their friends or family. Instead they would spend the rest of their lives on the run, constantly looking over their shoulders. Once the rising began, there was no going back. What made the *Marie Antoinette* mutiny so shocking was that when it began almost all of the crew were willing to rise up. They then handed their vessel over to their nation's enemies. By contrast, the so-called mutinies at Spithead and the Nore had been more like strikes than risings.

Inevitably, news of the mutiny spread around the ships anchored off Môle. Most of the sailors might have sympathised with the mutineers, as they knew how a sadistic captain could drive his crew to the brink. This would have been particularly true on board the *Hermione*, where many of the men might have felt that they too were suffering under a brutal captain. Discipline had already suffered thanks to the court martial of

Lieutenant Harris, and his replacement by an inexperienced youth who wouldn't stand up to his captain. Word of the mutinies back home would also have reached the fleet, despite attempts by the officers to keep the news from their men. As the days passed, and no word came of the schooner's mutineers being recaptured, a number of the *Hermiones* – men who had never considered rebellion – might have begun to harbour mutinous thoughts.

Meanwhile, life went on. After her return to Môle Saint-Nicolas, the *Hermione* underwent a careening. That involved getting at the underside of her hull to scrape off the barnacles and marine growth growing there. In a dockyard this was a simple process, but here the crew had to do everything themselves. The frigate was secured to the quay and then heaved over using ropes and tackles so she lay almost on her side. Then the crew set to, scraping the hull clean below the waterline, before the ship was turned around so they could get at her other side. It was hard, gruelling work, with men working both on the quayside and on stages or platforms secured to the ship's side. In the bustle, a seaman managed to sneak away, and deserted the ship. Jacob Fulga had only been on board for four months, having been press-ganged from a merchant ship. His successful escape must have inspired many of his shipmates to try their own luck, if they ever got the chance.

Finally, on Saturday 12 August, Captain Pigot was given fresh orders. Once again he was to lead a patrol in the Mona Passage, this time with the *Hermione*, joined by the 32-gun frigate *Renommée*, and the 16-gun brig *Diligence*. Once again,

Pigot would be in charge of the venture. They were to cruise the passage for up to three months, intercepting any enemy warships, privateers or merchantmen they encountered. It was another plum mission for Pigot – clear proof that he still enjoyed the favour of Vice-Admiral Parker. Fortunately, the careening had been completed by then and the frigate lay at anchor again. Taking on water, provisions, powder and stores took the best part of four days, but by Wednesday the 16th everything was ready and Pigot took his leave of the admiral. Neither man knew it yet, but it was the last time they would see each other. At 4.30pm that afternoon, the three ships weighed anchor and headed out to sea. *Hermione's* last patrol had begun.

Their route would take them down through the Windward Passage, and then along the southern coast of Hispaniola. Once past the south-western tip of Saint-Domingue, the three warships spread themselves out and began their hunt. Every day brought more strange sails to be chased and stopped, but all of these turned out to be either British vessels or neutral American ones. Early on Thursday 31 August, Commander Mends of the *Diligence* reported that his junior lieutenant had died late the previous evening. The cause was probably the 'yellow jack', as his body was buried over the side less than an hour after his death. Captain Pigot heaved to and sent over his master's mate, John Forbes, to serve as Mends's acting second lieutenant. Forbes was a former *Success* man, and an experienced seaman, but he had also testified in support of Lieutenant Harris at the recent court martial. The suspicion is that Pigot wanted rid of him – an act which inadvertently saved Forbes's life.

The next day, the squadron arrived off the southern end of the Mona Passage. Now the mission could begin in earnest.

They were soon rewarded with their first prize, a Spanish schooner sailing between San Juan in Puerto Rico and Santo Domingo. Pigot contributed to her prize crew, but gave orders that a midshipman from *Diligence* should sail her to Port Royal, almost 500 miles away to the west. No more enemy ships were sighted for almost a week, until on Wednesday 6 September they came across a six-gun Spanish packet. *Diligence* gave chase, and returned with her as a prize the following morning, after having to fight a brief engagement to force the Spaniard to stop. She too was sent to Jamaica with another prize crew. Then, on Sunday 10 September, they fell in with a cartel vessel bound for Môle Saint-Nicolas, with exchanged British prisoners of war on board. Pigot pressed the few British seamen on board, then sent her on her way.

So far the cruise had been moderately successful, but the weather had been unpredictable. White squalls kept sweeping through the Mona Passage, and some of these were surprisingly heavy. On 13 September, one of them damaged the spars and rigging of the *Renommée* so badly she had to be sent back to Môle, escorted safely past Santo Domingo by the *Hermione*. Therefore, when he returned to his station, Pigot was left with just the *Hermione* and the smaller *Diligence*. These squalls were not really surprising, as the Mona Passage was one of the most dangerous stretches of water in the Caribbean. A combination of sudden and unpredictable storms, frequent thunderstorms, changeable currents, ferocious swells and of course these unexpected squalls made this a challenging area to patrol. Then there were the enemy-held shores on both sides, fringed with rocks, reefs and shoals. Because of this, Pigot ordered that his two vessels should reduce sail at night – a very sensible precaution.

So it was that on the evening of Thursday 14 September, both *Hermione* and *Diligence* were sailing with their lower sails furled, and only their topsails set. To reduce sail further, in line with Pigot's orders, these topsails were reefed – partly furled, leaving about half of the sail still set, and the rest bunched up and tied using reef points. That evening, the captain and the first lieutenant were on the quarterdeck, and it was Lieutenant Reed who gave the order to begin reefing the topsails for the night. Each of the three masts was served by its own crew of up to a dozen topmen – some of the most experienced and agile seamen on board – whose job it was to run out along the yard, bunch up the sail, and secure it using the rope reefing points, which were sewn in horizontal lines across each sail. The work of each of these three teams was supervised by one of the ship's midshipmen. That evening, Midshipman Casey was in charge of the mainmast hands, and watched them race aloft.

The 19-year-old David O'Brien Casey was an interesting young man. He had joined the navy in 1789 as a captain's servant on board the Sixth Rate frigate *Hyaena*. In May 1793, the *Hyaena* was captured by the 40-gun French frigate *Concorde* off Saint-Domingue, and her crew taken prisoner. Casey was released, though, and shipped to Jamaica on a cartel much like the one Pigot had just intercepted. Captain Hills of the *Hermione* took him on as a midshipman, and he remained on board during part of Captain Wilkinson's time in command. He was eventually transferred to the Third Rates *Raisonnable* and *Swiftsure*, both flagships of Vice-Admiral Parker. From there, he became an acting lieutenant on board the frigate *Ambuscade*. There, however, he fell foul of Captain Twysden, who tried him for negligence. Although the charge was dismissed, he had to leave the frigate, and so Pigot, who sat on the disciplinary hearing, head-hunted the experienced youngster for his own midshipman's berth.

Until now, Captain Pigot had treated Casey well. In fact, the youngster owed his career to his new commanding officer. As a former *Hermione* man, Casey was well liked by the crew, and his experience had stood him in good stead in recent months. He had performed well during the *Ceres* grounding, and it was his advice on the placing of the pumps that helped Captain Otway refloat his ship. His stock with his captain and shipmates seemed high. Suddenly, though, all of that was dashed away. That Thursday evening, as Lieutenant Reed gave his orders, and the topmen raced aloft to carry them out, Captain Pigot could be seen pacing the quarterdeck, looking agitated. Later, some accused him of being drunk. He was an extremely mercurial character though, and this could simply have been his own bad mood getting the better of him. He had been shouting at the men, telling them to work faster. It was Casey's misfortune that his topmen were working directly above the captain.

A topsail was reefed by two groups of sailors. The topmen raced aloft, then the focsclemen on the deck hauled round the topsail yards using ropes until they were lying parallel to the wind. That took any strain off the sail itself. That done, the focsclemen hauled on the tackles, which raised the sail; a bit like raising a blind. The sail would then become bunched up as it reached the upper yard. The topmen, strung out along the yard, would then tie the sail at the reef points, which were sewn into the sail at regular intervals along a reinforced panel called a reef band. Then the men on deck would haul the tackles and the whole thing would be repeated, until all the required lines of reef points had been secured. It was a simple enough operation in good weather, but a dangerous one. It became even harder when a strong wind was blowing, or the captain down below was yelling at the men to work faster. That was when Midshipman Casey's world fell apart.

Just as the first lieutenant was about to order the topmen down from aloft, Casey spotted something amiss. One of the reef points hadn't been tied. Casey ordered one of his mainmast topmen to go back out along the yard to tie it. However, this drew the attention of the captain, who spotted the untied reef point, and the topman edging along the yard to fix it. As Casey later described it, Captain Pigot 'appeared to be greatly excited ... and got into a violent passion'. The captain unleashed a volley of curses, all directed at the unfortunate midshipman. As Casey put it later, Pigot used 'very harsh language'. He demanded an explanation. When Casey, sited in the maintop, began calling down his own explanation, Pigot 'instantly launched out in the most abusive and un-officerlike language, calling me a damned lubber, a worthless good-for-nothing, that I never did anything right, and used many other severe expressions'. It was a full-scale dressing down.

However, that wasn't the end of it. Captain Pigot had overreacted, but these things happen from time to time. To humiliate one of his officers – a highly competent one – in front of his men was bad for discipline on board, but in itself it wasn't unheard of. What followed, though, broke the bounds of rational behaviour. Pigot's lack of self-control and wild, impulsive temper got the better of him. When the first lieutenant ordered the topmen to come down from aloft, Casey returned to the quarterdeck. There, standing in front of his captain, he suffered another ranting barrage of curses and insults. But this didn't stop Casey from trying to defend himself. No sooner had he started to speak than the captain erupted. Pigot, red with rage, and shaking, yelled out the words: 'Silence Sir, or I will instantly tie you up to the gun and flog you!'

The shock of Pigot's words ran through the officers and men on deck like an electric charge. It was almost unheard of to beat or whip a midshipman, unless it was a token punishment, to a very young one. To flog a senior midshipman of Casey's age and experience was unthinkable. Casey mumbled a reply, saying this was cruel and undeserved. Incensed, Pigot ignored him, instead yelling back that Casey was under arrest. With that, the shaken young officer was sent below to his berth in the gunroom. There, he was left alone while his captain returned to his own cabin to calm down. If truth be told, both men were now in an unenviable position. Pigot must have known he had overreacted, but to back down would mean an immense loss of face on board. Casey, threatened with a flogging for a minor failing by one of his men, realised that he had irrevocably lost Pigot's favour, and was now completely at the mercy of a man whose reputation for cruelty was well deserved.

Eventually, Pigot called the first lieutenant, the master and the purser to his cabin. All of them had been on deck, but none of them had directly witnessed the incident develop. All they saw was the explosive finale. Undeterred, Pigot then sent for Casey. When he arrived, Pigot told him that he couldn't court-martial Casey, as these three other officers hadn't seen what happened. He went on to praise Casey's character and conduct, and added that until then, he had treated Casey 'like one of his lieutenants'. Casey tried to apologise for any offence, but Pigot would have none of it. Instead, he made his judgement: 'You go on your knees tomorrow morning.' In other words, in front of the whole ship's company, Casey had to kneel in front of his captain and beg his forgiveness. With that, Casey was sent back to the gunroom.

Later, during the evening watch, Lieutenant Reed summoned Casey on deck. There, he tried to persuade the midshipman to do what the captain ordered. Casey indignantly refused. The next morning other officers tried the same tack, but Casey remained resolute. After all, he had nothing to apologise for. As for his fellow officers, Casey said of them that none of them tried to change Pigot's mind. In fact, 'they all appeared to be greatly in dread of him'. So, as dawn broke over the Mona Passage that Friday morning, the tension in the ship was palpable. This feeling increased during the forenoon watch, until, just before six bells – 11am – the pipe was made for 'All hands aft to witness punishment'. Once the whole crew were assembled, including Midshipman Casey, Captain Pigot opened his copy of the Articles of War, and began reading them out.

The navy's familiar secular litany of crime and punishment was well known to everyone on board, but their reading added solemnity to the occasion, and an aura of authority to the captain. Pigot had everyone's attention. Then, turning to Casey, who was standing by the capstan, the captain issued his demand: 'For your contemptuous and disrespectful conduct yesterday evening, I insist on your going down on your knees and begging my pardon.' Pigot must have been sure Casey would accede to his demand. Clearly he didn't know the young man very well. Casey replied, assuring his captain that he meant no insult, and begged his pardon. That wasn't enough for Pigot. He retorted: 'I insist that you go on your knees.' Once again, Casey refused. For a moment, Pigot hesitated. He then said – bizarrely – that had Casey acceded, then he would have despised him for it. With that, Pigot ordered the master-at-arms and sergeant of marines to 'strip him and seize him up'.

The unfortunate Midshipman Casey was stripped to the waist in front of the assembled crew, and then bent over and tied to the bars of the capstan. That done, the boatswain, William Martin, stepped forward, with his cat-o'-nine-tails at the ready. Pigot ordered him to give Casey a dozen lashes. And so it began, watched by a shocked and silent ship's company. All of them were well used to floggings. No records of Pigot's floggings during his time in command of *Hermione* have survived. However, we can tell from his record while in charge of the *Success*, and subsequent events on the *Hermione*, that floggings of this kind were almost certainly commonplace on board. None of them, though, had ever been given to a young gentleman. This flew in the face of everything that held their floating community together. The dozen lashes complete, Pigot ordered Casey to be cut down. He now stood there, at attention in front of his captain, with blood running freely down his back.

However, Captain Pigot hadn't finished. And he intended to finish with a flourish. As Casey stood before him, he demoted him – effectively stripping him of his status as a young officer and gentleman, and reducing him to the level of the ordinary seamen who had witnessed his humiliation. Pigot added that Casey was to leave the ship at the first opportunity. Later, Pigot reportedly claimed that the very public humiliation of David Casey gave him more pain than anything else in his life. That morning, standing in front of his bloodied but unbowed subordinate, Pigot showed no sign of remorse. In contrast, after Casey slung his hammock forward of the midshipman's berth in the gunroom, the frigate's officers and men all showed him kindness. The officers, though, couldn't be seen to speak openly to him. None of them, it seems, was prepared to stand up to Pigot, despite his disgraceful treatment of one of their own.

The flogging of Midshipman Casey marked a real turning point on board the *Hermione*. Tensions had already been running high for some time, with friction between the *Successes* and the *Hermiones*. We can infer that Captain Pigot continued to flog and start his men for minor breaches of discipline, just as he had on the *Success*. For a time, Lieutenant Harris had helped bridge the growing divide between captain and crew. He alone had been willing or able to reason with him, and to advise restraint. His court martial was seen as an act of great injustice by the *Hermione*'s crew, and an example of their captain's ill will towards his officers and crew. When Harris was transferred off the ship, the last check on Pigot's behaviour had been removed. Now, the public humiliation of Casey exposed their captain for what he was – a petty and vindictive tyrant. The crew of the *Hermione* were fast approaching their breaking point. One more incident would tip them over the edge.

7

Murder in the Night

In the days that followed the flogging of Midshipman Casey even the least observant man on board could tell a new mood had settled over the ship. The men seemed resentful and sullen, and the usual joking and larking about had stopped. So had the sound of fiddle music which was usually heard from the lower deck after supper; instead, the men scowled, or whispered to each other. In the sick bay, a growing number of men reported sick with ailments, some showing the signs of the onset of scurvy. Others were simply trying to shirk their duties. It was clear that something was brewing. The only man who seemed oblivious to all this was Captain Pigot. Meanwhile, as *Hermione* and *Diligence* resumed their joint patrol of the Mona Passage, the routine of the ship continued as usual. The ship's bell sounded, the watches changed, the meals were prepared and eaten, and the crew continued their patrol. The *Hermione*, though, was like a clock whose mainspring had snapped.

———

Other little things had changed, too. In his cabin off the wardroom, the new marine officer, Lieutenant Robert McIntosh, was dying, smitten by yellow fever. All the ship's surgeon could do was to give him opium, to ease his suffering. So, command of the frigate's marines – traditionally a red-coated barrier between the officers and men – fell to their sergeant, John Plaice, who was less inclined than the lieutenant to risk his life in defence of the captain. For several days the patrol was uneventful, largely because the weather was bad, and visibility was poor. Dawn on Wednesday 20 September brought a slight improvement, though, and Pigot would have been hopeful that an enemy merchant ship or privateer would stumble across their path. At 11am, a strong breeze sprang up from the north-east, and the visibility improved. Half an hour later a signal broke out on *Diligence*'s masthead – a strange sail had been spotted to the north-east.

Pigot ordered the signal 'General Chase' hoisted, and both vessels turned towards the north. However, the *Diligence*, 3 miles off the frigate's starboard bow, was closer to the stranger than *Hermione*, and she could sail closer into the wind. So, the chase began. By noon the *Diligence* was well ahead of the frigate, barely in sight. At 1.15pm she signalled that the chase was an American, and by 2pm *Diligence* had overhauled her and, running his guns out, Commander Mends ordered the stranger to heave-to. When her master came on board, Mends's assessment was confirmed – she was a neutral – an American merchant schooner from Rhode Island, heading home from the Windward Islands. So, Mends let her go, and signalled the news to *Hermione*, still several miles away to the south. Pigot ordered Mends to rejoin him, and then the two warships turned away to the south-west – heading back

Captain Hugh Pigot of the *Hermione*, c.1797.
Although a good seaman, he had a volatile temper
and a brutal reputation.
(Stratford Archive)

Vice-Admiral Sir Hyde Parker,
Commander-in-Chief of the Royal Navy's
Jamaica Station.
(Stratford Archive)

A Royal Naval post captain commanded his ship
with absolute authority. He could make his ship a
happy one, or a living hell.
(Stratford Archive)

A British sailor of the period. Most of the
Hermione's crew were experienced seamen in their
20s or early 30s.
(Stratford Archive)

Toussaint L'Ouverture, the charismatic leader of the slave revolt on Saint-Domingue. Artist unknown.

(Hulton Archive/Getty Images)

Port-au-Prince, the capital of Saint-Domingue, and a deadly breeding ground for yellow fever.

(Boston Public Library)

Môle Saint-Nicolas, the Royal Navy's heavily fortified forward base in Saint-Domingue.

(Stratford Archive)

HMS *Hermione*, as she appeared under Spanish colours at the time of her cutting out.
A hand-tinted aquatint based on an original watercolour by Thomas Whitcombe.
(Corbis Historical/Getty Images)

A flogging on board a British warship during this period. On the *Hermione*, though, floggings were
carried out over the capstan. Engraving by George Cruikshank.
(Hulton Archive/Getty Images)

Port Royal, Britain's premier naval base in the Caribbean, and the site of the first trial and execution of the mutineers. View of Port Royal, Jamaica. Oil painting by Richard Paton.
(© National Maritime Museum, Greenwich, London)

A meeting of the Board of the Admiralty, in Whitehall, London, during this period. It was from here that the manhunt for the mutineers was directed. Print by Augustus Charles Pugin.
(Hulton Archive/Getty Images)

A British Sixth Rate frigate of 28 guns, similar to HMS *Surprise*. Illustration by William Mitchell from Charles Low, *Her Majesty's Navy* (London 1890–1893).

(Hulton Archive/Getty Images)

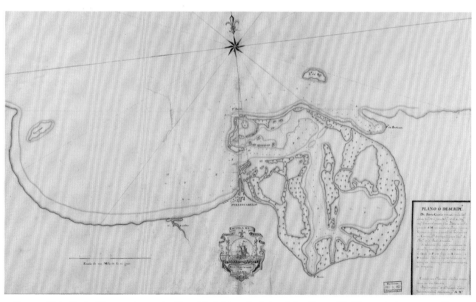

Puerto Cabello in Venezuala on the Spanish Main, the lair of the *Santa Cecilia*, and the scene of her dramatic cutting out. Denias, Francisco, and Real Escuela De Navegación, *Plano o descripcn. de Puerto Cavello*, 1757.

(Library of Congress)

Captain Edward Hamilton, who led the daring
cutting out of the *Hermione* at Puerto Cabello.
(Stratford Archive)

The cutting out of the frigate *Hermione* from
Puerto Cabello harbour. Artist unknown.
(Universal Images Group/Getty Images)

The cutting out of the *Hermione* was carried out from six small boats, with each crew allocated a
specific part of the frigate to assault.
(Stratford Archive)

A Royal Naval midshipman of the period. On the *Hermione*, one of these trainee officers was murdered by the mutineers, while another joined them.
(Stratford Archive)

A lieutenant in the Royal Navy, *c.*1797. All three of the *Hermione*'s lieutenants were brutally murdered during the mutiny.
(Stratford Archive)

A Royal Naval warrant officer of the period. Illustration by William Mitchell from Charles Low, *Her Majesty's Navy* (London 1890–1893).
(Hulton Archive/Getty Images)

A ship's carpenter. On board the *Hermione* the carpenter was 24-year-old Robert Price, a Welshman, who would later testify against the mutineers.
(Stratford Archive)

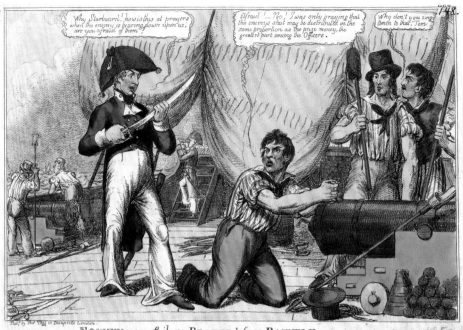

Why Starboard! how is this at prayers when the enemy is bearing down upon us; are you afraid of them?

Afraid! — No! I was only praying that the enemys shot may be distributed in the same proportion as the prize money, the greatest part among the Officers.

Why don't you sing Amen to that, Tom.

EQUITY or a Sailors PRAYER before BATTLE. *Consedcate of the Battle of Trafalgar.*

In this cartoon from the period, a British sailor prays that, in battle, the enemy shot will be proportioned in the same way as prize money – with most of it going to the officers. Charles Williams, *Equity, or a Sailor's Prayer before Battle*, 1805.
(The Art Institute of Chicago)

Portsmouth Point, now Old Portsmouth, where some of the last of the mutineers were caught.
Print by Thomas Rowlandson.
(The Metropolitan Museum of Art, New York)

to their old search area off the southern end of the Mona Passage.

Captain Pigot was clearly in a bad mood that day. He had been chiding his officers and men, as if they could make the frigate sail faster than she was already. At 4pm – the start of the dog watches – *Diligence* was back on station, and the two vessels were under easy sail, heading towards the Isla Saona, off the south-eastern corner of Hispaniola. Then, almost two hours later, a sudden squall could be seen, racing towards them from the north-east. Pigot, standing on the quarterdeck, ordered that the topsails be reefed. On all three masts, the young and agile topmen raced aloft, then out along the topsail yards. It was the same evolution that Midshipman Casey had overseen just six days before. By the time the men were working their way out along the yard the frigate was already rolling heavily. They began bunching up the heavy canvas in their hands as fast as they could, but it wasn't good enough for Pigot.

He began yelling and cursing at the men on all three masts, before leaning back and staring intently at the mizzen topmen, hurriedly lashing the sails at their reefing points, some 50 feet above his head. Reaching for his brass speaking trumpet, he raised it to his mouth, then bellowed out 'I'll flog the last man down!' The topmen froze, hurriedly finished their lashings, then scrambled back along the mizzen topyard towards the mast. Suddenly, one of the men lost his footing, and fell screaming towards the deck. A split second later two more also began to fall. The first of them struck the deck with a sickening thud, just a few yards from where Pigot was standing, still clutching his speaking trumpet. A second later, the two other topmen smacked into the deck. One of them,

Peter Bascomb, a young black sailor, landed on top of the master, Edward Southcott, who was standing nearby. The two men collapsed to the deck, as the helpless ship's company looked on in horror.

All three topmen were killed outright, their bodies crushed by the fall, their limbs jutting out at impossible angles amid spreading pools of blood. The master had been knocked unconscious, but he was still alive. The men standing nearby rushed to help him up. But Captain Pigot showed no contrition for the fatal accident his orders had caused. Quite the contrary. Instead, he looked disdainfully at the three broken bodies, then turned and looked for the boatswain. Seeing him, he barked out his next order: 'Throw the lubbers overboard!' Almost everybody on the deck or in the masts heard him, and stopped what they were doing, too stunned to continue. The boatswain remained frozen in shock. However, overhead, the mizzen topmen could be heard muttering in protest, and glaring angrily down at the deck. This was too much for Pigot. Ignoring the boatswain, he turned to his assistants Thomas Jay and Thomas Nash, standing just below the mizzen mast.

Captain Pigot then yelled out another horrific order – his third in just over a minute. Pointing up to the mizzen mast, he shouted: 'Boatswain's mates! Boatswain's mates! – Start all these men!' Recovering from their shock, the two young men had no option. They raced up the mizzen shrouds, one up each side, and when they reached the mizzen top they pulled out the knotted lengths of rope they each carried tucked in their belts. Edging onto the yard – one to port, the other to starboard, they began laying their starters across the heads and backs of the topmen. They couldn't protect themselves as they had to grip on to the yard or risk plunging to the deck like their shipmates. Even this wasn't enough for Pigot. His next order was that the boatswain should take the names of all of the mizzen topmen. His appetite for vengeance still wasn't sated. He ordered them all to be flogged the following morning.

As the topmen gathered angrily in the waist, they watched the boatswain and his mates carry each of their dead shipmates to the side of the quarterdeck, then pitch the bodies over the side. After splashing into the sea, they could be seen bobbing in the wake before sinking from view. The entire crew were still stunned by what they had just seen. In quick succession their captain had brutally given orders to flog the last man down – a threat they all knew he would carry out. Then, after this reckless order had caused the horrific deaths of three young men, Pigot had followed this by revealing his utter disregard for them, ordering their bodies to be callously thrown over the side like cattle. To add insult to injury, he had called these men 'lubbers', despite them being some of the best seamen on board. Then, after ordering their shipmates to be beaten, he promised to top this act of cruelty by ordering a mass flogging the next day. For most of the *Hermiones*, the tyrannical Pigot had gone a step too far.

With hindsight, it is easy enough to see that Pigot's fate was decided that evening. That night, those men not on watch would have discussed what they had seen, and slowly, horror would have turned to anger. From the testimony of men who were there, we know that there was talk of mutiny that night, and even of seizing the ship, to spare the backs of the mizzen topmen. In the end, though, the night passed without incident. Nevertheless, it was clear that discipline had broken down, and men who just a few weeks before had been resigned to living under their capricious and sadistic captain were now openly talking about killing him. But mutiny was a step that wasn't taken lightly. Afterwards, there would be no going back – no forgiveness by the navy, no return to Britain, and no happy reunion with family and friends. Although the minds of many were already made up, mutiny was such a drastic step that the men needed time to take it all in.

At dawn on Thursday 21 September 1797, *Hermione* was around 25 miles to the north-east of the Isla Mona, halfway between Santo Domingo and Puerto Rico. The winds were light but variable, swinging from the north-east to the north-west and back again. At 10.30am, just before all hands were called to witness punishment, signal flags flurried to the masthead of the *Diligence*, a dozen miles away to the north. Another sail had been sighted to the north-east. Pigot immediately ordered a 'general chase', and the two warships turned towards their prey. Any thoughts that this might have spared the mizzen topmen were soon dashed. After the *Hermione* steadied on her new course, and the topmen were back on deck, Pigot gave the order and the marine drummer sounded the call to muster. With that, the two boatswain's mates passed through the ship, ordering all hands to muster in the waist. Pigot was determined to have his mass flogging.

In all, 13 mizzen topmen were gathered by the capstan – all of the men who had survived the events of the previous evening. Once again, Pigot began by reading out the now deeply familiar litany of the Articles of War – a necessary precursor to any flogging. By now, though, the crew had become so brutalised that they knew every line by heart. Next, under the direction of the master-at-arms and the boatswain's mates, the men were led forward one by one – in alphabetical order – stripped to the waist, and lashed to the spars of the capstan. Then, taking it in turns, the two boatswain's mates gave them 12 lashes. By the time the last of the 156 blows had been struck, even Pigot would have been aware of the mood of the assembled ship's company. Many would have found it impossible to hide their anger and seething resentment for such an undeserved punishment. For some, it was the catalyst that turned their barely hidden rage into something much more deadly.

As the floggings went on, many of those watching the spectacle would have been largely unmoved by the brutality of it – they were used to that. No, it was the randomness of the punishment that kindled their anger. After the horrors of the previous evening, especially the throwing of the three bodies over the side, this mass flogging served to confirm their worst fears. Their captain was out of control. If these hard-working seamen could be flogged, and their shipmates terrorised so much that they fell to their deaths, then nobody on board was safe. Even those who had enjoyed Captain Pigot's protection would have felt the same way. Pigot had gone too far, and unless he was stopped, they would all suffer. The hands were dismissed, though, and the daily routine of a frigate at sea continued. But by now things were different. Although there were few visible signs of it, discipline on board had finally broken down. Self-preservation was all that remained.

Midshipman Casey was one of the few who didn't witness the mass flogging. He was confined to the gunroom. Later, he described it as 'a very severe punishment, I believe twelve or fourteen, took place in the usual way, at the public place of punishment'. The whole business had taken the best part of an hour. It only took around 40 seconds to administer each set of a dozen lashes. Then the man was unbound from the capstan spars, and the next one led forward. It was like a production line of inhumanity, with the master-at-arms, the boatswain and the boatswain's mates overseeing its smooth operation. So, every four or five minutes, a new young back would be laid open, until the pristine deck was flecked with blood. Pigot would have insisted that the punishment was completed by noon, as that was when the ship's bell was rung, marking the official start of a new day on board.

Pigot and Reed, and probably one of his remaining young midshipmen, would have been keen to take their noon sighting – using their sextants to measure the height of the sun at its zenith. Then they would have gone below, each separately using their readings to compute the ship's position. Normally, the master would have taken the noon sight, but he was still in his cot, recovering from his injuries. The bell also marked the start of the afternoon watch, and with it a change of the men on duty. The business of chasing that strange sail continued. A signal from *Diligence*, now several miles ahead of the frigate, revealed the chase was a privateer – a schooner, therefore probably French or Spanish. A little after noon the wind veered round to the north, and at 2.30pm they tacked, so that they were now following the privateer towards the north-east. They tacked again at 6pm, but the light breeze wasn't helping, so there was no real chance of catching her before nightfall.

Darkness came early in those latitudes. So, shortly before the change of watch at 8pm, the doubled-up lookouts were recalled from the mastheads. It was getting too dark for them to make out the privateer, over a dozen miles away to the north-east, although *Diligence* was halfway between the two, and the lookouts who took over for the evening watch were still able to make out her lights ahead of them, in the spreading darkness. At 8pm, Lieutenant Douglas handed over to the new officer-of-the-watch, Lieutenant Foreshaw, then retired to the wardroom to have his supper. The ship seemed to be settling down for the night, but then 30 minutes later Pigot ordered Foreshaw to call the other watch. He had realised that there was a good chance the privateer would try to work her way past them in the darkness. Therefore, he decided to split his forces – keeping *Diligence* in close pursuit, while tacking *Hermione*, then heading off towards the north-west under easy sail.

Tactically, this made perfect sense. It spread their net wider, and if the privateer tried to head south again, then it was likely she would try to avoid the dangerous looming shore of Puerto Rico in the darkness, and instead wear around to the west – towards the western side of the channel. If she did, with luck, *Hermione* might be able to find her there at dawn. As the light faded he signalled Commander Mends in the *Diligence*, telling him of his plan. While the men not on watch went below to rig their hammocks, Pigot remained on deck, just in case the privateer put in an appearance. It never did though, and at 10.30pm he went below, leaving Foreshaw in charge of the ship. However, before retiring he visited the gunroom to see how the injured master was coming along. Pigot had already given his night orders to Foreshaw and Reed, but he shared them with Southcott too. That done, he acknowledged the marine sentry outside the door, and went into his great cabin.

It was now around 10.45pm. Waiting for Pigot was his steward, John Jones, who helped the captain undress and change into his long white nightshirt. Then, after sipping a glass of wine, Pigot retired to his night cabin, just forward of the great cabin on the ship's larboard side. On *Hermione*, his cabins were really just one large space, divided into a suite of rooms by painted thick canvas screens. His duty done, Jones walked into the coach – a matching compartment on the starboard side, where he slung his hammock beside the captain's dining table. This led directly to the one door in or out of the captain's quarters. That was where Private Andrew McNeil stood guard, until he was relieved at midnight. Overhead on the quarterdeck, Lieutenant Foreshaw stood watch, accompanied by the master's mate, William Turner, who commanded the seamen of the watch, and the helmsman on the wheel, Thomas Osborn.

Below them in the waist were two lookouts, James Barnett to larboard and James Irwin to starboard. Barnett was one of the men who had been flogged that morning. Behind them, guarding the water butt, was Private Robert Newbold. Above them, in the tops of the three masts, were the seamen of the watch, who in theory were waiting for orders to take in or set more sail. Up there with them was a midshipman, John Wiltshire, who should really have been in his hammock in the gunroom. Instead, for some unknown reason, he was in the foretop. Perhaps he had an inkling of what was about to happen, and had decided to keep well out of the way. All in all, it looked like a normal night at sea on board the *Hermione*. In fact, things were far from normal. Down below, in the crowded and fetid lower deck, forward of the mainmast, a handful of men were preparing to rise up in bloody mutiny.

That evening, the hands who weren't on watch were talking among themselves, keeping their voices low to avoid drawing attention. Not all of them were intent on mutiny – far from it. For most of them, this would have been a line they weren't prepared to cross. It took a lot to sever all ties with the past – with family, loved ones and even country. A few, though, had already crossed that line, and were deciding what to do next. At 9pm – two bells in the first (or evening) watch – the order 'Lights Out' was passed through the ship. That meant all lanterns had to be doused, and the men were expected to climb into their hammocks and go to sleep. After all, at midnight the starboard watch would be called, and in theory the men needed to grab what sleep they could. But that night few of the men would have slept. Even if they weren't directly involved in planning a mutiny, many would have either known about it or would have sensed that trouble was brewing.

Some time after 'Lights Out' was called, James Allen, the Irish-born teenage servant to Lieutenant Douglas, broke into the gunroom spirit store, with the help of the gunroom steward William Anderson. He was just 11 years old, and hailed from Kent. Together, they filled a bucket full of rum from the gunroom cask and smuggled it forward to the forecastle. There, a small group of men had gathered, out of sight of the officer-of-the-watch and out of earshot of their shipmates, crammed together in the hammock-filled lower deck below their feet. Apart from the two boys, five men stood around the bucket. Two of them, Scots Gunner James Bell and topman John Smith from Yorkshire, were former *Successes*, and in their early 20s. Two more topmen, teenager David Forester from Kent and Joe Montell, an Italian, were there, together with John Farrel, a seaman from New York. According to witnesses, they soon became quarrelsome, as the rum took its hold.

Even without the stolen rum, this assembly was illegal, and if the officer-of-the-watch had found out, he would have roused the marines and arrested every one of them. This was a serious offence. By this stage, though, none of the assembled men were worried about that. They were all past caring. Fuelled by the rum, the muttered conversation became increasingly deadly. Soon all of them were committed: they would see the mutiny through. A few slipped below to gather some of their trusted shipmates – men who could be relied on to join them. Shortly after, 18 men were gathered there in the darkness of the forecastle. Now any talk about whether to rise up had ceased. The discussion was on how best to set about it. What they had to do now was to seize hold of weapons and rush the captain's cabin. Once the mutiny started, they were sure that their more reluctant shipmates would follow their lead and help them finish the job.

Enough cutlasses for the task were kept in the gunner's store located at the forward end of the lower deck, and therefore within reach. Probably Bell and the two boys broke into the store, and brought the weapons to the mutineers. By then their shipmates would have seen Captain Pigot go below, and so all they had to do was to stand by for the right moment. They waited until the ship's bell struck six bells – 11pm. It would be an hour before the change of watch, and when it was called, their assembly would be discovered. So the time had come to act. After arming themselves, and hurriedly exchanging last-minute instructions, they crept down onto the lower deck, and edged their way aft, between the hammocks of their shipmates. Some of the men there would have felt the mutineers brush past them, or saw them as they crept by, cutlass in hand. If they did, they kept quiet. Then the mutineers silently climbed through the hatch and onto the upper deck. This was their moment.

A knot of men rushed forward, taking Private McNeil by surprise. One second he was standing there, musket at his side, bayonet fixed, and counting the minutes until he was relieved, the next he was facing a small mob. One of them lashed out with his cutlass, slamming McNeil across the head with the flat of its blade. He fell to the deck, and others struck him too as he lay there. Before he lost consciousness, he heard a voice he recognised. It was John Jackson, a black sailor, and one of the crew of the captain's barge. Before everything went dark, he heard Jackson whisper to others to leave the marine alone. He then added: 'we'll go in and murder the captain'. Several of the men were armed with axes, and with that they began hacking at the door. Less than a minute later it splintered and swung open, watched by a fear-struck Jones, the captain's steward, tucked up in his hammock.

The mutineers ignored him as they ran past. In his night cabin, Captain Pigot had heard the commotion and struggled out of his hanging cot. Moments later, the mob burst through the door. Pigot didn't have time to grab his sword hanging on a hook on the bulkhead. Instead he grabbed a dirk – a small dagger – and turned to face his assailants, dressed only in his long white nightshirt. It was dark in the cabin, and this probably gave Pigot a momentary edge. The men could also see the glint of steel in his hand, which would have checked them for a second or two. Pigot yelled out for help, hoping the shout would reach the officer-of-the-watch on the quarterdeck above his head. He yelled out 'Where are my bargemen' as his assailants began moving closer. A voice cried out 'Here are your bargemen – what do you want with them, you bugger?' It was 24-year-old Hadrian Poulson who spoke, one of his chosen men of the barge crew whom Pigot hoped would protect him.

It was David Forester who struck the first blow, slashing the captain with his cutlass. Pigot stepped back and skewered his assailant in the leg. Then others found their courage, and began slashing or jabbing at Pigot, while others chopped down his cot, to get a better swing at him. Chairs were flung aside, and soon Pigot was surrounded. He was badly wounded at this point, his nightgown covered in blood. Still, he kept fighting. When the American seaman John Farrel came too close, Pigot stabbed him through the hand with his dirk. Seconds later though, Johann Phillips, a German-born sailmaker, jabbed at Pigot with the point of his cutlass, stabbing him through the stomach. It was a fatal blow. Pigot fell to his knees, then collapsed over the 12-pounder gun and carriage which took up much of the cabin. Faint from his wounds, he passed out, leaving the gaggle of mutineers uncertain of what to do next.

Pigot's shouts had indeed reached the ears of Lieutenant Foreshaw. Moments later, the lieutenant saw Private McNeil appear at the companionway, calling for him. When Foreshaw asked what was going on, McNeil replied: 'Sir! Some men have broken into the cabin! I think they're murdering the captain!' Until all this erupted, it seems that Henry Foreshaw had no inkling that a mutiny was under way. He soon found out though. He barked an order to the master's mate, William Turner, standing close by: 'Go down and see what's causing the noise in the cabin.' Turner glared back at him disdainfully, and retorted: 'If you want to know, you can go down yourself!' At that moment, with his normally responsible deputy of the watch turning on him, Foreshaw must have realised that the last vestiges of discipline had gone.

Foreshaw's only hope now was to find help. Desperate, he turned to the helmsman at the wheel, Thomas Osborn, and ordered him to steer towards the *Diligence*. He had seen her lights a few miles away only a few minutes before. Foreshaw's order had been clear: 'Put the helm up – wear the ship and steer for the *Diligence*.' The reply of the usually reliable helmsman, though, must have chilled him to the bone. Osborn spat back: 'I'll see you damned first.' Furiously, the lieutenant lashed out, striking Osborn's head. The helmsman, staggered, but kept gripping the wheel. He called for help, and seconds later it came. Several men were still lurking in the forecastle and they rushed aft, passing the captain's steward on their way to the quarterdeck. Jones, who had slunk away from the mutineers in the cabin, reckoned there were about 12 or 14 of them. Some of the men seized hold of the officer-of-the-watch, while the rest milled around, wondering what to do next.

Osborn's cry for help had also been heard by several of the mutineers in the great cabin, where they too were debating what their next move would be. Private McNeil had sneaked back down to have a look in, and saw the figure of the captain, propped against the larboard gun 'with his shirt torn and his body all over with blood'. A group of them raced up the companionway, passing McNeil as they went. These included Thomas Nash and Thomas Jay, the boatswain's mates who had started the topmen the day before, and flogged them that morning. Even more surprising was Patrick Foster, the captain's coxswain, and commander of his barge crew. He was a former *Surprise* man, a hand-picked favourite, chosen to accompany Pigot when he moved from the *Success* to the *Hermione*. Now, the 30-year-old coxswain from Waterford in Ireland had turned on his captain. On the quarterdeck, John Smith and James Bell were already holding Lieutenant Foreshaw when the others arrived.

It was clear that there were two groups of mutineers – those who had rushed aft from the forecastle, who were less enthusiastic about using violence, and the ones who had already attacked Pigot, and who probably felt they now had nothing to lose. The first group, led by Smith and Bell, had already told Foreshaw his life would be spared. The newcomers, led by Nash and Farrel, seemed hell-bent on killing him. When someone – probably Smith – asked what they planned to do with the young officer, Nash snarled back: 'Throw the bugger overboard.' Hearing that, Foreshaw began pleading for his life, reminding the mutineers that he had a young wife and three children at home. Jones, the captain's steward, heard him beg to be spared until morning, but none of the mutineers seemed to be listening. Instead, when the 16-year-old topman David Forester grabbed the officer from behind, the second group of mutineers closed in.

They began slashing at Foreshaw with their cutlasses and axes. The young officer wrenched himself free of Forester's grasp, and tried to defend himself with his arms. The men kept slashing and hacking at him, until he staggered back, coming up against the side of the ship. He struggled up and onto the bulwark and then fell over the side. That meant that the mutineers now had control of the ship. With that, Nash and five others went back down the companionway to the captain's cabin. They went into the night cabin, where, amazingly, they found that Pigot was still alive. He was leaning against his couch, his body covered in blood. In his New York accent, Farrel exclaimed: 'You bugger! Ain't you dead yet?' A defiant Pigot, shakily holding his dirk out in front of him whispered back: 'No you villain – I'm not.' The foremost of the mutineers – Farrel, Forester, Nash, Montell, Poulson and William Crawley, an Irishman – were all well-armed, and at that moment four of them began circling their wounded captain.

Seeing his three shipmates hesitate, Crawley cried: 'What four against one and still afraid?' With that he lunged forward and slashed at Pigot with his boarding axe. Spurred into action, the others leaped in, and Farrel sliced his cutlass into Pigot's already blood-soaked head. The captain sank down onto the deck, then struggled to get up again. He was begging for mercy now, but it didn't do any good. Armed with Private McNeil's musket and bayonet, Montell lunged at Pigot and sank the bayonet into his chest. With that, he said: 'You've shown no mercy yourself – Therefore you deserve none.' Pigot fell to his knees again, dropping his dirk. He looked up, and through a mask of blood he recognised one of his assailants. It was Forester, the teenage topman. Pigot exclaimed: 'David Forester – are you against me too?' These were his last words. The Irish youth replied: 'Yes I am you bugger!', and stabbed Pigot with his cutlass. This was probably the final killing blow.

Now the mutineers had to get rid of the body. They dragged Pigot's blood-soaked corpse to the stern windows, while a few of their shipmates broke the glass. Once the hole was big enough, several of the men picked up the body and tipped it through the stern window and into the sea, several feet below. At least one of them later claimed he still heard Pigot's cries as the body disappeared into the darkness behind the frigate's luminescent wake. The great cabin was a shambles, with broken glass, overturned furniture and a huge bloody trail stretching from the night cabin to the stern windows. But the mutineers didn't stand around to gloat. Instead, they hurried back on deck to see what was happening elsewhere in the ship. After all, they might have killed their captain and seized the quarterdeck, but the rest of the ship's officers were still very much alive. Most of the crew hadn't risen up with them. So, while they currently had the upper hand, things could change very quickly.

From the attack on the marine sentry to the death of the captain, the whole rising had taken no more than eight minutes. However, all the commotion would have alerted the officers, whose wardroom was directly below the captain's cabin, and that was the mutineers' next problem. One of the first to react was the master, Edward Southcott. Despite his injuries he struggled out of his cot and, still wearing his nightgown, he clambered onto a table in the centre of the gunroom, where an open skylight led to the upper deck. He began pulling himself through it, as for him it was the quickest way up. He later recalled that he had no idea the noise was caused by men seizing control of the ship. On the deck, he was spotted by one of the mutineers, Richard Redman, who exclaimed: 'Here's one of the buggers coming up!'

The 24-year-old cockney grabbed a trailspike from a nearby gun carriage and began beating the master's face and hands with it. Southcott grunted and fell back onto the table, before rolling off it onto the deck of the gunroom. He lay there, winded and injured, as other officers and midshipmen began to stir themselves. In the gunroom, the main area with its dining table lay amidships, and was flanked by small officer's cabins – each walled off using canvas screens. The dying lieutenant of marines lay in one, and the first lieutenant in another. The master, the second and third lieutenants and the surgeon all had their own cabins there. Further forward, divided by a screen, was the lair of the midshipmen and master's mates. Here too were the small cabins of the carpenter, the gunner, the boatswain and the captain's clerk. If these officers, midshipmen and warrant officers could gain the support of the marines and loyal members of the ship's company, they might still quell the rising.

One of the first to rouse himself was Midshipman Casey. Later, he recalled what happened: 'On the first alarm I was in my hammock asleep … being entirely unacquainted with the matter, and seeing some men near the gunroom, I called out to know what was the noise, or what the matter was, but received no answer.' So, he decided to investigate. He continued: 'I then got up in my shirt and went up the after hatchway.' That was close to the captain's cabin. 'I heard a dreadful noise issue from the cabin door, and I saw several of the crew running from the starboard side towards the cabin door. I again asked what the matter was, when two of the men, by the names of Farrel and Phillips, heard me call out.' They stopped to see who it was, and on seeing it was Casey, told him they were 'striking for Liberty', and advised him to go below and hide, or go back to bed, as they thought some of their shipmates would kill him. Judiciously, the unarmed Casey went below.

That, though, proved a mistake. When he returned to the gunroom – still in bare feet and wearing his nightshirt – he found the door blocked by a mob of armed and angry-looking men. He squeezed past, just before one of them, William Crawley, stepped inside brandishing a cutlass. He eyed up the officers gathered there and snarled out a deadly threat. According to Casey, the Irish sailor warned them 'that the first bugger who offered to move, or make the smallest resistance, they would put them to death'. Crawley and the men behind him looked like they were more than ready to do just that. Wisely, and deliberately, Casey clambered back into his hammock and lay down, even though his back was still covered in angry welts from his flogging a few days before. Then the mob departed, leaving a few of them at the open door, to make sure the officers did as they were told.

First Lieutenant Samuel Reed was in there, along with Second Lieutenant Archibald Douglas, the injured Master Edward Southcott, and McIntosh, the dying lieutenant of marines. So too was Marine Sergeant John Plaice, who had been maintaining a vigil at his officer's bedside. The surgeon and the purser also had cabins there. A few moments earlier, after he was attacked, Southcott had yelled out to wake up his fellow officers. Still in his nightshirt he grabbed his sword and stood at the door, only to see the same band of men Casey had encountered head towards him. Glancing behind him he found the gunroom was deserted – all of the officers had hidden in their cabins. So, as the mob of about 20 armed men surged towards him, he too stepped back into his small cabin. He couldn't do anything now, apart from hope for a miracle.

He quickly tucked his sword behind his sea chest, and lay down in his hanging cot. Overhead, he heard shouts, followed by someone yelling 'Hughie's overboard – Hughie's overboard! Huzzah – the ship is ours!' That could only mean Hugh Pigot – his captain – had been killed. This, then, was a full-scale mutiny, and having killed their captain, the mutineers could easily murder their officers too. All he could hope for now was mercy – the mercy of a blood-crazed pack of well-armed mutineers. At that moment, some ten minutes into the mutiny, its ringleaders could probably have called a halt to the violence. After all, Captain Pigot was the focus of their fury. Having hacked him to death and thrown his body overboard, the frenzied mob might have been sated. If this rising had been properly planned and led, the ringleaders might have just managed it. Instead, as Southcott feared, the whole situation was fast descending into chaos, and the blood-letting had only just begun.

8

The Evil that Men Do

There was a brief pause in the mayhem, almost as if the mutineers were drawing breath, or steeling themselves for what lay ahead. There was still no real leadership to the revolt, although there was a hard core group of mutineers who seemed to be at the forefront of the rising. So far, no more than around 35 to 40 men had taken part in the mutiny. With a ship's company of around 150 men, that represented just a quarter of the crew. The rest of the *Hermione* men were just as surprised by the sudden outburst of shouting and violence as the officers and midshipmen had been. Now, though, as the crew struggled to understand what was going on around them, they would find themselves dragged into the orgy of bloodshed, whether they wanted to be or not.

———

Up in the maintop, John Brown was one of the few men on watch who fully understood what was going on. After all, he had already seen the mutineers gathering in the forecastle, and decided he wanted no part in what they were planning. He was still on watch, and so he had returned to his post.

He had heard all the shouting and commotion on the quarterdeck, when Lieutenant Foreshaw was hacked down. Now, as the sounds of struggle had abated, he decided to climb down to see what was happening. As he reached the deck he came across a group of men around a large arms chest. Many of them were former *Successes*. James Bell had hacked the chest open with a boarding axe and was busy passing out the weapons. He spotted Brown and called out threateningly, declaring: 'Here's one of them'. By that he meant men loyal to the captain. However, some of his companions vouched for Brown, and so Bell handed him a musket.

Later, Brown claimed he had to take it, or risk being killed. Bell told him to use it to guard the after hatch, and not let anyone on deck he didn't know. Others would have found themselves in a similar position. In the darkness of the lower deck, amid a sea of men in hammocks, many had no idea what was causing all the commotion. So, when the mutineers first barged their way into the gunroom, James Duncan had been taken by surprise. He was posted outside it, guarding a beer barrel. As he passed, William Crawley threatened to knock Duncan's brains out if he didn't keep out of the way. He did as he was told. A few feet from him, the marine guarding the gunroom simply backed away crying 'Mercy'. Struggling out of his hammock nearby, the captain's cook, John Holford, thought the ship was on fire, but soon realised it was a mutiny. But now, as they hadn't stepped in to protect their officers, all three men were implicated, just as much as Crawley, Bell and the others.

For a few brief minutes, hiding from the mob in their cabins, the officers and midshipmen might have thought they'd been spared. After all, the mutineers had already warned them to stay put, or risk being killed. But then, having armed themselves with more weapons, the mob returned and this time they were after blood. Some of them were shouting as they came, yelling out: 'Where is he? Where's the bugger?' They seemed to be hunting Lieutenant Douglas, one of the captain's favourites, and a man who shared Pigot's love for the lash. When the mob had first appeared, Archibald Douglas had leaped out of his cot and run into the next cabin, where the marine lieutenant lay in his death bed, watched by the loyal Sergeant Plaice. Later, the sergeant recalled the moment: 'When I first saw him, he was naked. He said "Lord Sergeant, what is the matter", then he crept under the officer's cot.' He must have thought he had found a safe hiding spot.

When the mob went away, Douglas came out from his hiding place and went back to his cabin to put on a dressing gown. Other officers were stirring, too, but when they heard the mob returning they bolted back into their cabins. Douglas went back under the dying marine's cot, watched by a bewildered Plaice. Seconds later 20 or more mutineers barged into the gunroom, led by Joe Montell, his clothes splashed with Pigot's blood. The first lieutenant, Samuel Reed, jumped onto the gunroom table, planning to climb to safety through the skylight. Montell was quicker, though, and lashed out with a boarding axe, cutting Reed in the face. The officer fell back onto the deck, where he was trampled on by the mutineers coming in behind Montell. They were still yelling out 'Where's the bugger?' and 'Where's Douglas'. This was a lynch mob, pure and simple. Finding his cabin empty, they slashed at his cot and belongings, before searching the place more thoroughly.

Sergeant Plaice recalled what happened next: 'At this time there were about 20 or 30 of the mutineers in the gunroom ... I heard them say, "The bugger is gone – we cannot find the bugger!'" Many of them left to search the ship, but a few were more methodical. One of the searchers was the teenager David Forester who, like Montell, had been one of those who had first attacked Pigot. He had a lantern with him, as well as Pigot's sword, and he went through the wardroom from cabin to cabin. Others were doing the same, and it was another youngster, Douglas's 14-year-old servant James Allen, who caught sight of part of his master's dressing gown underneath McIntosh's cot. According to Plaice, he yelled out: 'Here he is! Here he is!', and a moment later Forester arrived with his lantern, followed by a group of vengeful mutineers, yelling: 'Come out you bugger!'

Plaice was still in the cabin, but he was brushed aside. Douglas tried to crawl out, or he was dragged, and then pulled to his feet before being shoved into the gunroom. Later, Plaice relived the horror of what happened next: 'I suppose there were twenty tomahawks, axes and boarding pikes jagged into him immediately in the gunroom'. Douglas was stabbed at least 20 times, while trying to protect himself with his right arm, and crying out for mercy. His attackers replied: 'You bugger – we'll show you mercy!' As Plaice watched in horror, even Douglas's servant had a go, yelling out: 'Let me have a go at him' before swinging his axe at his master. According to Plaice, as he struck him the boy cried out: 'He shan't make me jump about in the gunroom any more'. At that moment, Douglas slipped free, and tried to run, but only managed to go a few steps.

He headed forwards, to the midshipmen's berth, and so it was Midshipman Casey who saw what followed. Lieutenant Douglas was coated in blood, his gown hanging in ribbons about him. As Casey watched, 'I saw him seized by several of the crew. Those men fell on him with different weapons, and left him, apparently dead, on the gratings of the after hold.' Casey added: 'I was so shocked that I turned my head away.'

Archibald Douglas had been a highly unpopular officer, largely because, thanks to him, dozens of the crew had been flogged since he joined the ship. Now that their blood was up, they began looking for his accomplice in much of this – a midshipman named Charles Smith.

This was really who Forester had been looking for. He caught sight of the youngster and grabbed him. Smith wriggled free, but before he could escape Forester cut at him with Pigot's sword. Having dealt with Douglas, many of the others now turned on Smith, stabbing and hacking at him until he fell to the deck close to Douglas's body. This wasn't far from the main hatchway, and as he listened, Casey heard men on the upper deck call down 'Hand the buggers up! Launch the buggers.' Sure enough, the mutineers grabbed hold of Douglas's body, and carried him to the hatchway ladder. At that moment Casey heard the blood-soaked body groan slightly, which meant that, almost unbelievably, Archibald Douglas was still alive. Still, he was passed up, then dragged through the hatch by his heels. Moments later, Midshipman Smith followed. As Casey put it, the two officers were handled 'as though they had been two dogs'.

Once they had been brought out onto the upper deck, the bodies were surrounded by a ring of jeering mutineers, with others behind them yelling 'Cut the buggers! Launch the buggers!' or 'Heave the buggers overboard!'. One of them was the Irishman, William Crawley. He pushed his way forward, and according to the captain's steward, John Jones, he yelled out: 'Let me have another stroke at him before he goes!' With that, he sunk his axe into Douglas's skull so hard that the handle splintered with the force. Next, Douglas's horribly mutilated body was dragged to a nearby open gunport and thrown through it, into the sea. Moments later the smaller carcass of Midshipman Smith splashed into the sea too, bundled through the gunport by Forester and a seaman, John Fletcher, who had recently been given a hard flogging, on Smith's insistence. With the killing of Pigot, Douglas and Smith, the mutineers had wreaked a bloody revenge on their three worst oppressors.

That then, might have been the end of it. With their bloodlust satisfied, there was a chance the mutineers would spare the other officers. Many would have wanted nothing more than to stop the killing spree there. Others, though – a hard core of the more fervent mutineers – had other thoughts. Then, moments after the two bodies had been pitched over the side, someone cried out, and pointed aft to the quarterdeck. There, clambering over the ship's side by the mizzen shrouds, was the bloodied figure of a dead man. It was Henry Foreshaw, the third lieutenant. Having attacked the officer-of-the-watch and bundled him over the side, many of the mutineers would have forgotten about him. Now, though, he was back, battered and bloodied, but seemingly very much alive.

It seemed Foreshaw hadn't fallen overboard after all; instead the starboard mizzen chains had broken his fall. They were the thick baulk of timber attached to the outside of the hull, which formed the base for the ratlines of the mizzen mast. Foreshaw had become lodged in the chains securing the ratlines to this timber, and lay on the ledge the timber made, trying to recover his strength. Eventually he hauled himself back on board, only to be spotted when he clambered over the gunwale and stepped down onto the quarterdeck. In response, several armed men ran aft to surround him. Foreshaw cried out for mercy, exclaiming: 'Good God men, what have I done to you, that I should be treated in this manner?' A few of them felt the killing had gone too far, and as Foreshaw was a popular officer, they agreed to spare him. For a moment, it looked like the young officer would survive, but then he was spotted by two of the main ringleaders of the mutiny – Thomas Nash and John Farrel.

They pushed their way forward and Nash grabbed Foreshaw by the wrist of his right hand. With that, he exclaimed: 'Foreshaw you bugger! Are you not overboard yet?' He continued: 'Overboard you must go, and overboard you must go!' With that, he pulled on Foreshaw's arm, extending it out along the edge of the gunwale. The badly wounded officer was too weak to resist and could only watch in horror as Farrel raised his axe and struck. The New Yorker's axe cleaved through the lieutenant's wrist, cutting the hand clean off. Foreshaw screamed, and as blood pumped from the stump he was bundled along the sloping deck a few feet to the break in the quarterdeck, where steps ran down the starboard side of the hull. There, he was unceremoniously heaved over the side, still screaming. This time, the mutineers watched him hit the water, and bob away out of sight into the dark.

With Captain Pigot dead, and two lieutenants and a midshipman also killed, there would be no turning back. The leading mutineers – those who had a hand in the murders – would all be keenly aware of that. Now a group of them gathered on the quarterdeck to discuss what to do next. They included four of the captain's murderers – John Farrel, Thomas Leech, Thomas Nash and Richard Redman. Also taking part in the discussion was the master's mate, William Turner, who, together with Thomas Osborn at the helm had stayed at their post, as well as at least one other, John Elliot, a 26-year-old seaman who, like Redman, was a former *Success* man. Others might have chipped in, as Boatswain's Mate Thomas Jay and Gunner James Bell were also nearby. The first decision to make was which direction Osborn should steer the ship. All through the mutiny, the *Hermione* had stayed on her old course, heading towards the north-east, and the coast of Puerto Rico.

The real danger was the *Diligence*. The lights of Commander Mends's brig had still been within sight at 11pm, when the mutiny had begun. She would still be out there in the darkness, as both ships were on the same course. The first decision was therefore pretty simple. They had to change course, or else come daybreak the *Diligence* would soon realise that something was wrong on board the *Hermione*. So, encouraged by Nash, the mutineers decided to turn away and head south. That meant calling all hands to turn the ship about. This of course was a real problem. Until now, most of the crew hadn't been involved in the mutiny, but now they had to be called on deck. The risk was that they would refuse to help the mutineers, and with too few of them to sail the ship, the chances were that the *Diligence* would find them, and the mutiny would fail. Still, there was no real option; they had to take the risk. So, Nash told his fellow Boatswain's Mate Thomas Jay to go below and rouse all hands.

It was now probably a little after 11.40pm – 20 minutes before the change of the watch. Following the mutineers' order, Jay went through the ship, piping his boatswain's call, and yelling out: 'Every man to his station to about ship!' On the quarterdeck, the knot of mutineers would have held their breath. Then, the hands began to pour onto the upper deck, and climb aloft to their assigned places. They might have known what was going on, but most would have been confused, and, on hearing these old familiar orders, they simply followed them. These few minutes were crucial to the success of the whole bloody enterprise. Then, as Master's Mate William Turner gave the order, the men tugged on their ropes, Osborn turned the wheel and the *Hermione* began a graceful curving turn. Once she had steadied on a southerly course, the entire crew were now implicated in the mutiny; as they'd helped the mutineers, they were now literally all in the same boat.

Most of the crew must have realised that. By midnight, many of them had joined forces with the mutineers, and busied themselves breaking into the ship's stocks of alcohol – the spirit store, and the captain's and gunroom's stores. Many would have felt frightened and intimidated at the sight of their armed and blood-splattered shipmates. Many would have sympathised with them, but wouldn't have been willing to cross the line into mutiny. Now, though, whether they liked it or not, the die was cast. As for the ringleaders, they had overcome their first big hurdle. By midnight the *Hermione* was now running before the wind – heading southwards with the wind astern of her. Every minute put them further away from the *Diligence*, and the immediate threat of their horrific crime being discovered. That bought the ringleaders of the mutiny time – enough to figure out what to do next.

By all accounts there were 20 of them by now. Thomas Nash had evolved into something akin to their leader, although there was still no hierarchy. Richard Redman was emerging as his leading deputy, though, and according to John Jones, the late captain's steward, it was Redman who turned aside from the group and addressed William Turner, still standing on the quarterdeck, as nobody had relieved him when the watch changed. The group had been discussing the vexing problem of command, and after more muttering, according to Jones, Redman turned and called out to Turner: 'Officer, here you are!' Effectively, the mutineers were placing him in charge of the running of the ship. Then, while Thomas Jay and James Bell stayed with Turner, probably to make sure their newly recruited fellow ringleader did what he was told, the remaining 16 of them went below, to the bloody shambles that was the captain's cabin. There, they would thrash out what to do next.

The Ringleaders

Name	Position	Age	Nationality	From Success or not
James Bell	Quarter Gunner	21	Scottish	Former *Success*
William Clarke	Able Seaman	–	English	
Henry Croaker	Gunner's Mate	31	English	Former *Success*
Lawrence Cronin	Surgeon's Mate	35	Irish	
John Elliot	Able Seaman	26	English	Former *Success*
John Farrel	Able Seaman	–	American	
David Forester	Maintopman	16	English	
William Herd	Able Seaman	–	Scottish	
John Innes	Able Seaman	27	Scottish	Former *Success*
Thomas Jay	Boatswain's Mate	30	English	Former *Success*
Thomas Ladson	Able Seaman	30	English	Former *Success*
Thomas Leech	Able Seaman	–	–	
Robert McReady	Maintopman	23	Irish	Former *Success*
Joseph Montell	Maintopman	–	Italian	
Thomas Nash	Boatswain's Mate	25	Irish	
Hadrian Poulson	Able Seaman	24	Danish	
Richard Redman	Able Seaman	24	English	
John Smith	Foretopman	22	English	Former *Success*
William Turner	Master's Mate	–	English	
Michael Whatman	Carpenter's Yeoman	24	English	Former *Success*

Now that the *Hermione* was heading away from the *Diligence*, the ringleaders' next big problem was what to do with the remaining officers. A deck below them, still in their cabins, and effectively held there as prisoners, were ten men. First Lieutenant Samuel Reed was there, wounded from the blow he had received to his head when he had tried to escape. He had been tended by the ship's surgeon, Hugh Sansom, and told to lie down in his cot. In theory Sansom was also tending the lieutenant of marines, Robert McIntosh, but according to Sergeant Plaice, who still sat with him, he was past help and was expected to die within hours. The master was there, Edward Southcott, who had also been injured and was now in his cot. Stephen Pacey, the purser, was in his cabin, as was Midshipman David Casey, who was still suffering the after-effects of his flogging. His fellow midshipman, John Wiltshire, was nowhere to be seen – the likelihood is that by now the impressionable 13-year-old boy had joined the mutineers.

Also under guard were the warrant officers: the gunner, Richard Searle; the boatswain, William Martin; and the carpenter, Richard Price. With them was Martin's wife Fanny, who looked after the young midshipmen, as well as John Manning, the captain's clerk. According to John Mason, the Irish carpenter's mate and a former *Success* man, he went looking for the carpenter and found him in the gunner's cabin on the starboard side just forward of the gunroom door. He was openly weeping. Searle was there, still naked after waking up to the sound of the commotion outside. Mason had still been with them when Lieutenant Douglas and Midshipman Smith were butchered, just a few feet outside their door. He decided to stay in the cabin for a bit. As he put it later:

'I was frightened, and wanted to get out of the way.' On the larboard side, the boatswain and his wife were also hiding in their cabin, next to the one occupied by an equally fearful captain's clerk. Like the others, they didn't dare to set foot outside their little canvas and wood cabins.

Back in the captain's great cabin, the mutineers couldn't agree what to do with their officers. One group, including Nash and Redman, were in favour of leniency. They felt the killing had gone as far as it needed to. The others, including the bloodthirsty teenager Forester, were all for killing all of the prisoners. That way, they argued, nobody would be left to testify against any of the mutineers if they were ever caught. In the end the meeting broke up without any clear decision being made. Nash then went down to the gunroom, where he assured Midshipman Casey that, if he had anything to do with it, his life would be spared. This wasn't particularly reassuring as in the past half hour several seamen had barged into the cabin and threatened both him and his fellow officers. Nash recommended that for his own safety Casey go up on deck. He did, but once he got there, Casey decided it looked even more dangerous than his cabin. So, he went below and clambered back into his hammock.

In the gunroom, the tension mounted. Nash and others had posted sentries to protect the officers but every few minutes drunken mutineers tried to barge in, or jeered down through the open skylight, threatening to 'kill them all'. By now many of the mutineers were drunk, including a few of the ringleaders. According to John Jones, Redman had ordered him to open up the captain's store room on the orlop deck, where Pigot's wine was stored. Once inside, Redman used Pigot's sword to slice off the neck of a bottle of Madeira, and took a large draught of it. He passed out a few bottles to his shipmates, then decanted the rest of his bottle into a tankard. Then he went back up to the gunroom. There he pressed a drink on the master, who immediately recognised the sword. Next, Redman visited the boatswain and his wife and forced more drink on them. As the only woman on board, Fanny Martin was terrified.

A few minutes later, Nash and Farrel appeared, and together with Redman they began arguing over who they should spare. Jones heard them when he followed Redman up from the captain's store room. Someone – possibly Farrel – was heard saying: 'they might as well be hung for a sheep as a lamb'. Somehow, a decision was made. Seconds later Nash, as spokesman for the mutineers, opened the gunroom door again and told the surgeon and the purser that the ship's company had decided to put them to death. Casey tried reasoning with Nash, but it did no good. Then, at least for the moment, the officers were left alone, except for their guards and the jeering mutineers peering through the skylight. It was clear by now that, fuelled by copious amounts of alcohol, the mutineers were veering more towards murder than clemency. In the gunroom, and the cabins just in front of it, the captives were keenly aware that their fate now lay in the hands of a drunken mob.

It was then, at some time between 12.30 and 1am, that their fate was decided by an Irish Republican. On most frigates, the surgeon usually had an assistant to help him deal with amputations, operations and all the grisly tasks that needed an extra pair of hands. Medical knowledge was less important than strong hands and an even stronger stomach. On the *Hermione*, the surgeon's mate was Lawrence Cronin, a 35-year-old seaman from Belfast. He'd been promoted into the job by Pigot, which allowed him to berth with the midshipmen and master's mates. Although we don't know what his relationship with Hugh Sansom the surgeon was like, from what followed we can guess that it wasn't a cordial one. It was then, after that short lull in the chaos, that Cronin walked into the gunroom and shouted up to the men around the skylight to gather round. It seemed he wanted an audience for what he planned to say.

Soon, everyone was waiting expectantly, while more men crammed into the gunroom itself, or jostled for a space on the flats outside, where the warrant officers and midshipmen had their cabins. Cronin jumped onto the gunroom table and pulled a piece of paper out of his pocket. He had prepared a speech. In their cabins, Reed, Southcott, Casey and the others were able to hear every word. He announced he had something to read out. Then he began, stating: 'I have been a Republican since the war [began]', before going on to say that he thought this rising was a very right and good thing. He continued, arguing that they needed to put all of the remaining officers to death. It was no use just killing one of them. The men began cheering at this, and no sooner had Cronin finished than several of them began their deadly chant again: 'Hand them up! Pass the Buggers up! Kill them all!' For the prisoners in their cabins or ordered to sit in the gunroom, it must have seemed that their final moments had come.

As Casey later put it: 'The scene now became dreadful, and the greatest confusion prevailed. All were more or less inflamed and excited by spirits'. He added that the exception seemed to be many of the ringleaders of the mutiny, who were relatively sober, and who counselled for clemency.

The mob, though, were now baying for blood. Moments later, a knot of men burst into the gunroom and shoved the sentries aside. These included two of the more bloodthirsty ringleaders – Joe Montell and David Forester – as well as two seamen and two marines. They grabbed Stephen Pacey, the purser, bundling him out of the gunroom door and up the accommodation ladder to the upper deck. There, he was stabbed repeatedly, and then punched and kicked when he fell to the deck. Montell and the others then pulled him up, dragged him to a gun port and threw the dying man into the sea. However, that was only the start of the frenzy. Having been warned before by Nash, the surgeon, Hugh Sansom, knew he would be next.

Sure enough, when Montell and his accomplices returned to the gunroom they found the doctor there, steadying himself against the mizzen mast, which passed up through the gunroom. Beside him, his 14-year-old servant, James Hayes, was dancing a jig with delight, watched with smug satisfaction by Cronin. Like the purser, the surgeon was an unpopular figure on board, as he was seen as a toady to the captain. The terrified doctor was grabbed by Montell and the others and soon met the same bloody fate as Pacey. Reportedly, he was still alive when he was pitched over the side, despite having been stabbed repeatedly. A few weeks before, the young Hayes had been punished for stealing from his master and, although no records survive, he had probably been thrashed by the boatswain's mates. Now he had his revenge.

It was now clear that, despite the earlier assurance of men like Nash and Redman, the first lieutenant, the master, and possibly even the remaining midshipmen would be slaughtered. The lives of the warrant officers – the boatswain, the carpenter and the gunner – were also hanging in the balance. Sure enough, when Montell and his cronies appeared, they made for the first lieutenant's cabin. They hauled the door open and found Samuel Reed lying in his cot. He was still dazed from the head wound he had suffered an hour earlier at the hands of Montell and his axe. Since then, the surgeon had stitched up the wound, bandaged it, and helped the lieutenant into his hanging cot. Now Montell was back to finish the job. He and his 'snatch squad' grabbed Reed, carried him to the upper deck, stabbed him and threw him over the side. So far the crew had killed their captain and all three of their naval lieutenants. The lust for blood, though, had still not been completely sated. There was still one more lieutenant on board.

While Montell and his 'snatch squad' were busy congratulating themselves on a job well done, more violence erupted from the gunroom. This time the target was Robert McIntosh, the lieutenant of marines. The door of his cabin was yanked open and two of his marines shouldered their way past Sergeant Plaice. Patrick Field and a private known as 'Happy Tom' grabbed the blanket their officer was lying on. While a sailor, James Hannah, kept Plaice at bay, and other sailors moved in to help, the marines lifted the blanket, and used it as a makeshift stretcher. The blanket was badly soiled – the fever-wracked McIntosh had already lost control of his bodily functions, and the dying man was also frothing at the mouth. Still, McIntosh was carried onto the upper deck, where the fever blotches on his skin were clearly visible, and then, like the others, his body was heaved into the sea, along with the soiled blanket.

For many of the crew, that would have been a particularly shocking act. It was clear, given the involvement of some of his marines themselves, that McIntosh wasn't a particularly popular officer. Still, he wasn't expected to last through the night, and the mutineers hadn't needed to kill him. However, this was all about making a clean sweep of it, as Lawrence Cronin had demanded, and there was little place for humanity. The only senior officer left on board was the master, Edward Southcott, who until this point had been protected by the sentries posted by Nash outside his cabin. Now, though, it looked like they wouldn't be able to save him. His door was yanked open and as Southcott put it: 'There were eight or ten men in my cabin to take me out, and the gunroom was full of them.' They began dragging him out, but this time the onlookers peering down through the skylight called out for help. Moments later two mutineers – probably Nash and another ringleader – intervened, and earned Southcott a reprieve.

But the killing didn't end there. While all this had been going on, Richard Redman had kept on drinking the captain's Madeira, and had been biding his time. Now he made his move. After gathering together a few half-drunk men, ones suitably inspired by Cronin's speech, he headed to the flat outside the gunroom and pulled open the door to the boatswain's cabin. Inside, William and Fanny Martin sat huddled together on a bench. Redman cried out: 'By the Holy Ghost! The boatswain shall go with the rest!' With that he grabbed the boatswain, and he and his followers bundled him up on deck and threw him over the side. Sergeant Plaice claimed he heard the boatswain cry out for help as he floundered in the water. The real reason Redman had killed him was soon apparent. He returned to the cabin, and spent the rest of the night there with the boatswain's widow. Faced with a drunken, dangerous and lecherous man, soaked in blood and armed with a sword, she was in no position to resist.

The tenth victim of the evening was John Manning, the captain's clerk. He had been hiding in his cabin next to the boatswain, and as a favourite of the captain he knew he wasn't particularly liked. This time, the 'snatch squad' consisted of David Forester, helped by Adam Brown, James Hannah and William Marsh. John Jones, the captain's steward, watched them drag Manning from his cabin and up on deck. Ignoring the young man's pleas for mercy, they pitched him out through a gun port and into the sea. With that, and for a time at least, the bloodlust was over. For Southcott and the handful of prisoners who remained, it had all been a terrifying ordeal. As Casey put it, during that last hour: 'the language, noise and scene altogether was horrible'. Now, after Southcott's reprieve, the master was left alone in his cabin, with sentries posted outside it, but Casey was ordered onto the quarterdeck, together with the two remaining warrant officers, Searle, the gunner, and Price, the carpenter.

Earlier that evening, before the final burst of violence, Nash had asked Casey if he wanted to take command of the ship. Casey had refused, and the boatswain's mate hadn't pressed the issue. Now, as the midshipman and the two other prisoners stood at the after end of the quarterdeck, Nash tried again. He called Casey forward, then turned to William Turner, the master's mate, who had been running the ship all evening. No doubt Nash had discussed the matter with his fellow ringleaders, and so his words carried their collective authority. He said: 'Mr. Turner – you are to consider yourself captain of the ship while she is in your charge.' He then added: 'You, Mister Casey, are to be the first lieutenant.' Once again, Casey refused, and once more Nash accepted the midshipman's decision, and sent him below to his cabin, where he would be guarded by sentries. If Casey had accepted, the authorities would have branded him a mutineer. Now, though, he would wonder if his decision would cost him his life.

So, by around 1.30am, the frenzy of killing came to an end. It had all begun less than two-and-a-half hours before, when the rising was spearheaded by a small band of men driven to commit murder in order to end what for them had become a living hell. By killing their captain they had merely swapped one form of torment for another. They knew perfectly well they were now outcasts, and would be hunted men for the rest of their lives. These men, along with a few others, had become the ringleaders of the mutiny. It was others, though, for the most part, who had seen this rising take on a horrific life of its own. Once the majority of the ship's company were involved, the mutiny had become an excuse for a string of murders fuelled more by revenge, or fear of retribution, rather than a fight for freedom. A few had even used the mutiny to settle old scores. As the bloodlust abated, all of them would have begun thinking about what to do next, and how to avoid the wrath that would surely follow in its wake.

9

The Spanish Main

For what remained of the night, the situation continued as volatile as ever. For the master and midshipman, confined in their cabins, and the carpenter and gunner, huddled in a corner of the quarterdeck, it didn't look like they would see the sunrise. Despite being guarded by sentries, their lives depended on the whims and caprices of a drunken mob. Once the last wave of violence was over, the ringleaders had discussed their fate, and decided to spare the lives of the remaining four officers. But this wasn't the end of it. Throughout the night, and the morning that followed, the four men expected to be killed at any moment.

————

Later, David Casey recalled what he went through that night. As he lay in his hammock, he kept hearing gangs of men outside his door, and expected them to burst in at any moment and drag him on deck like the others. As he put it: 'My life was repeatedly debated, and for some time hung in the scales. I was subsequently told by my friends that I was twice or thrice condemned, and on the point of suffering.' Fortunately, though, those same friends among the mutineers – men like Nash – did what they could. Even then, as the midshipman put it: 'It was with the greatest difficulty that I was saved.' Ultimately it was these friends who saved him: 'Two or three of them always kept near me during the night, as a protecting guard, and removed me occasionally from place to place for more safety.'

Edward Southcott had a similar time of it. As he recalled: 'A great many times during the night, until half past eleven o'clock next morning – I suppose twenty times – they attempted to take me out and put me to death, and were stopped by others desiring them not to do it.' So, like Casey, the master had friends among the crew. One of these was John Edwards, the ship's quartermaster, who wasn't an active participant in the mutiny. He and Southcott had always got on well, and now he and a few shipmates did what they could to save his life. The same would have been true of Gunner Richard Searle and Carpenter Richard Price. What these four men had going for them was popularity. Unlike most of those who had been murdered, they had been well liked by the crew and had tried to stand up for the men in the face of Pigot's injustices. When the time came, that helped tip the scales in their favour.

Slowly, the first streaks of light appeared on the eastern horizon. The exact position of the *Hermione* is unknown that morning, as her log books and charts were later deliberately destroyed by the mutineers. However, the previous evening the ship was to the north-east of the Isla Mona, which lay in the middle of the Mona Passage. Both the *Hermione* and the *Diligence* were heading in a north-easterly direction, towards the coast of Puerto Rico. They were probably midway between the island and Punta Rincón on the Puerto Rican coast when the mutiny erupted. They then turned south, so that when dawn came a little after 6.20am on 22 September they would have been out of the Mona Passage, about 30 miles south-east of the Isla Mona, and 20 miles from Los Morillos, the south-western corner of Puerto Rico. The coast would still have been in sight astern of them, off their larboard quarter.

The mutineers' biggest worry was that the *Diligence* was still in sight. Instead, dawn revealed a grey, overcast and slightly blustery day, and an empty horizon. The wind was still blowing from the north, so they kept running southwards, away from the *Diligence*, and into the Caribbean. They were making reasonably good progress, but after talking to his fellow mutineers, the acting captain William Turner ordered the topgallants to be set, to increase their speed a little. By then some semblance of watch-keeping had been restored. Now, instead of their usual officers, leading mutineers commanded their shipmates in the tops. This time, though, they were leading by example, using experience and persuasion rather than fear to get the work done. There would be no more flogging the last man down on this ship.

However, the problem was that the drinking continued unabated. Groups of men were gathered around half barrels of rum or wine on the open deck. Watching all this was John Jones, the captain's steward, who, together with his son Gabriel, took no part in the mutiny. Instead he watched everything, and took mental notes. He saw men who, just the day before, had been feigning injury or illness now capering about, and drinking heavily. He even saw Richard Redman emerge from the boatswain's cabin, after spending the night with his widow. Above all, he noted who were the leaders of the mutiny, and who were their willing supporters. Most of the crew still hadn't taken an active part in the rising, and so Jones noted who these men were too. One day soon, he hoped, he would be able to tell his story to the British authorities.

As the ship was running southwards, with the wind coming from astern, there wasn't any need to trim the sails or perform any other challenging tasks. That left the crew with time on their hands to discuss what to do next, where they should go and, above all, what to do about their remaining four officers. Actually there were five, but Midshipman Wiltshire had joined the mutineers during the night, and so the young teenager was now officially one of them. They also kept on drinking, and according to Jones, the majority of them became exceedingly drunk as the morning wore on. Meanwhile, the words cried out by Lawrence Cronin the previous evening still rang in their ears – they needed to kill all of their officers, or risk leaving witnesses behind who could testify against them if they were caught. Dead men tell no tales.

By 11.30am, the mood had darkened enough for another lynch mob to form around the rum barrel. After working themselves up into a frenzy, they picked up their weapons and, together, they went down to the gunroom. This time, they brushed Elliot's guards aside and seized hold of the master. He had been expecting it for several hours, so he was dressed and ready. The mob dragged him up the companion ladder to the upper deck, and then aft to the quarterdeck. The word went through the ship that the master was to be put to death. The small knot of drunken agitators soon swelled into an angry crowd. Many were yelling out 'Kill the buggers!' and other blood-curdling exclamations from the night before. Edward Southcott had no doubt that his time had come. He might even have been resigned to it. Then, completely unexpectedly, the whole situation changed.

Suddenly, a small group of the ringleaders shouldered their way to the front of the crowd, and the baying, drunken crowd of armed men grew quiet. They probably included Thomas Nash, Thomas Jay and John Elliot, although Southcott only mentioned the bleary-eyed Richard Redman. The men spoke, arguing that the master had been fair to the men, and deserved a trial. If some saw the need to put Southcott to death in cold blood, after they had already taken control of the ship, then there were others who wanted to spare him, as he had treated them well over the past five months, since he joined the ship. Redman demanded a show of hands. So, what had begun as a simple murder had now become a kangaroo court. Consequently, a bewildered Southcott found himself on trial for his life, with a simple vote deciding if he would live or die.

Then came the vote. The first round was for those who wanted to spare the master. For Southcott, the tension must have been unbearable. Amazingly, a good number of the men raised their hands. As Southcott put it later: 'a great part of them held their hands up'. Then, the vote was called for those who wanted him killed. A number of hands flew up, but not as many as before. So, as a result of a democratic show of hands, it looked like Southcott's life had been spared. Redman confirmed the result, and then, amazingly, the crowd gave three cheers. With that, a mightily relieved Southcott was led aft to the captain's blood-soaked cabin, where he was confined.

Effectively, this also helped save the lives of Casey, Searle and Price. While the latter two were confined in their cabins off the gunroom flat, Casey was put in the captain's great cabin. All four men were guarded, as much for their own protection as to prevent them from escaping. In the great cabin, Southcott and Casey were told to sit on opposite sides of it, and they were forbidden to talk to each other, unless the guards were able to hear what they said. During the days that followed, all four men were given food and drink, and allowed to take exercise on the upper deck, but only when an armed man accompanied them. The main thing was that, against all the odds, they were still alive. Their lives had been spared because of their popularity. However, it was a decision which ultimately would cost some of the mutineers their lives.

This leniency raised another problem: it went in the face of Lawrence Cronin's bloodthirsty advice of the previous night. The danger now was that once the four officers were released, they would be able to tell the authorities who the ringleaders were, and who had blood on their hands. Inevitably, it was Cronin who came up with a plan. He decided to administer an oath which would bind everyone on board, including the four officers. It was important that this included everyone, not just the minority who had spearheaded the mutiny. Otherwise the whole thing wouldn't work. Many would have been reluctant to give their word, as it would further implicate them in the mutiny. However, they also realised that they didn't really have a choice. Whether done willingly or not, this oath would be morally binding, and, in drafting it, Cronin probably drew on his experience of similar Irish Republican pacts.

One of the main elements was that everyone on board had to protect their shipmates. Cronin worded it so that they agreed 'not to know one another, in any part of the globe, man or boy, if they should meet, nor call each other by their former names'. So, Cronin was already looking ahead, to the necessary diaspora of the mutineers. It finished with: 'This is my oath and obligation, so help me God.' To make sure they were bound by it, Cronin himself supervised the oath-taking by the four officers. All of them said the words, even though they had already sworn a far more binding oath to the Service, and to the upholding of naval discipline and the Articles of War. They had to say the words, though – they had no choice. In the end, everyone on board swore Cronin's oath, including the crewmen who refused to have anything to do with the mutiny – a small group who included John Jones.

That done, the ringleaders set about distributing the plunder gathered from their victims. A few of them had already helped themselves to some things – the captain's sword for instance, or Lieutenant Douglas's clothes. The ringleaders kept the bulk of the booty for themselves, including the personal money of the captain and the murdered officers, as well as watches, a gold ring, silver goods such as spoons, breech and shoe buckles, tankards and even a teapot, as well as a pair of pistols. David Forester took one of Pigot's shirts and a pair of his stockings, while others also claimed their share of clothes. Even then, there was a certain amount of grumbling, as some of the ringleaders felt short-changed, and others were jealous of the plunder being distributed among such a small clique.

Meanwhile, the *Hermione* continued to head out across the Caribbean. During their brief exercise periods on deck, both Southcott and Casey noted that the drinking seemed to continue unabated. As Casey put it: 'The ship was in the greatest possible confusion during the passage, many of the crew continually in a state of drunkenness and frequently fighting.' It was clear, though, that the small inner circle of ringleaders were now in charge. They also seemed to take little interest in the general carousing. Casey said: 'But for the steady good conduct of some of the principal mutineers, we must have suffered.' Southcott concurred, and gave examples of life on board during that period. He watched a marine, Private John Pearce, throw his scarlet uniform over the side, complete with its pipe-clayed crossbelts and gaiters. It was a small, private act of rebellion, and a mark of a life reborn.

The problem facing the mutineers now was where to go. In theory, every coast was hostile and every harbour barred. Clearly any British port was out the question, as was any held by a British ally, such as the Dutch island of Curaçao. The United States of America was neutral in the war, and might well harbour them, although as a country which relied heavily on seafaring, the Americans probably wouldn't take too kindly to mutineers. The most likely prospect, then, was to take the *Hermione* into a port owned by one of Britain's enemies. In September 1797 that really meant France or Spain. They could take the frigate into a port like San Juan in Puerto Rico, or Santo Domingo, or even a French port in Saint-Domingue. However, that meant traversing waters which were frequently patrolled by the British. That would be too much of a risk.

For the same reason, the mutineers could effectively rule out the French-held islands in the West Indies, as the region was a battleground fought over by French and British forces. No, it was much more sensible to continue south, and put in to a Spanish port somewhere on the Spanish Main. Essentially, this encompassed the northern coast of South America, from Cartagena in the west to the island of Trinidad in the east. Of course, the *Hermiones* had already been there. Earlier that year they had cruised off the Venezuelan coast, and had lingered there when the *Ceres* ran aground off the Gulf of Triste. So, naturally, the crew thought of those waters, and the Spanish port of La Guaira, which served as the harbour of the region's capital, Santiago de León de Caracas. After some debate, the ringleaders decided to make La Guaira their destination, just over 400 nautical miles away to the south.

The problem was getting there. The most experienced navigator on board was the master. So, Nash was sent to ask him for his latest position – his noon sun sight. He replied that as he'd been laid up in his cabin for the past few days, he had no real idea where they were. Pigot and Reed would have taken their own readings at noon the previous day – just after the mass flogging. However, their readings couldn't be found, as the ship's log and captain's log had already been destroyed, along with the *Hermione*'s muster book. So, William Turner, who knew the rudiments of navigation, demanded Southcott hand over his notebooks. Using them, and the ship's charts, he was able to work out their approximate position, to the south of Puerto Rico.

From there, he could lay on a course to the Spanish Main, taking account of prevailing wind and currents. In theory, they would make landfall off La Guaira.

In theory the port lay five easy days' sail away. The wind was favourable – one the mariners called 'a soldier's wind', meaning it blew them where they wanted to go, so even a landlubber or a soldier could reach his destination without too much trouble. There was little chance of them meeting a British warship that far out in the Caribbean, or for that matter in the waters off the Venezuelan coast. So, the men could relax, and the drinking, fighting and skylarking continued as they sailed southwards. During these late September days, according to Casey, the leading ringleaders had taken to calling themselves 'lieutenants', and a few of them kept pressing him to join them, so that when they reached La Guaira, he could take up service with the Spanish navy. Casey saw this as a sign that at least some of the mutineers hoped to do the same if they were given the chance.

Some of the *Hermione*'s crew, though, were less optimistic. One of them, the ship's butcher, James Perrett, confessed to Richard Price that he was sorry for what had happened, and was crying. Perrett had a wife and family back home, and now he expected he would never see them again. Others in the crew would have been in a similar position and would have felt the same way. However, only a couple of them approached the four officers, as Perrett had done. Throughout this period, only four members of the crew steadfastly refused to have anything to do with the mutiny. These were Sergeant Plaice, the ship's cook William Moncrieff, John Holford the captain's cook and John Jones the captain's steward. None of them knew what would happen to them when they reached their destination, as their evidence would be as damning as that of the officers.

Finally, a little after dawn on Sunday 27 September, the lookouts in the foretop spotted the mountains of the Venezuelan coast ahead of them – the Cordillera de la Costa. They were just a few hours away from their destination. On board the *Hermione* the mutineers began fevered preparations for their arrival. First of all, they needed a cover story, and a good one. None of Europe's maritime powers liked mutiny, even if the mutineers were from a rival navy. Mutinies set a bad example, and so mutineers were viewed with extreme suspicion. They had betrayed their country and their navy; therefore, they were worthy of contempt. To most naval officers and state officials, they were little better than pirates. If it came out that the *Hermione* mutineers had murdered ten of their officers in cold blood, then there was a good chance that the Spanish authorities would simply arrest them and try them as criminals.

So, that morning, Cronin, Nash, Elliot, Redman and the others concocted their story. The first part of it was easy. The *Hermione* had been ruled by a sadistic, brutal captain who had driven his crew to breaking point. That was true enough. However, although they would claim the mutiny took place in the Mona Passage, they then veered from the truth by claiming that all of the officers had been put into a boat laden with provisions, about 30 miles off the coast of Puerto Rico. To bolster their tale of woe, Cronin insisted that they add that they had been ill-fed, and hadn't been paid for more than four years. Then, freeing themselves from oppression, the crew had voted unanimously to hand the frigate over to the Spanish authorities. That done, they hoped to enjoy the benevolence and protection of His Most Catholic Majesty, King Carlos IV of Spain. Cronin's letter was as flattering as it was inventive.

La Guaira was a bustling port of some 5,000 people. First founded in 1567, it soon grew into a maritime gateway to the province. Behind the port lay the mountains, which served to protect the region's capital of Santiago de León de Caracas, or Caracas for short. The road curved up into the mountains and then through a narrow pass to reach the city, several miles inland. Although somewhat exposed, a large underwater bank some miles out to sea protected the port from the worst of the region's storms. It was also well protected by city walls, forts and well-placed coastal batteries. In charge of La Guaira was the port's governor, Don José Vásquez y Téllez. He would be the man the mutineers had to impress with their story. Essentially, the fate of the *Hermione* and everyone on board her now lay in his hands.

As they approached the port under a white flag, the *Hermione* anchored offshore, just out of reach of the Spanish guns. Then the jolly boat was lowered from the frigate and three 'delegates' clambered in, armed with another white flag. These were all key ringleaders of the mutiny – William Turner, John Elliot and Thomas Leech. The Spanish-born Antonio Francisco, one of the *Hermiones*, also joined them, to act as the interpreter. Before embarking, the three ringleaders were shaved by John Jones, and washed, did up their hair and put on clean clothes. Once ashore they were taken under escort to meet Don José Vásquez, and after formal introductions had been made they presented Cronin's letter. The governor read it, and it appears he took the delegates at their word. He offered the mutineers his protection, at least for the moment, and told them he would consult his superior in Caracas.

Don José Vásquez may have been easily duped, but he was no fool. He knew that the mutiny of the *Hermione* was something of a windfall for the Spanish, as it deprived their enemies of a fine ship, and all being well it could be used to reinforce the Spanish fleet. However, as he told Francisco the interpreter, the final decision about what to do with the frigate lay with the captain-general of the Province of Caracas, Don Pedro Carbonell. So, Don José sent the mutineers' petition to Caracas by hard-riding messenger, together with his own covering letter. The reply came the following day. Walking down to the waterfront, Don José met Turner and his men by their boat, and through Francisco he told them what the captain-general had decided.

For the present the *Hermione* would remain in La Guaira, protected by the port's formidable defences. A delegation from the frigate would journey to Caracas the next day, to meet the captain-general and work out the terms. This, though, was expected to be a mere formality, as would the granting of royal assent on the arrangement by the Spanish Crown. Meanwhile, the *Hermiones* would be able to enjoy the freedom of the port, and, to sweeten the deal, Don José was prepared to pay every man on board a sum of 25 Spanish silver dollars (or pesos), by way of a subsistence allowance. The British would later describe this as 'blood money'. The meeting with the captain-general went well. Don Pedro agreed to the terms, pending royal assent, and Don José even visited the *Hermione*, as she lay snugly under the port's guns. It seemed that the Spanish had bought the mutineers' story.

Edward Southcott, who overheard all this, later reported that 'the main point that interested the listening mutineers was that the captain-general undertook not to hand them over to the British'. This promise of official Spanish protection was crucial. Waiting for the Spanish Crown to approve the whole arrangement could take months. In that time it was more than likely that the true story of the mutiny might leak out. This meant that, whatever happened, they should be safe from British retribution. However, this promise was still dependent on one more meeting, to be held over the next day or so in Caracas. There, the captain-general and his junta, or governing council, would meet to ratify all these provisional decisions and decide what was to be done with the *Hermione*.

Meanwhile, the port's governor told the mutineers they would be housed in naval barracks on shore – a standard practice in the Spanish navy. His officers also took the mutineers' four prisoners ashore – Edward Southcott, David Casey, Richard Price and Richard Searle – as well as the ship's cook, William Moncreiff. All along, the Orcadian cook had refused to support the mutiny, and before they entered port, he had demanded that William Turner add his name to the list of prisoners. The list was duly handed over to Don José Vásquez, and the five men were now taken ashore and imprisoned in the port's main fortress. At the same time, several of the crew who were sick or injured were also taken ashore, to the port's hospital.

Meanwhile, the captain-general's junta met on 3 October, and ratified his provisional decisions. As well as Don Pedro, the junta consisted of the powerful *Intendante* (a combination of provincial administrator and treasurer) Don Estevan

Fernandez de Leone, and two generals. This meant that the *Hermione* would officially be accepted into Spanish service. The mutineers would be offered asylum, and the protection of the captain-general. They would also, pending royal approval, be considered the subjects of King Carlos IV. At the meeting, the junta decided to rename the *Hermione*. Now she was a Spanish ship, she would need a Spanish name. So, they named her *Santa Cecilia* after an early Christian martyr, a name shared by a Spanish frigate destroyed by the British earlier that year off Trinidad. At dawn the following morning, the red and gold Spanish flag was raised over the former *Hermione*.

It seemed that this cosy relationship between Spanish officials and the former *Hermiones* was set to last. However, over the next few weeks rumours about what had happened during the mutiny began to spread. Part of the captain-general's agreement was that the mutineers would remain in the province until the king's assent arrived. They soon found their money wasn't lasting, and without a knowledge of Spanish their employment options were limited. Many found themselves carting stone to build the port's new hilltop fortress, the San Carlos, or else mining salt a few miles out of the town. Both jobs were little more than hard slave labour, the men toiling in the heat for food rather than money. The lucky ones were the 25 mutineers whom the captain-general had asked to remain on board, to help move the frigate to another port up the coast. They at least would be paid a wage.

The conversion of the *Hermione* into the *Santa Cecilia* would take a little more than a change of name. The mutineers had already got rid of all the bloodstains, and the stern window could easily be repaired, but the Spanish *Armada Real* did things a little differently from the Royal Navy. Proper cabins would have to be installed, the sails and rigging replaced to suit the Spanish style, and her armament would need to be overhauled and converted to conform to her new owner's requirements. Then the ship had to be provisioned and crewed. The junta felt that this could best be done in the smaller harbour of Puerto Cabello, 65 miles to the west of La Guaira. As preparations for this short voyage got under way, another Spanish vessel, the merchant schooner *San Antonio*, was about to slip out of La Guaira, bound for Santo Domingo. She was destined to play an important part in the story.

Master and Commander Robert Mends of the brig *Diligence* had last seen the *Hermione* on the evening of the mutiny – Thursday 21 September. As he put it in his official report: 'The last time that I saw her was at eleven o'clock at night on the 22 September. We were both in chase of a privateer off Mona, the weather extremely dark and gloomy.' He added: 'I apprehend it was at this time that the abominable purpose was effected.' It was true – he might have got the date wrong by a day in his hastily penned letter, but he was certainly right about the time the mutiny began. The *Diligence* was still within sight of the *Hermione*'s lights when the mutineers had struck. In hindsight, he must have wished he had known what was going on, so he could have intervened and saved the frigate, her captain and nine of her officers.

In fact, some of his crew may have seen her a little later. At 12.30am, the master, Charles White, spotted the whiteness of a distant sail in the darkness, roughly where he expected the *Hermione* to be. Within 30 minutes, though, it was no longer in sight. Then, at dawn the following morning, they spotted another strange sail, far off to the south-east. This might have been the *Hermione*, or it might have been another ship altogether. The *Diligence* turned to give chase, but the vessel began to pull away from him, and by noon it was out of sight. After that the *Diligence* resumed her patrol of the Mona Passage, and Mends was confident that the *Hermione* would reappear. She never did, and as the days passed he became increasingly worried.

On 29 September the *Diligence* was running low on water, so Mends put in to the Bahía de Ocoa, a deserted anchorage on the southern coast of Santo Domingo. After refilling his water casks he returned to the Mona Passage. The brig was due to return to Môle Saint-Nicolas by late October. There had been a real shortage of prizes during the cruise, but then, just as he was about to head home, Mends's luck changed. On Monday 16 October he captured the American schooner *Sally*, which had herself been taken a week before by a French privateer. Then, four days later, they spotted two vessels, one of which turned out to be a neutral Danish sloop, which was sent on her way. The other craft was the Spanish schooner *San Antonio*, eight days out from La Guaira. After meeting her master, Captain Mends was finally able to find out what had happened to the *Hermione*.

This news of the mutiny would have shocked Captain Mends to the core. He pressed the Spanish master for details, and then, as the *Diligence* sped back to Môle Saint-Nicolas with the grim tidings, he began drafting his report. It began: 'It is with inexpressible pain I inform you of the fate of His

Majesty's ship *Hermione*, the uncertainty of which to me, had long been a source of the most mortifying reflections'. He described capturing the *San Antonio*, adding that she had sailed from La Guaira. Then he continued: 'I am informed that the *Hermione* arrived at this latter place on the 26th of last month, at 3pm, having been run away with by her crew, who, not content with such atrocity, attended to it the last, the most horrible of human actions – a general indiscriminate slaughter of their captain and officers.' So, the fate of the *Hermione* was now known. Her crew had risen up in bloody mutiny.

The account wasn't as accurate as it could have been. The Spanish master told Mends that the surgeon had been spared, and a master's mate, who hid themselves during the rising. He added that the dead amounted to around 40, including most of the marines and six women. He continued: 'It appears that Captain Pigot about the time of going to bed was murdered by his coxswain, who was nominated commander afterwards'. These inaccuracies say much about the extent of the blood-curdling rumours circulating in La Guaira around the time the *San Antonio* set sail. It seems like some of the mutineers had been unable to keep their secret, or more likely, Southcott had told the authorities the real truth. This explains Mends's closing line: 'The Master of the Spanish schooner informs me that the Mutineers are held in the utmost detestation at La Guaira... the scorn and contempt of everyone.'

Mends learned something else too – something almost as troubling as the revolt of Pigot's crew. The Spaniard had told him that: 'it seems from the declaration they [the mutineers] gave at La Guaira, that there had been a correspondence held with the *Diligence*'s crew to this end, and had we not separated, they would have taken us along with them'. Was this true? Had his own crew plotted to rise up along with the *Hermione*'s that night? Mends was a popular and experienced commander, and he decided to tackle this accusation head-on. He mustered his crew, told them about the mutiny, then asked them directly. Their collective indignation told him everything he needed to know. They even said they would have recaptured the frigate if they had known of the mutiny at the time. Mends believed them. His own crew were loyal, and he could trust them to a man.

Mends's duty now was obvious. He had to pass on his grim tidings to Vice-Admiral Parker as quickly as he could. Then, Parker might be able to do something about the *Hermione* and the mutineers before they were both spirited away by the Spanish. He took the *San Antonio* under tow, and ordered his prize crew in the *Sally* to follow him. Before noon on Friday 20 October he was speeding his way to Môle Saint-Nicolas. Shortly before 2am on 31 October the *Diligence* dropped anchor close to the *Queen*, Parker's flagship. Mends was rowed over, and on greeting the flag officer he insisted that the admiral be roused from his sleep. This was news that couldn't wait. Minutes later a surprised Sir Hyde greeted Captain Mends, read his report and quizzed him about its contents. Then, without losing a minute, he called in his clerk and dictated his orders. There wasn't a moment to lose.

Vice-Admiral Parker's journal records, in the clerk's beautiful copperplate hand, what Sir Hyde's immediate reaction had been. A few days before, he had sent Captain Ricketts and the frigate *Magicienne* to the Mona Passage, to relieve the *Hermione*. Now he ordered Mends to take on stores and water, then chase after Ricketts. He would expect to find the frigate 'between Altavilla and Cape Roco, on the SW end of Puerto Rico'. Together, they would sail at once to La Guaira, carrying a letter for the Spanish governor there from the British admiral. As Parker put it, Ricketts was to 'use his best endeavours to procure the company of that ship [*Hermione*]'. That was his first priority. He realised the Spanish would keep the *Hermione* if they could. He was quite sure, though, that they would do the proper thing and hand over Captain Pigot's murderers.

Parker himself would put to sea, to rendezvous with Ricketts off Monte Christi, on the northern coast of Santo Domingo. If Ricketts failed in his mission, then the *Diligence* was to speed 'an account of his proceedings' to Parker. That way, he might still be able to intervene, and strike a bargain with the Spanish authorities. Next, Parker had the unenviable task of telling the Board of the Admiralty about the mutiny. He included a copy of Mends's report. They would be sent in the next fast packet bound for home. In a second letter, written a few days later, he added that it was of great importance that 'the perpetrators of the piracy be brought to consign punishment'. He recommended that the government should even approach the Spanish Crown 'to have the villains delivered up'. Parker expected that, faced with such a heinous crime, the Spanish king would do the right thing.

He also wrote to the British naval commander on the West Indies Station, as well as all British governors in the West Indies and the Caribbean. All of them were sent an account of the mutiny and asked to show no mercy to the mutiny's ringleaders. Parker even urged that other lesser mutineers might be spared, if they were willing to turn King's evidence against their leaders. Parker even wrote to Robert Liston, Britain's minister in the United States, as he feared some of the mutineers might make their way there. Sir Hyde Parker was in no doubt that the king, the Admiralty and the British people would demand nothing less than the ruthless hunting down of these mutineers, murderers and pirates who had brought such shame to the Service. Now, the full weight of the British state, and the might of the Royal Navy, would be devoted to hunting the mutineers, and then bringing them to justice.

10

The Manhunt

The news finally reached the Admiralty in London on 13 December. The board released a statement about the mutiny two days later. At the time, the only account available was the version told to Captain Mends of the *Diligence*, which, if it were even possible, was more horrific than the truth. The British public were outraged, especially as the press embellished the story, to make it even more sensational. Press and politicians demanded that every effort be made to hunt down the mutineers and hang them en masse. The Board of the Admiralty needed no telling, particularly after the recent mutinies at Spithead and the Nore. So, their priority was the recapture and trial of the mutineers. However, they also hoped that at some point the navy would be able to recapture the *Hermione*, and so wipe out the bloody stain the mutiny had left on the navy's honour and reputation.

When they first arrived in La Guaira, the mutineers had hoped to hand over the frigate and then disperse, using false names to sign on as seamen on any merchant ship they could. However, as mentioned above, the captain-general had foiled this scheme by insisting they remain in the province. Although some found subsistence work labouring on the new fortress or mining salt, many couldn't even do that, and were reduced to begging on the streets of La Guaira and Caracas. A few, though, were luckier than their shipmates. Despite not being on the official list of prisoners, the captain's steward, John Jones, begged permission to serve the officers, and so became a prisoner of war. Several other crewmen who had taken no part in the mutiny tried this too, including six marines, but the Spanish refused. Bureaucracy demanded that they should have made the demand when the *Hermione* first arrived in the port.

When the *Hermione* officially became the *Santa Cecilia*, the captain-general demanded that William Turner select 25 British seamen to accompany the ship to Puerto Cabello. The rest of the temporary crew would be made up of Spaniards. Turner volunteered for the job himself, as did five of the ringleaders – James Bell, John Farrel, Thomas Jay, Robert McReady and Thomas Nash. Turner then recruited the remainder from among the other mutineers. So, they remained on board when their shipmates went ashore to their new accommodation in the naval barracks. Later, two more batches of the mutineers were forcibly shipped to Puerto Cabello, to help speed up the work of preparing the frigate for Spanish service. However, at least they were paid for their efforts, even if it was just 12 Spanish dollars per head.

Then, in early November, the men were suddenly confined to barracks while Spanish troops searched the streets of La Guaira for any of them who were still at large. Effectively they were being imprisoned. The reason soon became clear. The Spanish were about to lift an embargo which prevented the numerous American trading ships in port from sailing. The governor of the port didn't want the mutineers absconding before the king's reply arrived. This was also when he drafted the men to augment the work parties in Puerto Cabello. These draftees included John Holford, the captain's cook, and his son John the Younger, as well as the topman James Barnett, another former *Success* man who still bore the scars of Pigot's mass flogging from seven weeks before. All of them were housed in the fortress of Castillo San Felipe at Puerto Cabello, as if they were prisoners rather than free men.

However, after a few weeks, the Spanish authorities eased their restrictions and the mutineers in La Guaira were free to go where they pleased. The reason for this was that, by then, they had become an embarrassment to the Spanish authorities. On 5 December the *Magicienne* and *Diligence* arrived off La Guaira, and under a flag of truce Captain Mends was sent ashore with Vice-Admiral Parker's letter. Don José Vásquez sent it to the captain-general, so Don Pedro Carbonell now knew that the mutineers hadn't cast their officers adrift as they had claimed. This confirmed the rumours which had been circulating for weeks – the mutineers had blood on their hands. Still, he had already offered them his protection and felt he couldn't go back on his word. So, calling a meeting of the junta, a reply to Parker was drafted, expressing his official apologies but saying that his hands were tied until the king made his ruling.

So Mends returned empty-handed. Vice-Admiral Parker was furious with this Spanish attitude. In his report to the Admiralty he railed against 'the false policy which has actuated the government of that country in the protection of these atrocious villains'. Then he added that the mutineers were now 'dispersing themselves in different parts'. In other words, it would be hard to bring the mutineers to justice if they became scattered around the Americas. Sure enough, this dispersal was exactly what Don Pedro had in mind. By lifting his restrictions on the movement of the mutineers, he hoped the embarrassment of their presence on his provincial doorstep would solve itself. Several of them, together with the widowed Fanny Martin, were issued with permits allowing them to travel to North America. While a few planned to stay in Venezuela, most of them intended to leave the province.

Those who could signed on with merchant ships. A few mutineers managed to take passage to the Dutch island colony of Curaçao, 150 miles away to the north-west. This was a much busier port than La Guaira, and under false names most of them managed to find work on Dutch, American, Danish or French merchantmen. These included John Mason, the carpenter's mate, and John Elliot. Both men eventually joined the crew of the French privateer *Petite Magicienne* ('Little Magician') whose captain was planning to operate from Santo Domingo. Others, though, had to go on any ship they could find. John Holford and his son, on their return to La Guaira, joined James Bell and a group of mutineers who rowed to Cumaná, a port 150 miles away to the east, where they signed on to a Spanish merchant vessel, serving for food but no wages. Still, it was better than no work at all.

When the work on the *Santa Cecilia* was finished the British mutineers were let go, and most made their way back to La Guaira on foot. Holford and his son were among them. However, Joe Montell, who had had a hand in killing five officers, and mutineer Antonio Marco managed to sign on with the French privateer *L'Espoir* when she put in to Puerto Cabello. Also on board the privateer was David Forester, the 16-year-old maintopman who had the most blood on his hands from the mutiny, and a French-born shipmate, Pierre D'Orlanie. A few mutineers found work on small fishing boats or coastal vessels, and so were able to work their way along the Spanish Main in search of better opportunities. A few chose to stay put on land. The rabble-rousing Irish Republican, Lawrence Cronin, for example, stayed on in La Guaira, running a business, while a few of the marines joined the local military garrison.

Inevitably, this made it much harder for the British to track down the fugitives. Almost all of them now had aliases, and although lists and descriptions were posted in all British-owned ports in the Caribbean, and back home, it was unlikely any of the mutineers would be stupid enough to set foot in any port where they might be recognised. The big risk for the Admiralty was if they made it to the United States of America, where it was probable that the strong anti-British sentiment in the young country would make it unlikely the mutineers would be returned to the British, even if they were identified. The best chance was through random searches. Following the Admiralty's orders, in the wake of the mutiny the Royal Navy stepped up its policy of stopping and searching neutral ships. With luck, the search party might find one or more of the mutineers among the neutral's crew.

The odds, though, were stacked in the mutineers' favour. First, there were no shortage of havens for them to hide in, from Newfoundland down to Brazil. Naturally, most would gravitate to one of the larger seaports, and from there ships could sail just about anywhere, including Europe, Africa or even the Far East. By crossing to the Pacific coast a whole new range of opportunities would open up. Merchant ships visiting the Caribbean were often short of crew thanks to disease, and so experienced seamen would usually be taken on without too many questions being asked. Even if a mutineer were unlucky enough to be stopped by an official in a British-operated port, or by a British boarding party, in the days before photographs, it would be extremely hard to tie up a vague written description with a particular individual. So, the British authorities needed luck, and plenty of it.

Eventually, the Admiralty's manhunt bore fruit. The first catch was the German-born sailmaker John Slushing (originally Slussing), a 40-year-old Prussian from a village outside Danzig. That November he joined the 17-man crew of a six-gun Spanish privateering schooner called the *Casualidad* ('Chance'), which left La Guaira bound for Spain on 2 December, her small hold filled with cocoa. On 17 January 1798, west of Cape Finisterre, the schooner was intercepted by the British frigate *Aurora*. Despite giving his alias of John Henson, Slushing was identified as a *Hermione* man and taken on board the frigate. During the subsequent voyage to Lisbon and then Portsmouth, Slushing wrote out a four-page statement, which would be used against him at his court martial. However, he would have to wait almost a year for this, as the Admiralty gathered more evidence.

For almost four months, the only version the British had of the mutiny came from the master of the *San Antonio*.

Now, for the first time, Slushing's statement told something akin to the real story. It was through him that the Admiralty first learned that not all of the officers had been killed, and began to pull together a list of who the main ringleaders were. This, then, was a real breakthrough. Copies of Slushing's confession were hurriedly distributed around the fleet. Meanwhile, back in the Caribbean, other mutineers began to fall into Vice-Admiral Parker's net. He had sent almost every available ship to sea to take part in the hunt, partly to widen the search, but also to avoid an outbreak of yellow fever in Môle Saint-Nicolas.

On 1 March, six weeks after Slushing's capture, Parker's flagship *Queen* was cruising off Santo Domingo in company with the 74-gun Third Rates *Carnatic* and *Valiant*. A strange sail was sighted, and Parker sent Captain Crawley in the *Valiant* off in pursuit. After a five-hour chase, the *Valiant* overhauled a 16-gun French privateer and forced her to haul down her colours. She turned out to be the *Petite Magicienne*. A copy of the Slushing statement still hadn't reached the Jamaica squadron, so the boarding party didn't have much to go on. However, they found a number of British seamen among the 88-man crew. Then, one of them stepped forward and spoke to them in a Belfast accent. He identified himself as John Mason, former carpenter's mate on the *Hermione*. The 30-year-old then pointed the finger at four of his shipmates. He claimed all four of them were *Hermione* mutineers.

On board the *Queen*, now lying off Môle Saint-Nicolas, Mason named his former shipmates as the Genoese Antonio Marco, the French Pierre D'Orlaine, and two of the ringleaders – John Elliot from Kent and Joseph Montell from the Italian-speaking part of Switzerland. Better still, Mason dictated a detailed statement – the first such account of the mutiny that Parker had heard. It would take another three weeks for a copy of the Slushing statement to reach him, so this was the first the British admiral knew that four of the frigate's officers were still alive, and imprisoned in La Guaira. Mason named the main ringleaders, including Turner, as well as Bell, Cronin, Farrel, McReady and Nash. However, he denied having played any part in the mutiny himself. He recalled the way most of the crew cheered the captain's murder though. He also named Montell as one of Pigot's murderers.

On Saturday 17 March, a court martial was held on board the 64-gun *York*. It was formed of five captains, with Captain George Bowen acting as court president, assisted by William Page, the deputy judge advocate. The court heard Captain Mends's account from the previous October, as well as Captain Crawley's report of the privateer's capture. Following this, the court heard Mason's deposition read out. Then Lieutenant Harris was called in. *Hermione*'s old first lieutenant identified all the men as former *Hermione* men. That done, they demanded that Mason deliver a verbal report, before questioning him about the mutiny. The deliberation which followed didn't take long. The mutineers were all guilty of murder by the killing of Pigot, piracy by taking the *Hermione* into a Spanish port, and taking up arms against their king through joining the privateer. There was never any real doubt about the outcome.

Two days later, at 9am on Monday morning, a yellow flag was hoisted and a four-gun salvo fired, to attract the attention of the sailors in the other ships in the fleet. Then,

Pierre D'Orlaine, John Elliot, Antonio Marco and Joseph Montell were hanged from the main yardarm of the *York*. Afterwards, their bodies were cut down and taken ashore, where they were suspended in gibbets, as a warning to other would-be mutineers. They would hang there until their bodies were reduced to bare bones. This warning wasn't as melodramatic as it sounded. A few weeks before, a mutinous plot was uncovered in the frigate *Renommé*, and four ringleaders were arrested. Their plan was to murder their officers and sail the frigate into Havana. Three of them were later hanged for it.

So, Vice-Admiral Parker had had his first public trials and executions, bought at the cost of letting John Mason turn King's evidence, and then being pardoned for it. Interestingly, shortly before his death Montell confessed to killing Captain Pigot and Lieutenant Douglas, but offered mitigating circumstances for Elliot, who, afterwards, helped protect the master, Edward Southcott, from harm. However, the word of a self-confessed murderer wasn't enough to save Elliot's life. For Parker, this whole affair had given him two useful leads. The first was that Mason had identified some of the main ringleaders of the mutiny. These would become his leading targets. Then there was the news that the master, a midshipman and two warrant officers were still alive, and being held in La Guaira as prisoners of war.

Parker immediately dictated a letter to Don José Vásquez in La Guaira, demanding the release of the four officers, as well as the return of the ringleaders he could now name. However, by then the prisoners had already been released. Unbeknown to Parker, Rear-Admiral Henry Harvey commanding the Leeward Islands Station had already written to the port governor and secured the release of the British officers. So, on 30 March Southcott, Casey, Searle, Price and six loyal *Hermiones* were put on board the Spanish cartel *La Bonita*, which then sailed for the West Indies. On 11 April the *Hermione* survivors were received on board Harvey's flagship *Prince of Wales*, moored off Fort Royal in Martinique. Now, after all of their long ordeal, they were safe at last. They soon had the chance to have their revenge.

When they were interviewed by the admiral, Southcott and Casey learned that two suspected *Hermiones* were being held in the flagship's brig. A week before, the frigate *L'Aimable* had captured two small French privateers off Puerto Rico, *Le Triomphe* and *Le Chasseur*. Among the French crews they found two British seamen, who had been brought back in chains to Martinique. Southcott was able to identify them as Thomas Leech and William Mason, both from his old frigate. So, on Monday 1 May, a court martial was held on board the 74-gun *Alfred*, and the two seamen were horrified to discover that not only was Southcott present at the trial, but all the surviving officers, and several former shipmates. During the trial, Leech, the serial deserter but a favourite of Captain Pigot, was identified as one of the men who had killed the captain, and who had then become one of the ringleaders of the mutiny.

The *Hermione's* officers gave evidence, as did the other *Hermiones*, including Sergeant Plaice, the cook, Moncrieff, and McNeil, the marine sentry. McNeil's evidence was damning, as he was able to place Leech among the men who had stormed the captain's cabin. All of them, though, while naming Leech as a leading mutineer, couldn't recall seeing William Mason involved in anything. The topman protested his innocence, saying he was on watch in the maintop when the mutiny occurred, and hadn't come down until it was all over. In the end, the court ruled that Leech would hang for his crimes, but Mason would be acquitted. Two days later Leech swung from the *Alfred's* yardarm. The *Alfred* then left Martinique bound for home, and the *Hermione's* officers sailed with her. Sergeant Plaice and his three loyal marines, though, were kept in Fort Royal, in case they were needed to identify any more mutineers.

Meanwhile, off Môle Saint-Nicolas, Vice-Admiral Parker was dealing with his own trio of mutineers. Three former *Hermiones*, William Benives, William Herd and William Hill, had been arrested six weeks before, when they stepped ashore in Jamaica. They had all been in Curaçao when a small Spanish cartel vessel came in. When she sailed again, bound for Guadaloupe, the three mutineers were aboard, having signed on as crew. Once at sea the British newcomers seized control of the vessel, then took her into Port Morant, in the south-east corner of Jamaica. Realising they were from the *Hermione*, the British authorities handed them over to the navy, who duly shipped them off to Parker, now back in his old anchorage.

Parker planned to try them as mutineers, but he lacked hard evidence. He knew they had been on board at the time, but so far nobody had named any of them as active participants in the rising. So, the men were held in irons, until the admiral could figure out how to deal with them. Fortuitously for him, the solution came in the shape of another *Hermione* man, John Brown. The Scottish topman had signed on to a British merchant ship, but she was stopped and boarded by a British privateer, the *Benson*. When Brown was named as a former *Hermione* man, the privateer captain took him with them, then put in to Kingston, where he handed Brown over to the authorities. Like the others, Brown was clapped in irons and sent to Parker. On the way he wrote a detailed statement, protesting his innocence. Not only did the admiral believe him, but he also persuaded Brown to turn King's evidence.

In Môle Saint-Nicolas, Brown's character was attested to by the *Hermione*'s former master's mate, John Forbes, who had transferred to the *Diligence* shortly before the mutiny. So, in return for his freedom, Brown was allowed to point the finger. His written statement made interesting reading – it described how David Forester had tried to recruit Brown and his fellow maintopman George Walker into the mutiny, and he had seen them gathered in the forecastle, drinking their stolen rum. Then, from the maintop, he saw the mutiny develop. He went on to name 25 leading mutineers, and added that Midshipman Wiltshire had known about the mutiny before it happened, but rather than tell his fellow officers, he hid in the foretop to save his own skin. It was a damning indictment.

This meant that, now, Vice-Admiral Parker had his star witness at the trial of Benives, Herd and Hill. The court martial was held on Friday 5 May, the same week as the one held off Fort Royal. Both Forbes and Brown were called on to identify the men, and confirm they were all on board at the time of the mutiny. Then, Brown was asked about their involvement in the mutiny. Brown said he didn't know about the others, but named Herd as an active participant. Herd protested his innocence. Brown also added that Benives had been almost blind at the time – a common symptom of scurvy. When questioned, Brown admitted that he had no real proof about Herd – it was just hearsay. Still, despite the men having given themselves up – an indication of innocence – the court declared all three men guilty. All three of them were hanged from the main yardarm of the *Carnatic* at 9am the following morning.

When the *Alfred* arrived in Portsmouth, Southcott and the others were ordered to attend a court martial into the loss of the *Hermione*. It was held on board the 64-gun *Director*, moored off Sheerness on 9 August. The court's president was none other than Captain William Bligh, a man who knew a thing or two about mutiny. He was the same Bligh who had commanded the *Bounty* in 1789 when his crew mutinied and set him adrift in a boat. Eight years later, when commanding the *Director*, his crew mutinied off the Nore, and set him ashore. Given his experience, Bligh was very understanding. He exonerated Southcott, Casey, Searle and Price of any blame for the mutiny, or the loss of their ship. Also on trial was the Orcadian ship's cook, William Moncreiff, who had refused to support the mutiny. He too was acquitted. Now, at last, the four officers and the cook could get on with their lives, even though the horrors of that night would stay with them forever.

By now, the Admiralty had a growing dossier on the mutineers. Each new arrest and confession produced more scraps of evidence, and the testimony of the surviving officers and loyal crew greatly added to the pile. By late summer the

Admiralty were pretty much aware of who the instigators of the mutiny had been, who the main ringleaders were, and who had committed each of the ten murders. It had detailed descriptions of the mutineers, down to details of height, age, weight and complexion. Best of all, good identifying evidence such as tattoos, distinguishing marks or injuries were all recorded, and the details circulated around the fleet. That meant that, as the first anniversary of the mutiny approached, and given that most of the mutineers would seek employment as seamen, the chances were still high that more of them would be brought to justice.

In fact the first of them had already been caught. In April, off Puerto Rico, a British privateer captured a Spanish xebec – a vessel with lateen-rigged rather than square sails. On board were two former *Hermiones*: the captain's cook, John Holford, and his son John the Younger, now 13 years old. This was the ship they had boarded in Cumaná, working for food but not wages. They were taken to Kingston, where they gave the authorities a detailed written statement. Despite protesting his innocence, the cook from Surrey and his son were then sent to Vice-Admiral Parker to stand trial for mutiny. They were held in a prison on shore in Môle Saint-Nicolas while Parker gleefully arranged to hold another court martial. Before it sat, though, the defendants were joined by another old shipmate.

That same month James Irwin from the Irish port of Limerick had signed on to an American schooner in La Guaira. She was on her way to New York when she was intercepted by the British 28-gun frigate *La Tourterelle* while approaching the Mona Passage. A boarding party was sent over, looking for British seamen to impress, and Irwin was taken on board the frigate and signed on to the ship's muster. However, he was identified as a former *Hermione*, put in irons and taken to Môle Saint-Nicolas. So now Parker had three *Hermiones* to try. The court martial was convened on 23 May on board the 74-gun *Brunswick*, flagship of Parker's deputy, Rear-Admiral Richard Bligh. The two men and the boy were tried together, with evidence supplied by several former *Hermiones*: Lieutenant John Harris, Master's Mate John Forbes and Boatswain Thomas Harrington.

Also there were John Mason and John Brown, the mutineers who had turned King's evidence. Bligh had presided over Harris's one-sided court martial, but this time around he was scrupulously fair. The three had already admitted they were on board when the mutiny happened. That was never in dispute. However, Holford was adamant that neither he nor his son had had anything to do with the mutiny. Brown and Mason confirmed this – both Holfords had steadfastly refused to take part. So they were found not guilty. James Irwin, though, had been on watch when the mutiny began, and had done nothing to prevent the murder of Lieutenant Foreshaw. So he was sentenced to hang, but, as he took no active part, Bligh delayed the execution, pending a plea for mercy being sent to the Crown. In the end, Irwin had his sentence commuted to the living death of penal servitude in Australia.

Vice-Admiral Parker was incensed. He had promised the Admiralty that he would set an example, and now here was his deputy setting two mutineers free and showing mercy to a third. His argument was simple. The three *Hermiones* were on board when the mutiny took place. So, unless it could be proved that they had tried to stop it, or registered their innocence by becoming prisoners of war then they should all hang as mutineers. Effectively, he was arguing that as a 12-year-old boy hadn't stood up to two score of drunken and well-armed mutineers, he deserved to hang. Not content to stop there, Parker then wrote to the Board of the Admiralty, demanding that his deputy Rear-Admiral Bligh should be dismissed for his leniency, or else he would resign himself. The Admiralty knew the two admirals were already barely on speaking terms. Sensibly, they quietly ignored Sir Hyde's frothing letter.

In his letter to the Admiralty, Sir Hyde had expressed the need for 'imposing discipline by the terror of exemplary punishment in this momentary crisis'. In other words, he wanted the punishment for mutineers to be so draconian that others would be too terrified to follow their example. So, when two *Hermione* mutineers fell into his clutches, he made sure that no leniency was shown. Thomas Charlton and Adam Lynn were serving on an American brig when they were captured by a French privateer. She was then captured in her turn by the British ship-of-the-line. The pair were found guilty on board the *York* on 7 August. They were hanged three days later, and then their corpses were hung in gibbets on Gallows Point, just outside Port Royal harbour. This was where the bodies of pirates such as 'Calico Jack' Rackam and Charles Vane had been displayed 80 years earlier. Parker was making his point.

Parker's next prisoner was John Coe, a *Hermione* from Norwich who had signed on with a French privateer, *La Fleur de Mer*, when she put in to La Guaira. She made it safely through the Mona Passage, and in September she had reached the Bahamas Channel – an excellent cruising ground. There she captured the American brig *Ring Boston* of New York, which was on her way to New Orleans. Coe formed part of the French prize crew charged with taking her to a friendly French port in Saint-Domingue. However, off the northern coast of Cuba they were intercepted by the British frigate *Aquilon*. Together with a handful of others, Coe jumped into a boat and tried to make it to the shore, but they were captured before they reached safety.

The frigate's commander, Captain Boys, thought his English prisoner might be a former *Hermione*. So, Coe was taken back to Port Royal, where he was formally identified. The court martial was held on Rear-Admiral Bligh's flagship, *Brunswick*, on 8 December. As a *Hermione* mutineer turned French privateer, the outcome was never in doubt, and two days later Coe was hanged from the yardarm. By noon his body was swinging from a gibbet on Gallows Point. For Parker this marked a satisfactory end to what had otherwise been an unsettling year. He was back in Port Royal, as in October the navy had finally abandoned Môle Saint-Nicolas in the last stage in a phased withdrawal from Saint-Domingue. After six years and with over 100,000 British lives lost to disease, the British had finally signed a peace treaty with Toussaint L'Ouverture and washed their hands of the blood-soaked French colony.

The next crop of *Hermiones* were the Cornish Gunner's Mate Henry Croaker, and two seamen, Thomas Ladson from Kent and Peter Steward. All three of them were taken from an American brigantine, which had been stopped and searched in the Mona Passage. They had joined her in Jacmel on the southern coast of Saint-Domingue, after taking passage there from La Guaira in a Danish schooner. Again, Bligh presided over the court martial on board his flagship *Brunswick*, and to Vice-Admiral Parker's continued fury he was scrupulously fair. One of the three, Steward, transferred from the *Adventure* shortly before the mutiny, had been suffering badly from scurvy. Thanks to John Holford the Younger, who helped identify the men, it emerged that Stewart was unable to walk at the time of the mutiny. Afterwards, he had spent three months in the hospital in La Guaira. So, he was acquitted.

For Croaker and Ladson, though, there would be no mercy. Both former *Successes* had been involved in the mutiny from the very start, and Brown, the Holfords and Mason confirmed this. Effectively, both were among the ringleaders, although only as followers rather than instigators or murderers. However, their guilt was clear and both men were condemned to death. Two days later, on 17 January 1799, the pair were hanged from the *Brunswick*'s yardarm, and their bodies then added to those swinging from the gibbets on Gallows Point. That meant that by the end of that January, 16 months after the mutiny, a total of 20 former *Hermiones* had been caught and tried. Of these, 13 of them had been hanged, one transported to Australia, two allowed to turn King's evidence and four acquitted. Parker hoped many more executions would follow during the course of the year.

He was still adamant that terror was the best form of deterrent. After the mutinies at Spithead and the Nore, the Admiralty could only agree with his sentiments. The *Hermione* mutiny had been so brutal that there would be little mercy shown by the navy, regardless of any mitigating circumstances. After all, not only had the crew mutinied, but they had also then handed their frigate over to the enemy. In time of war, this was nothing short of treason. There was also the matter of public perception – the press at home demanded action, and nothing spoke louder by way of response than a string of well-publicised hangings.

These trials didn't just take place in the Caribbean. In fact, just two months after the last court martial at Port Royal, five former *Hermiones* – Jacob Fulga, James Perrett, Richard Redman, John Slushing and John Williams – were tried for their lives in Portsmouth, the very centre of Britain's naval power. Therefore, the trial would be front-page news, with press and public baying for vengeance. This, though, would be no show trial. This public scrutiny meant that the navy was careful to show that proper justice was being done. The way these five former *Hermiones* landed up in Portsmouth reflects the way the mutineers were now spreading out around the world. It also demonstrated the Royal Navy's broad reach during the 'Age of Nelson'.

The oldest was the gunner's mate, John Williams. He had been pressed into the *Hermione* from the *Mercy* of Liverpool, when both ships were in Port Royal in the summer of 1797. He was on board when the mutiny took place, but he never joined the mutineers, save for swearing their oath. When the frigate reached La Guaira he was taken to the Spanish naval hospital, as he had become lame. While there, he told Richard Price, the carpenter, that he planned to return home and give himself up. So, he left La Guaira on a Danish merchantman, but she was captured by a British privateer, as the Dane had been operating between Spanish ports, which violated her neutral status. She was taken to Tortola but, being British, Williams was set free. He signed on to the *Mona*, a merchant ship from Liverpool, and returned to his home port in her.

In Liverpool, he met the father of Lieutenant Foreshaw, and told him of his son's death, while assuring the man that he had taken no part in the mutiny. As he was married, and had three sons, he probably visited his family too, but this wasn't recorded. Then, after admitting himself to hospital for an operation on his damaged leg, he hobbled over to the City Chambers and turned himself in. He continued to protest his innocence as he was transported in chains down to Portsmouth.

Another *Hermione* who really was innocent was Jacob Fulga. He had deserted from the ship at Môle Saint-Nicolas, two months before the mutiny, and had been on the run ever since. Despite changing his name, some 18 months later, in January 1799, he was arrested in Portsmouth, after being identified as a former *Hermione*.

An even bigger haul was the capture of Richard Redman – a ringleader, and the murderer of both Captain Pigot and the boatswain, William Martin. In late July 1798, in company with James Perrett, Redman left La Guaira on board the Spanish merchant ship *L'Edad d'Ora*. She was bound for La Coruña, with a cargo of cocoa. However, on 6 September, when almost within sight of her destination, she was intercepted and captured by the British frigates *Aurora* and *Nymphe*. When the *Aurora's* prize crew appeared, Perrett gave himself up and named Redman as a *Hermione* mutineer. Both of them were duly taken to Portsmouth to stand trial.

The fifth man on trial for his life was the Prussian sailmaker John Slushing, who had also been captured by the *Aurora* six months earlier. It was his detailed statement which had given the Admiralty their first true account of the mutiny.

The court martial was finally convened on 15 March 1799. It was held on board the 44-gun *Gladiator*, the port guard ship and flagship of Rear-Admiral Charles Pole, deputy to the Commander-in-Chief Portsmouth, Admiral Sir Peter Parker. Attending it were several key witnesses: Edward Southcott and David Casey, the carpenter, Richard Price, and John Jones, the captain's steward. All of the five prisoners were identified as former *Hermiones*, but thanks to the evidence of these witnesses, two of the accused men were acquitted. Richard Price was able to confirm that John Williams was completely lame at the time of the mutiny, and couldn't possibly have taken part in the rising. Southcott and Casey both testified that Fulga had deserted before the frigate sailed for the Mona Passage, and so while a deserter, he was innocent of mutiny or murder. So, both men were returned to service in the navy.

The ship's butcher, James Perrett, was more of a problem as, while it was agreed by all four witnesses that he hadn't take part in the mutiny, Southcott told the court that after it Perrett had spoken to him about the murdered officers and had shown shocking disrespect. Perrett, though, claimed he was 'as innocent as a child unborn'. He added that he had been asleep when the mutiny broke out, and he wasn't aware of what had happened until it was too late. This was probably true – as a 'waster', with no set watches, he would usually have been in his hammock at 11pm at night. As further evidence of his innocence, he reminded the admiral and his court that he had voluntarily given himself up to the officer from the *Aurora*, and that he had also identified Redman at the time, naming him as one of the principal mutineers. So, despite his show of disrespect, he, like the other two, was acquitted.

The Prussian sailmaker Slushing (or rather Slussing) was much more straightforward. While none of the witnesses had seen him during the actual mutiny, afterwards he was very much to the fore, drinking with the leading mutineers, and celebrating with them. The most damning evidence against him was that he shared in the division of the spoils from the dead officers' effects. According to Jones, he was given some of the captain's silver plate. In his own defence, Slushing claimed he was asleep when the mutiny took place, and so couldn't prevent the murders. However, he was clearly supportive of the mutineers, and regarded himself as one of them. If not guilty of actual mutiny, he was certainly involved in handing the frigate over to a foreign power – something the Admiralty viewed as an act of piracy. Thus, Slushing was condemned to death.

The final prisoner was Richard Redman. After Perrett had pointed him out as one of the main ringleaders of the mutiny, Redman had written a letter in his own defence, which he read out in court. In it he claimed he had great affection for Captain Pigot, and as a former *Success* he saw himself as one of the captain's favourites. Redman wrote that the first he knew about the mutiny was when it was all but over, and he was subdued by threats, which prevented him defending his officers. He even claimed to have tried to save the boatswain. This, of course, was pure fabrication. Southcott identified him as the man who hit him over the head with a trailspike as he tried to climb through the gunroom skylight to see what was happening. That alone was enough to condemn him to death.

Of course, there was even more damning evidence to come. While there wasn't any proof that he'd killed Captain

Pigot, John Jones had seen him among the men who broke into the captain's cabin, and later he was spotted with blood on his clothes. Even more damning was Southcott's observation that, in the gunroom afterwards, Redman had been carrying the captain's sword in his hand. Jones also told the court how Redman had forced him to break open the captain's store room, and described how he had drunk the captain's Madeira, and passed the rest of it to his shipmates.

Finally, it was Jones who told the court how, rather than defending the boatswain, William Martin, Redman had dragged him from his cabin, in front of Martin's terrified wife. Afterwards, Jones stated, the drunken and blood-stained Redman had spent the night with the grief-stricken Fanny Martin in the boatswain's cabin.

There was little doubt about the outcome, and after a brief deliberation the court martial's president Rear-Admiral Pole called the prisoners and witnesses back into his great cabin. The judge advocate read out the verdict on the admiral's behalf. Three of the accused – Jacob Fulga, James Perrett and John Williams – were acquitted. The other two, though, Richard Redman and John Slushing, would be hanged from the flagship's yardarm. One of the court members, Captain Sir Edward Pellew, recommended an unusual step. He suggested that the court should order that sentence be carried out immediately, to increase the effect it had on other sailors in the fleet. Pole agreed, and so, despite the pleas of Redman and Slushing, the two mutineers were executed just an hour after being condemned. It was a clear signal that, if caught, the mutiny's ringleaders could expect nothing but the most merciless vengeance.

It can be argued that the arrest of these five mutineers demonstrated the vigilance of the navy in hunting down the fugitives. In fact, it also highlights just how much luck was involved. A year earlier, before the diaspora of mutineers had started, the chances of finding them had been higher. Now that they had spread further afield, the navy, as well as British officials around the world, had to be especially vigilant, as the mutineers might turn up just about anywhere. For the British authorities, this also highlighted a worrying new development. Evidence suggested that by 1799 several of the *Hermione* mutineers had reached the United States of America. Others had been taken from American ships. This then, added a new diplomatic element to the manhunt. Even Vice-Admiral Parker, though, wasn't expecting his search for mutineers to spark a full-scale diplomatic incident.

An International Incident

Since 1793, the Royal Navy had been fully stretched in what had almost become a global war against Revolutionary France. Naval victories over France's allies at Camperdown and St Vincent in 1797 and a crushing defeat of the French at the Nile in 1798 went some way to re-establishing Britain's naval supremacy. However, after six years of war the navy was short of manpower. Despite the work of the press gangs and the justices in supplying unwilling recruits, the Admiralty was hard-pressed to crew its ships. Experienced seamen were in especially short supply. So, the navy stepped up its policy of searching neutral ships for men it could press into service. While this angered all the neutral powers, it was especially resented in the United States, where the economy was heavily dependent on maritime trade.

So, as American politicians such as Secretary of State Thomas Pickering became increasingly antagonistic to Britain, her merchants and sea captains were equally happy to sign on Royal Navy deserters, regardless of their past. By 1799, according to the testimony of Joe Montell, at least ten former *Hermiones* had found their way to American ports, and many were now sailing under the new American flag. The Admiralty realised this, and so it ordered that, wherever possible, neutral American ships should be stopped and searched, not just for prime seamen who lacked the paperwork which could protect them, but also for mutineers. By stepping up the scale of this stop-and-search policy, it was inevitable that Britain's hunt for the *Hermione* mutineers would fuel the growing sense of American national outrage. It also created a diplomatic crisis which came close to causing a war.

———

The British stop-and-search policy was based more on *force majeure* – one of the benefits of being the world's largest naval power. During the French Revolutionary Wars and the Napoleonic Wars the Royal Navy freely stopped neutral vessels on the high seas, and despite the protests of neutral countries, they got away with it. In the United States, though, there was a growing intolerance of the policy. Thomas Pickering described these searches as 'a constant irritation in the public mind'. Even worse was the pressing of seamen from American ships into British service. Often, according to Pickering, this was done despite their proof of citizenship. In fact, fake proof of American citizenship was a commodity that was easily bought in the larger American ports, as was the issuing of 'Protections' by American customs collectors which, in theory, protected the seaman from impressments.

While the officers leading British boarding parties would prefer to press genuine British sailors, they were also happy to widen the net to include anyone who lacked the paperwork which might prove their nationality, or guarantee their safety from impressment. Even American protection certificates were often viewed with a critical eye, and the naval officer in charge of the boarding party had to make up his own mind about whether the certificate was genuine or fake. Of course, it wasn't just American seamen who suffered. The muster books of the *Hermione* contained sailors from a range of countries or states: Denmark, France, Genoa, Hanover, Norway, Portugal, Prussia, Spain and Sweden, as well as the United States of America. Many of these were neutral states, but that hadn't stopped the navy from pressing these men into naval service.

So throughout the spring and summer of 1799, British frigates continued to patrol the waters of the Caribbean, and neutral ships continued to be stopped and searched. Most neutral captains regarded this as a something they had to endure. Others, most volubly American masters and ship owners, saw it as a violation of their rights and liberties on the high seas. Bad feeling already existed between Britain and America. The ease with which a major incident had arisen over the Jessup affair a few years before reveals just how strained international relations had become. In 1812, this same stop-and-search policy would lead to war between the two countries. For now, though, all it did was fuel American resentment, and in 1799, with a US presidential election the following year, and given the right circumstances, it could easily become an important and emotive election issue.

However, for the Royal Navy the policy served three useful purposes. First, it limited the maritime trade of Britain's enemies and other maritime powers. Second, it was a useful tool in the drive to impress more seamen into the service.

Finally, it was still one of the best means the Admiralty had to capture the *Hermione* mutineers. An example is the case of James Barnett. In early June 1799, the frigate *Maidstone* was patrolling the Florida Straits, watching out for ships trying to slip into Cuban ports, and also carrying out stop-and-search missions in this busy 90-mile-wide waterway. On Monday 3 June, a sail was spotted to the west, off the coast of the Florida Keys. It turned out to be a neutral vessel – the American schooner *Polly*, on her way home to Boston from Jamaica. Her papers were in order, but eager for more men, *Maidstone*'s Captain Donelly ordered the pressing of three British seamen from her crew.

The patrol continued, and more neutral ships were stopped and searched, and more men pressed. By then, though, Donelly had become concerned that at least one of them – a 17-year-old topman – might have been a former *Hermione*. So, when the *Maidstone* returned to Port Royal in mid-July, he arranged for the men to be inspected by three of their former shipmates. John Mason, John Brown and the two Holfords were all serving in Parker's flagship the *Queen*, and so the three eldest of them were sent over to the frigate. Two of them didn't recognise the young man, although they thought he looked familiar. Perhaps the teenager had aged a lot over the past two years. Holford, though, was able to identify him as James Barnett, a former topman from the *Hermione*. So, thanks to the stopping of the *Polly* of Boston, Vice-Admiral Parker had another mutineer to put on trial for his life.

The court martial of James Barnett was held on Friday 23 August on board the *Brunswick* as, once again, Rear-Admiral Bligh was presiding over the trial. First of all, the three former *Hermiones* repeated what they had said on the

Maidstone – the youth looked familiar to Brown and Mason, but they couldn't place him. The captain's cook, John Holford, could though, and said that Barnett was from Chatham, and a main topman on the *Hermione*. It seems strange that his fellow topman, John Brown, claimed not to recognise him, but he might have been trying to protect the youth.

When asked to speak, Barnett said he had taken no part in the mutiny, but hadn't resisted it either. In La Guaira he had worked at the salt pans at Macuto, breaking salt rocks in return for food. Then, together with the Holfords, he had travelled to Cumaná in an open boat, before signing on to the same Spanish xebec as they did. In Barcelona, 30 miles down the coast, he had signed on to a Danish ship, before switching to the *Polly*. He stressed he was just 15 at the time of the mutiny, and had taken no part in it. Still, in the unforgiving eyes of the navy's Articles of War he was as guilty as any adult. Inevitably then, the ashen-faced youth was sentenced to death, but at least the execution was delayed pending the King's Pleasure – a plea for leniency based on Barnett's youth. He was eventually pardoned by royal decree in late November, and the teenager resumed his naval service as a topman.

In an attempt to solve some of the diplomatic problems between Great Britain and the United States, diplomats negotiated a treaty, setting out the terms of the countries' legal and commercial relationship for the next decade. The brainchild of John Jay, the US chief justice, it was designed to finally sort out all of the unfinished diplomatic business left over from the American War of Independence. The fine-sounding Treaty of Amity, Commerce and Navigations was signed in the American capital of Philadelphia in June 1795, and ratified by both countries the following February. Unofficially, it was known simply as the Jay Treaty. Despite its undoubted benefits for American trade, it was a divisive treaty in the United States, as it was bitterly opposed by the Jeffersonian Republicans, who preferred strengthening ties with Republican France rather than with Britain.

While the treaty never properly dealt with the problem of British impressment, it did encourage the British to show greater leniency when dealing with American ships. More relevant was Article 27 of the treaty, which covered the arrangements for extradition between the two countries. This wasn't particularly contentious, even for the Jeffersonians, as in theory it suited both countries. It declared that after the flight from one country to the other by a murderer or forger, the subject would be returned to his home country. However, it added that this would only happen if sufficient evidence was provided by the country applying for the extradition. In other words, the applicant couldn't just demand extradition on suspicion of a serious crime – it needed to provide proof. Thanks to the *Hermione* mutiny, these new extradition laws were about to be tested.

It all began in early February 1798, when the American brig *Hannah* returned to its home port of Wilmington, Delaware. She had recently been to Santo Domingo, where a British-born seaman calling himself Simon Marcus had joined her crew. In conversation, though, he revealed that he was a *Hermione* mutineer. Regardless of what individual Americans might think, this was not only an act of mutiny – it was also piracy. So, Marcus was duly detained by the local authorities. The American press had displayed a morbid fascination for the *Hermione* mutiny and the hunt for the mutineers. So, when Fanny Martin, the widow of the frigate's boatswain, read about Marcus's arrest, she decided to have her say. On 16 February she swore a deposition which identified Marcus as one of the mutineers. She even supplied a description of him, so there is no room for doubt that she knew who he was.

A copy of the widow's deposition reached Sir Robert Liston, Britain's minister to the United States. It stated that Mrs Martin had 'certain knowledge' that Marcus was one of the mutineers. So, Liston decided to put the diplomatic cogs into gear. On 19 February he wrote to US Secretary of State Thomas Pickering, a man he knew well. Despite Pickering's notable anti-British sentiment, the two men were on cordial terms. The letter requested that the mutineer be extradited to Britain. Pickering in turn told the US president, John Adams, although he also warned the president that the widow's letter hadn't directly implicated Marcus in any of the murders of the *Hermione*'s officers. The application for extradition was still pending the president's decision three weeks later when Liston learned that three more *Hermione* mutineers had been arrested.

In early February, the American brigantine *Relief of New York* was preparing to sail from Santo Domingo, when her master was approached by three British seamen, looking for work. He hired them, but during the voyage he learned that, despite their aliases and back stories, they were actually *Hermione* mutineers – John Evans, Joannes (or Johannes) Williams and William Brigstock. When he reached his destination – the small port of Perth Amboy, New Jersey – he explained his suspicions to the local authorities. The men were arrested and thrown into the jail in nearby New Brunswick. There, on 10 March, they were charged with 'feloniously murdering on the high seas' their captain and officers, and then 'piratically delivering up' their ship to the Spanish. So, just three weeks after Liston had filed his extradition plea, he had another extradition request to prepare. He filed it on 29 March.

To back up his request, Liston enclosed another statement from Fanny Martin, identifying Brigstock as a mutineer. Although Williams was a Swede, he was still a *Hermione*, and therefore a candidate for extradition. Evans was British, so that didn't present any problem, but Brigstock was an American, pressed into the *Success* before being transferred to the *Hermione*. Still, to make Liston's life easier, all three men had admitted they were on board the frigate when the mutiny took place. So, Pickering agreed that if there was sufficient evidence to satisfy US Attorney General Charles Lee, then all the prisoners would be turned over to the British. By then, though, the extradition request for Simon Marcus had been withdrawn. Liston discovered from the other three mutineers that Marcus hadn't been on board the frigate at the time of the mutiny.

Like Pickering, Charles Lee was no friend of the British, but his legally trained mind spotted a flaw in Liston's argument. The mutiny had taken place at sea, and so it didn't occur in a place of British jurisdiction. The United States was therefore under no legal obligation to hand over the prisoners. Besides, as Brigstock was an American citizen, he could only be tried in an American court. Therefore, Lee argued, the men had been charged, and should be tried, but there would be no extradition – this would take place on American soil. Liston was forced to concede the point. So, on Thursday 5 April 1798, the trial began in Trenton, New Jersey, 28 miles to the north-east of Philadelphia, on the opposite side of the Delaware River. That meant it would be held before an all-American jury. Presiding was Supreme Court Justice Samuel Chase, assisted by Robert Morris of the federal district court.

When the proceedings began, all three defendants were charged with piracy rather than mutiny. In addition, though, following evidence supplied by Fanny Martin, William Brigstock was named as one of the men who had murdered the frigate's officer-of-the-watch, Lieutenant Foreshaw. Therefore he was charged with inflicting 'a mortal bruise' on the lieutenant. The only non-American testimony was given by Fanny Martin, who confirmed all three were former *Hermiones*. That at least was straightforward. The court then considered nationality. Brigstock was described as a New Yorker, but formerly a British subject. Effectively then, he was a US citizen. The other defendants, John Evans and Joannes Williams, were both recorded as being 'late' of Great Britain. That really didn't bode well for Liston.

Mrs Martin was followed by six witnesses for the defence, all testifying to Brigstock's character. He was portrayed as a good American citizen who had been pressed into service with the Royal Navy. Despite all the written evidence supplied by Liston and Parker, the court decided there wasn't enough evidence to prove beyond reasonable doubt that the three defendants had all participated in the mutiny, or the handing of their ship over to the Spanish. So, after just 20 minutes of deliberation, the jury declared the men not guilty of the charge of piracy. That only left Brigstock's charge of murder to be dealt with. The court decided this needed a separate trial. So, while Evans and Williams were acquitted and released, William Brigstock was taken back to his cell in New Brunswick.

This was extremely disheartening for the British minister. Liston blamed the decision on the Attorney General, whose interpretation of the law when it came to extradition was, he thought, motivated by politics rather than justice. Meanwhile, from his jail cell, Brigstock had enlisted the help of a New York Congressman, Edward Livingston, who was a staunch opponent of British impressment. He was planning to intervene on behalf of Brigstock when the whole case against the seaman fell apart. On 1 June, Liston received a bombshell of a letter from Vice-Admiral Parker. After questioning the *Hermione* witnesses, it turned out that Brigstock had opposed the mutiny, and the murder of the ship's officers. His stance had even resulted in him being victimised by the mutiny's ringleaders. He had certainly never attacked Lieutenant Foreshaw. So, he was innocent of both mutiny and murder.

Parker's letter also questioned the credibility of Fanny Martin. Her accusation of murder had been a falsehood – one that wasn't supported by any other *Hermione*, or repeated in any statement from a captured mutineer. In other words, she had been lying. The reason is unclear, but she also told other untruths. The biggest one is that she accused the gunner's mate, Henry Croaker, of murdering her husband, the boatswain, William Martin. The 31-year-old Cornish gunner had certainly been a ringleader of the mutiny, and he had even received a share of the plunder from the murdered officers. However, he wasn't a murderer, and he certainly didn't kill Martin. Perhaps Fanny was trying to protect

Richard Redman, which suggests their union after Martin's death wasn't as spontaneous as it first seemed. So, the grieving widow was at best an unreliable witness. At worst, she was guilty of perjury.

On receiving the letter, Secretary of State Pickering spoke to President Adams, who told him to drop all charges. Therefore, on 8 June, Pickering wrote to the New Jersey courts requesting that William Brigstock be released by command of the president. So, Brigstock walked free. Liston's letter also shared fresh information about Simon Marcus, the young seaman who had been arrested in Wilmington. He had already learned from Parker that Marcus had left the *Hermione* before the mutiny, and now he could supply Pickering with written evidence to back this up. This too was another instance of Mrs Martin misleading the court, as she had accused Marcus of being on board the frigate at the time of the mutiny. Sir Robert Liston must have vowed that next time a *Hermione* mutineer was identified on American soil he would make sure he had got his facts right, and enough evidence to guarantee an extradition.

In fact, it was just a matter of weeks before the next mutineer was caught on American soil. John Watson, a quarter gunner on the *Hermione*, had arrived in Virginia by way of La Guaira and Curaçao. There he had joined the US Navy and joined the crew of the 38-gun frigate USS *Constellation*. A month after the Brigstock case collapsed, Watson was identified as a *Hermione* mutineer and sent ashore at Norfolk, Virginia, under armed guard. After a meeting with Colonel John Hamilton, a former Loyalist who acted as the port's British consul, a local magistrate ordered Watson to be thrown into the local jail. However, a crowd had gathered, and Watson addressed them, declaring he would mutiny again 'rather than be confined on board a British vessel'. It seems Watson was then spirited away to safety before he ever set foot behind bars. At least Liston was spared another humiliation.

———

Thanks to the US Attorney General's rigid definition of the 1795 treaty terms, it now looked like no *Hermione* mutineer could ever be extradited from the United States. Therefore, Sir Robert began a campaign of lobbying American politicians like President Adams and Secretary of State Pickering, both of whom, he knew, had no love for mutineers and traitors, wherever they came from. He also enlisted the diplomatic help of Lord Grenville, Britain's minister for foreign affairs, who had helped draft the treaty in the first place. He was helped by the boom in commerce that resulted from the Jay Treaty, as American merchants now had access to lucrative British markets. Also, a 'quasi-war' had erupted between the United States and France over war debts so, as a result, relations with Britain had mellowed somewhat and Adams and Pickering put pressure on Attorney General Lee to review his stance.

The result was that the next time a *Hermione* mutineer was arrested on American soil, provided there were no serious questions over his citizenship or origins, it was now far more likely that he would be extradited into British custody, to stand trial for his crimes. For President Adams, though, this was a double-edged sword. The following year – 1800 – would see the country's fourth presidential election, and so Thomas Jefferson's Democratic-Republicans were doing whatever they could to undermine John Adams's Federalist administration. British impressment remained a hot issue, and Jefferson's supporters used the press to whip up indignation. The aim was to make Adams look weak, and the sense of outrage even spanned the party divide. Sir Robert Liston would have to tread very carefully indeed when the next mutineer came within his grasp.

The chance came on Wednesday 20 February 1799. That morning a young American seaman knocked on the door of Benjamin Moodie and asked to see him. Moodie was one of Britain's two consul generals in the United States, and lived in Charleston, South Carolina. The seaman turned out to be William Portlock, an 18-year-old Virginian-born sailor on the American schooner *Tanner's Delight*. The schooner had arrived in Charleston from the Caribbean three weeks before. Portlock told the consul that one of his shipmates, Nathan Robbins, had been one of the mutineers on the *Hermione*. The previous Christmas, when the schooner was in Santo Domingo, Portlock had overheard Robbins in a harbour tavern drunkenly boasting to French privateersmen that he had once been a boatswain's mate on the British frigate. Young Portlock had no doubt that Robbins had been telling the truth.

Naturally, Moodie had the detailed list of the mutineers the Admiralty had compiled, complete with names, ages, duties and a description. After checking the list again, Moodie was convinced he had found his man. The height, the long black hair, the hairy arms and torso and the age, as well as the Irish accent all fitted Moodie's description of Thomas Nash. If he was right, then his extradition would be a real coup. Nash, after all, was one of the main ringleaders of the mutiny, and was linked to the murders of both Captain Pigot and Lieutenant Foreshaw. However, as he was deeply aware of the strength of anti-British feeling in the country, Moodie did everything by the book.

First, he took Portlock to the city's Federal building, where the youth swore an affidavit outlining what he'd heard. Then, Moodie saw Judge Thomas Bee, the Federal judge for the South Carolina District. He asked Bee if Robbins could be arrested and detained, pending an extradition appeal. The judge agreed, and within the hour Robbins was arrested and thrown into Charleston jail. However, he wasn't prepared to simply hand Robbins over to the British. After consulting District Attorney John Parker, Bee was reminded of the Attorney General's recent ruling in the Brigstock case. In his view, extradition wasn't an option unless it was approved by the president. The problem, of course, was the definition of Article 27 which claimed Britain's jurisdiction didn't extend to the high seas.

So, Moodie needed help. He wrote to both Sir Robert Liston in Philadelphia and Vice-Admiral Parker in Port Royal, telling them what he had done, and requesting that the admiral send him someone who could identify the prisoner. Therefore, Parker sent John Forbes, formerly a master's mate, and now a Royal Navy lieutenant. On Wednesday 17 April he arrived in Charleston in the ten-gun cutter HMS *Sprightly* and was able to attest that Nathan Robbins was really Thomas Nash, former boatswain's mate of the *Hermione*, and one of the most notorious of the mutineers. Robbins, of course, denied everything.

The next step was a formal request for an extradition, in line with Article 27 of the Jay Treaty. Liston sent it to

Pickering, complete with a copy of the affidavits of both Portlock and Forbes, the Admiralty's official description of Nash, and a no-holds-barred account of his crimes, courtesy of Vice-Admiral Parker. It was as watertight an application as Liston was ever likely to get. He also mentioned Judge Bee's reluctance to help, and his insistence that ultimately the decision to extradite or not lay with President Adams. It seems that, for once, Pickering was supportive. For a start, this time he didn't seek the advice of the Attorney General. Instead, on 15 May he wrote directly to President Adams, who had gone home to Massachusetts for the summer. He asked for Adams's ruling, but he also gave the president the benefit of his own opinions on the case.

Pickering wrote: 'The only legal question was whether an offence committed on a public ship-of-war on the high seas was committed within the jurisdiction of the party demanding the offender'. He then added: 'I am inclined to answer in the affirmative.' In other words, when it came to Article 27 of the treaty, Pickering was willing to treat the deck of a British warship as being just as much a piece of sovereign territory as a patch of British soil. After all, he argued: 'On the high seas, her [Britain's] officers have and exercise a particular jurisdiction on board their own ships.' This contradicted Attorney General Lee's opinion, but it worked both ways – the decks of a US warship could then also be classed as American territory, which might be a useful ruling in the future.

Today, such considerations seem arcane, as like embassies on foreign soil, a nation's warships, according to international law, enjoy sovereign immunity. This is slightly different from sovereign territory, which is what was covered in the Jay Treaty. However, it wasn't until 1812 that the US Supreme Court recognised the notion of sovereign immunity. Thirteen years before this ruling, Pickering, Lee, Moodie and therefore President Adams were very much in uncharted legal waters. Still, Pickering was adamant that supporting the British in recovering the mutineer was the right thing to do, therefore he finished his letter to Adams by saying: 'I respectfully submit my opinion that the Judge of the District of South Carolina should be directed to deliver up the offender.' So, Pickering was ready to support Moodie.

The plea clearly worked. From Quincy, Massachusetts, John Adams replied by return, saying: 'I have no doubt that an offence committed on board a public ship-of-war on the high seas, is committed within the jurisdiction of the nation to whom the ship belongs.' Then he injected a note of caution: 'How far the President of the United States would be justifiable in directing the judge to deliver up the offender is not clear'. Still, he had already made his decision. He finished: 'I have no objection to advice and request him [Judge Bee] to do it.' So, Robbins, or rather Nash, would be handed over. On 3 June, Pickering wrote to Judge Bee, informing him of the British application for extradition, then telling of the president's 'advice and request that Thomas Nash may be delivered up'. This time, it looked like the British were finally going to get their man.

It was at this point that fate intervened in the shape of Abraham Sasportas, a merchant and pillar of both Charleston's Jewish community and the city's circle of freemasons. Sasportas was an ardent Jacobin, a supporter of the French Revolutionary movement, and he traded regularly with Saint-Domingue, where his brother had an office. As a staunch abolitionist, Sasportas often found himself at odds with the South Carolina establishment. He was also the French Republic's commercial agent in Charleston, until the quasi-war brought an end to French trade. When he heard of Robbins's arrest, Sasportas visited the prisoner and offered him his support. He then wrote to the city's authorities, claiming that Robbins was a bona fide American citizen, and he even had a certificate to prove it. This, of course, was a real game-changer, given the widespread outrage in the country over British impressment.

Sure enough, the document duly surfaced. It was dated 20 May 1795, and issued in New York. He added that, in 1797, while sailing in the brig *Betsey* of New York, Robbins had been pressed against his will into the *Hermione*. Above all else, he claimed he wasn't Thomas Nash. Sasportas then arranged for Robbins to be taken under guard to Charleston's Federal building, where he swore an affidavit that claimed he was a native of Danbury, Connecticut, and after being pressed he remained on board the *Hermione* until after the mutiny – a rising he had no hand in. The president's 'advice and request' had been made with one major proviso – that 'such evidence of his criminality be produced' by the British to justify their extradition claim under the laws of the United States, and the state of South Carolina. This new development threatened to wreck the whole tidy arrangement.

On the surface this new evidence of American citizenship sounded very convincing. However, Lieutenant Forbes remained adamant – Robbins was a false name. The prisoner was definitely Thomas Nash, a 26-year-old from Waterford in Ireland, a former master's mate on the *Hermione*, and both a mutineer and a murderer. Nash had joined the frigate in December 1792, and on the day the certificate of citizenship was being signed, he was in the *Hermione*, which was busy bombarding Port-au-Prince at the time. Somebody was lying.

Then, Alexander Moultrie stepped in. A colonel during the War of Independence and a brother of a war hero, he had become a lawyer after the conflict and rose to become South Carolina's Attorney General, but fell from grace in 1792, when he was impeached for embezzling public money. His brother William, though, rose to become the State's governor. In mid-July, Sasportas hired Moultrie to represent Robbins in the forthcoming court hearing ordered by Judge Bee. Alexander Moultrie should have been delighted to help. After all, he was an ardent Jeffersonian Democratic-Republican, and he saw this case as a heaven-sent opportunity to humiliate Adams's Federalist administration. However, Moultrie resigned before the hearing, as he thought the case was unwinnable. So, at the last minute, Sasportas hired William Johnson, a prominent Charleston lawyer with an impressive local pedigree.

However, on the morning of the hearing, on Wednesday 23 July, Sasportas and Johnson discovered that Robbins had hired a lawyer of his own – none other than Alexander Moultrie. It was almost as if the three men were jostling for the right to speak for Robbins.

Johnson immediately resigned, while a third lawyer, Samuel Ker appeared, to join this ad hoc defence team. They led with Robbins's affidavit claiming he was from Danbury, Connecticut. Ker argued that this proved that Robbins, a US citizen, had been forced into British service, and therefore he had a right to regain his liberty, even if that meant using violence. Moultrie pitched in by declaring Moodie's affidavits as nothing more than suspicion. The whole defence centred around Robbins's claim of US citizenship trumping any claims the prosecution made, and the defendant's constitutional rights.

This defence might have worked if the defenders had been better prepared. Instead, the prosecution's lawyer John Ward easily dismissed any discussion of Robbins's rights and liberty. This matter was solely governed by Article 27 of the treaty, not an individual's rights as a US citizen. Ward argued convincingly that Britain enjoyed jurisdiction on board its own warships. While he didn't question the ins and outs of the British use of impressment, he argued that if Nash really was an American, then this evidence would have come to light much sooner – not at the last minute. In effect, Ward was shifting the burden of proof onto the defence rather than the prosecution. When the court reconvened the next day, Judge Bee waded into the defence. He accused them of appealing to passion rather than sticking to the facts. The Jay Treaty wasn't on trial – only this solitary extradition request.

Bee reminded the defence team that nationality didn't make any difference to extradition. Even if Robbins was an American citizen, he would still be liable to extradition to stand trial for murder. The judge even went further, questioning this last-minute claim of citizenship, produced after making no mention of it despite spending several months in an American jail. As this wasn't a jury trial – merely an extradition hearing, Judge Bee then delivered his verdict: 'I do therefore order and command the marshal to deliver the body of the said

Nathan Robbins, alias Thomas Nash, to the British consul.'
So, Benjamin Moodie finally had his man. Before the hearing
the cutter *Sprightly* had returned to Charleston, with a file
of marines on board. So, when the manacled prisoner was
handed over to him, Moodie had him marched down to the
harbour and bundled aboard the British ship.

Three days later, on Saturday 27 July, the *Sprightly* slipped
out of Charleston, bound for Jamaica. It seemed that during
the two-week voyage the last vestiges of Nathan Robbins
dropped away, and the prisoner reverted to being the Irish-
born sailor Thomas Nash. It was just as well, as two days
after his arrival, on Thursday 15 August, Nash stood trial for
his life. This time, though, there would be no last-minute
claims of citizenship, or the inflaming of passions. This was
a very stolid display of naval justice. The court martial was
convened on board the 74-gun Third Rate *Hannibal*, lying
off Port Royal, Jamaica. It was presided over by Captain
Tyrrell Smith, commander of the *Hannibal*, and his board
consisted of no fewer than five more highly experienced post
captains. Expecting criticism in the American press, Vice-
Admiral Parker wanted to be sure he wouldn't leave himself
open to charges of legal impropriety.

The proceedings began with the reading out of charges –
mutiny, desertion to the enemy, delivering the *Hermione* to the
Spanish, and murder. Then, Lieutenant Jump of the *Sprightly*
recounted what had happened in Charleston, and confirmed
that the accused had been legally extradited. Next, the accused
man was formally identified as Thomas Nash. The witness
here was his old shipmate John Mason, the carpenter's mate
who had turned King's evidence. Mason, though, had never
seen Nash murder Captain Pigot or Lieutenant Foreshaw.

Then, John Brown verified the prisoner was indeed Nash, and testified about Nash's part in the murder of Foreshaw. He told how Nash participated in the initial attack on the lieutenant, and told his fellow mutineers to 'Heave the bugger overboard'. It was pretty damning evidence, and enough to hang him, but more was to come.

The next witness was John Holford the elder, Captain Pigot's cook. Holford readily identified Nash, but didn't name him as one of the mob who had stormed past him to murder the captain. Instead, he recounted the moment when Foreshaw reappeared over the side of the frigate, his face still streaming with blood. Holford recalled: 'I saw Thomas Nash come running down the ladder from the quarterdeck. He advanced towards Lieutenant Foreshaw immediately and caught him by the right wrist, and said "You bugger Foreshaw. Are you not overboard yet"?' Holford continued: 'They got him upon the gangway and immediately hove him overboard.' It also emerged that in the division of plunder from the murdered officers, Nash received a pocket watch. It was now clear that Nash was not only one of the main ringleaders of the mutiny, but he was also the man who murdered Foreshaw.

The board deliberated, but for some reason the verdict was only formally given two days later, on the morning of Saturday 17 August. Inevitably, Nash was found guilty and condemned to death by hanging, then his body was to be hung in chains. The execution took place on Monday morning, with Nash strung up from the fore yardarm of the frigate *Acasta*. Afterwards, according to the court martial board's instructions, his body was wrapped in chains and iron bands and hung from the waiting gibbet on Gallows Point, next to the decaying remains of Nash's shipmates. During his final few days, Nash 'confessed himself to be an Irishman', thereby belying his alleged American citizenship. He also warned the crew of the *Acasta* 'to take timely warning of his fate'. In other words, he was advising them not to turn to mutiny, or else they would face the same grisly fate.

Back in Philadelphia and Charleston, Liston and Moodie fully expected the news of the execution to cause some form of outcry. Even they, though, were unprepared for the full extent of the furore. While some newspapers presented the facts, others, mainly the Republican-leaning ones, piled on the vitriol, screaming that this was a public affront to the American people, and that Robbins, an American citizen, had been let down by the judiciary and the Federalist administration. Sir Robert Liston tried to extinguish some of the flames by publishing details of the clear identification of the man as the Irish-born Nash rather than the American-born Robbins, the irrefutable evidence that Nash was a murderer, and Nash's own confession of nationality and guilt after the court martial. It did little good. Instead, Nathan Robbins was being turned into an American patriot and a martyr to liberty.

The real issue here was the election of 1800. By stirring up feeling over the Nash-Robbins affair, the Jefferson Democratic-Republicans were able to portray President Adams's administration as complicit in his execution by a foreign power. The fact that Nash-Robbins was a mutineer and murderer were conveniently ignored. Instead, according to one frothing article, he 'was ignominiously put to death because he was an American citizen'. It was scandalous of course, but in the United States of the time, the press had immense influence on public opinion, and therefore on the outcome of elections. In that election, held in late 1800, President Adams and his Federalists were roundly defeated by the Democratic-Republicans. So, Thomas Jefferson became the country's third president. His victory was achieved in part by the execution of an Irish-born mutineer on board a British warship.

12

The *Surprise*

The execution of Thomas Nash on 17 August 1799 marked a turning point in the manhunt for the *Hermione* mutineers. It had now been almost two years since the mutiny, and while no doubt more of them would be caught, the navy was also embroiled in a war, and so it had other priorities. In Port Royal, Vice-Admiral Parker had his own problems. While the British had left Santo Domingo, they were still embroiled in fighting in the French islands of the West Indies, and in combating attacks by enemy privateers. He was expecting to be recalled to Britain soon, as his time in Jamaica was almost done. Before he left, though, he had an outstanding problem to deal with. The *Hermione* was still in Spanish hands, and intelligence reports suggested she would soon be ready to put to sea. Before he left for Britain, Parker was determined to recapture her, and so efface the shame of the mutiny.

———

In the late afternoon of Thursday 17 September, Parker summoned Captain Edward Hamilton to his flagship and gave him the orders that might well set this in motion. They instructed Hamilton: 'To proceed with the *Surprise*, and cruise between the Aruba and Cape St. Roman (taking care to prevent your station being known at Curaçao), and use your utmost endeavours to capture the *Hermione* frigate loading at Porto Cavallo [Puerto Cabello], and intended to sail early in October for the Havana.' Hamilton, who commanded the Sixth Rate frigate *Surprise* of 28 guns, was one of Parker's favourite frigate captains, and certainly one of his most successful. Still, asking him to sail 750 miles into enemy waters and then to fight and capture a larger and better-crewed frigate was a tall order, even for a commander used to success.

Clearly Edward Hamilton thought so too. When he was in Sir Hyde's cabin on board the *Queen*, he suggested cutting out the *Hermione*. Essentially, that meant sending several of the ship's boats into Puerto Cabello to 'cut out' the captured frigate from under the noses of the Spanish. Obviously, this was a highly risky undertaking, as the harbour was heavily fortified and, as the frigate's boats could only carry a hundred men, the attackers would be greatly outnumbered. Hamilton even, supposedly, asked Parker for extra boats and men, but the admiral turned down the request, as he deemed the venture 'too desperate'. So Hamilton was left with one option – patrolling the waters off Aruba until the *Hermione* appeared, and then taking her in a sea battle. Even that was a risky undertaking.

Why Parker chose Hamilton and the *Surprise* for this mission is perplexing. After all, he had other frigates, and most of them were larger, carrying 32 or even 36 guns. The *Surprise* was smaller and less well armed than the *Hermione* had been before the mutiny, and now, if the usual Spanish practice was followed, she would also carry a much larger crew. Hamilton would have to rely on good seamanship and gunnery to win the day; that and a great deal of luck. That said, Edward Hamilton was probably the most fortunate captain on the Jamaica Station. He and the *Success* had arrived in the Caribbean in October 1798, and Parker had given them a string of independent cruises off Cuba, Hispaniola and Puerto Rico. In the past year or more the *Success* had captured or destroyed over 80 enemy vessels, and her captain, crew and the admiral had earned themselves a small fortune in prize money.

The frigate spent the next day taking on water, powder and stores – enough for several weeks. In the Spanish Main, where the entire coast was in enemy hands, there would be little chance to put in somewhere quiet to take on more water. This then, would be the main limiting factor on Hamilton's cruise. Parker's intelligence sources had told him that the *Santa Cecilia* – the old *Hermione* – was almost ready to put to sea. In mid-October she would leave Puerto Cabello, bound for Havana in Cuba. There she would join a powerful Spanish squadron under the command of Commodore Don Francisco Montes. Almost certainly, this meant that she would sail along the safest and quickest route between the two ports – which meant passing through the Aruba Channel. That, then, was where Hamilton would lie in wait for her.

At dawn on Saturday 20 September the *Surprise* slipped out of Port Royal harbour and headed out into the Caribbean. On the way they would have passed Gallows Point, where the bodies of several mutineers still hung from their gibbets. The south-westerly wind was favourable enough and, once

Jamaica fell away astern, the frigate's master, Thomas Made, was able to steer towards the south-east – an almost direct course towards their destination. Hamilton intended to make his landfall around Punta Gallinas and Bahia Honda, some 120 miles due west of the island of Aruba, on the far side of the Gulf of Venezuela. Then he planned to follow the coast until he reached the Aruba Channel. Ideally, he could snap up some Spanish merchant vessels along the way. Then the *Surprise* would begin her vigil, cruising the channel until the *Hermione* turned up.

They made landfall off Bahia Honda early on Tuesday 1 October, after a fairly swift 11-day voyage. Almost immediately the frigate's lookouts spotted their first victim. She was a small schooner, lying in the lagoon that was tucked behind the Punta Gallinas. So, Hamilton ordered three boats to be lowered – two cutters and the gig – and a 40-strong cutting out expedition was sent in, led by the frigate's first lieutenant, John Busey. It was a long haul through the winding entrance to the lagoon, but by mid-afternoon the prize was lying alongside the frigate. She turned out to be the *Nancy*, a French schooner, her small hold filled with sacks of coffee beans. Hamilton sent her to Port Royal, crewed by a midshipman, a master's mate and eight experienced seamen.

Hamilton was in no hurry, as *Hermione* wasn't due to pass through the Aruba Channel for at least another four weeks. So he lingered off the mouth of the Gulf of Venezuela, and even headed into it, towards the bottleneck at its southern end, which led to the Lake of Maracaibo. It was there, 130 years earlier, that the great buccaneer Henry Morgan had led a crippling raid on the Spanish Main. Now Hamilton, a keen reader of maritime history, was ready to strike his own blow against Spain's colonies. For the moment though, no more prizes presented themselves, and so at noon on Sunday 13 October, the *Surprise* arrived at the western end of the Aruba Channel. It was just 14 miles wide at its narrowest point, so it was unlikely anything could slip past them, at least in daylight. Therefore, what Hamilton should have done was to lurk there in mid-channel, waiting for his prey.

Instead, he decided to take a closer look at the Dutch-held island of Aruba. Just before dawn on Monday, they approached Bahía de los Caballos (now Oranjestad) on the island's south-western side, and spotted a large schooner. Despite his orders to stay in the main channel, Hamilton decided to cut her out. Still, he had no chance of doing it in daylight, and so he stood off until nightfall. A little after dusk, they approached the anchorage and lowered two boats. Lieutenant Busey led the attack, and all went well until they set foot on board the schooner. The Dutch crew fought back, and in the struggle Busey was shot and badly wounded. He died a little after midnight, shortly after their return to the *Surprise*. The prize, the 80-ton schooner *Zwakkeling* ('Lame Duck') of ten guns, wasn't worth the life of a good officer. Besides, the Dutch on Aruba now knew a British warship was operating in the area.

For the rest of Tuesday the *Surprise* stayed out of sight of the island, cruising the middle of the 15-mile-wide channel. With Aruba off their larboard beam and the Cabo San Roman at the head of the arid Península de Paraguaná to starboard, they were in an excellent position to intercept any ship heading towards them from the east. However, Hamilton noted the strong current flowing through the channel from east to west. That would work in the *Hermione*'s favour when she appeared, speeding her passage through the bottleneck. This didn't suit Hamilton at all. He also had another problem. After capturing the *Zwakkeling*, he expected that vessels from Aruba would try to make the 50-mile journey eastwards to Curaçao, and let their fellow Dutch colonists know about this new threat to their shipping. So, he had to guard against the *Hermione* and watch out for local Dutch boats too.

The *Surprise* remained on station in the Aruba Channel for several more days. The *Hermione* never appeared. Nor, it seems, did very much else. On Sunday 20th they caught a Spanish schooner, *La Manuela*, which they sank after letting her crew take to their boat. It was now becoming clear that something was wrong – the *Hermione* didn't seem to be sticking to the schedule suggested by Vice-Admiral Parker's intelligence sources. So Captain Hamilton reached a decision. If the *Hermione* wasn't going to come to him, then he would go to her. He decided he had to try to look into Puerto Cabello, 150 miles to the south-east. If the frigate was still there, then he would know he hadn't missed her. There was also the danger that word had reached the Spanish port that a British frigate was in the area, which would result in the Spanish taking another route to Cuba. Therefore, moving closer to the port reduced the risk of letting the *Hermione* slip by.

So, that night, Hamilton ordered the master, Thomas Made, to set a course for Puerto Cabello. The wind was favourable, and by dusk on Monday they were less than 20 miles from the port. Hamilton didn't fancy getting any closer during the day, as the risk he'd be spotted from the shore was too great. Instead he hoped to intercept a vessel coming out of Puerto Cabello, so he could interrogate her crew. Unfortunately for him, by dawn the wind had died altogether, leaving them becalmed in an empty sea. Then the lookouts spotted a sail.

A vessel was hull-down to the south-west, and seemed to be heading to Puerto Cabello. It was more than likely that her crew had spotted the becalmed frigate. Worse, the vessel was under canvas, and seemed to be picking up a light wind. If Hamilton didn't do something, then she would reach port ahead of the *Surprise* and warn the Spanish. There was only one possible solution.

It was now 6am. Hamilton gave the order for the ship's boats to be lowered and crewed with the frigate's strongest seamen. They were armed, too, and so the plan was to row after the ship and intercept her before she reached Puerto Cabello. The boats set off, but the prize was at least 10 miles off, and gradually pulling further away; it promised to be a long, hard row. Then, at 7am, when the boats had covered 6 miles, they saw the waves move away to the south-west. A light breeze was springing up, and a few minutes later it overtook them. The frigate began to move through the water, and while their speed was less than a slow walking pace, it was better than nothing. Gradually, though, the wind freshened, and the *Surprise* picked up speed. However, the chase was now south-west of them – directly to windward. That meant tacking regularly, zigzagging their way towards their prize.

At noon they had caught up with their boats, which was just as well as the sun was directly overhead and the rowers were exhausted. Hamilton ordered the boats to be recovered, then resumed the chase. Little by little it was clear they were overhauling the chase. The only questions now were whether the wind would hold, and whether they would reach her before they came within sight of Puerto Cabello. In fact the wind strength increased during the early afternoon, and by 2pm they were within hailing distance. They could see the coast of the Spanish Main to the south – another half hour and they would have been easily visible from the shore. A boarding party was sent over, and it turned out the prize was a neutral Danish schooner, sailing from Curaçao to Puerto Cabello. Hamilton used a shot across the bows to persuade the Danish master to turn back and return to Curaçao.

The problem was that the Danish schooner might double back and try to slip back into the Spanish port. Or, she might head somewhere else along the coast – La Guaira for instance. By turning her away, all Hamilton had managed to do was buy some time. He still didn't know if the *Hermione* was in Puerto Cabello or not. Had he missed her? Had she taken a different route to Cuba? His worst fear, of course, was that she had slipped through the Aruba Channel after the *Surprise* had left her station. So he had another decision to make. Should he head back to the Aruba Channel, to continue his patrol in accordance with his orders, or should he press on with his risky idea of trying to find out if *Hermione* was still in port. If she was, what should he do about it? Captain Hamilton had a lot to think about that evening, as the *Surprise* edged away to the north, keeping out of sight of the land.

———

At that moment, 25 miles to the south, His Most Catholic Majesty's frigate *Santa Cecilia* – formerly the *Hermione* – was indeed getting ready to set sail. For the past two years she had languished in Puerto Cabello. Until now, her only voyage under the Spanish flag had been the short one up the coast from La Guaira. Now, finally, she was ready to join the *Armada Real* – the Spanish navy. When the *Hermione* had arrived in La Guaira in September 1797, the region's governor, Captain-General Don Marmion, recognised the frigate for what she was – an opportunity to strengthen the naval defences of the Spanish Main. So the frigate was given a new name and a new flag, and sent up the coast to Puerto Cabello, a port with better facilities than La Guaira. So far so good. However, Don Marmion quickly realised that fitting her out would take men and money – both of which were in short supply.

He never thought it would take another two years to prepare her for Spanish service. According to the port's shipwright, all she needed was a few repairs to her hull – stripping off her copper below the waterline to get at the timbers underneath. Then, once she had been careened, she had to be re-rigged, and then armed and manned. All this would take time – perhaps until the end of the year. Instead, the frigate would languish in the port for two years. The worst of it was that this delay was wholly avoidable. It was simply the result of in-fighting between the two leading members of the Venezuelan junta – the captain-general, Don Marmion, and the *intendant*, or financial controller, Don Estevan Fernandez de Leone. While this argument raged, and letters were sent by both to Spain asking for help, support and money, the *Santa Cecilia* lay abandoned, her planking splitting in the summer heat.

The problem began when Don Marmion saw there was no money available to cover the repair and operating costs of his new frigate. In response, he decided to pay for it out of the budget allocated for privateering. That, though, was the devolved responsibility of Don Estevan. So, her captain, Don Andreas Caperuchiavi, answered to the intendant, not the captain-general. Don Marmion was responsible for the funding and operation of warships in Venezuelan waters, but privateers – which presumably the *Santa Cecilia* now was – fell under the control of his rival Don Estevan. The result was, while the two Spanish nobles argued over budgets, the frigate herself was all but abandoned. Even if either man had the funds to get her ready for sea, a lack of suitable seamen kept her rotting in port.

The months went by, and still the *Santa Cecilia* remained in Puerto Cabello. In early 1798, Don Marmion thought he had solved the problem when he received royal approval and funding for the repairs. He even appointed his own captain, a merchant captain from La Guaira, who brought along his own crew. Still, Don Estevan refused to hand over control of the frigate without formal instructions from Spain. The standoff would have continued, but that summer the Spanish secretary of the navy finally stepped in. Admiral Don Juan de Lángara sent a King's officer, Don Ramón de Eschales y Gaztelu, to take command of the frigate's repair, and to speed up the work. Don Estevan's obstruction continued, but now, officially, the *Santa Cecilia* was firmly under the control of the *Armada Real*. So, at long last, things started moving.

The frigate was hauled up onto the beach and careened over the winter. Her copper sheathing was replaced, and by the spring, once she was back in the water, work began on her sails and rigging, which had suffered from a year and a half of neglect. The frigate's British guns had been removed, overhauled and replaced after the ship was re-rigged. While there wasn't any chance of re-boring them to conform to slightly different Spanish shot sizes, *Hermione* had enough supplies to last Captain de Eschales for the foreseeable future.

By the time she was re-armed, six Spanish 6-pounders were added – four to her quarterdeck and two to her forecastle. That gave her a total of 26 12-pounders and 12 6-pounders. The Spanish, unlike the Royal Navy, included carronades in the total. So, with them added, the 32-gun *Hermione* was duly transformed into the *Santa Cecilia* of 44 guns.

Now the *Santa Cecilia* needed crew. And they were on their way. Over the spring and early summer, batches of Spanish officers and men were sent out from Spain. Other seamen were recruited from the ports of the Spanish Main. By September, Captain de Eschales had 321 officers and men under his command, augmented by 56 infantry and 15 gunners, drafted to the ship by the captain-general. Interestingly, this was almost double the crew Captain Pigot had had in the *Hermione*. The frigate finally had the men it needed. It was just as well, as in late September, de Eschales had orders to take her to Havana, to join the squadron forming there under Commodore Don Francisco Montes. On 7 September, Captain de Eschales told Don Marmion that he expected to sail for Cuba by the middle of the month. He had no idea that *Surprise* was now lurking in wait for him, just over the horizon.

On board the *Surprise*, Captain Hamilton had a lot on his mind. It was now the evening of Wednesday 23 October, and after driving off the Danish schooner, the frigate had stood away from the coast, which at dusk had been little more than a faint smudge on the southern horizon. He had two clear choices. The first was to return to his patrol area in the

Aruba Channel and wait there until the *Hermione* appeared. That was the prudent course. The other choice – a far more risky one – was to find a way to attack the *Hermione* as she lay at anchor in Puerto Cabello. Hamilton felt the Spanish would soon learn that the *Surprise* was lying in wait for the Spanish frigate. They would therefore delay her sailing until the coast was clear. So, as he saw it, the bolder of the two courses – cutting out the *Hermione* from the Spanish port – was probably the only one which offered any real chance of success.

That evening, as the frigate ghosted along under light winds, Hamilton ordered the acting first lieutenant, William Wilson, to bring him the frigate's watch and quarter bills and muster books. The captain knew his crew well, but these helped remind him of everyone's strengths and weaknesses. Then, with pen, ink and paper, he began drawing up his plan. He worked on it well into the night, and then, after grabbing what sleep he could, he called for Wilson to report to his cabin, along with six other officers. All of them would play a key part in what was to come. Once they had gathered, he outlined his plan. While the ship's master, Thomas Made, would remain in charge of the *Surprise*, five other officers would command one of the ship's boats in the attack, with the marine lieutenant accompanying them. Hamilton himself would lead the attack and take command of the sixth boat.

Hamilton divided his six boats into two 'Divisions', each of three boats. The six boats could hold 100 men – less than a third of the numbers on board the *Santa Cecilia*. Still, Hamilton had no other option. Vice-Admiral Parker's intelligence reports had the *Santa Cecilia* moored by the bow and stern, with her stern facing the entrance to the harbour.

The First Division would board the frigate on her starboard side, the side facing the bay, while the Second Division would do the same on the larboard side, directly under the guns of the port's main fortress, the Castillo San Felipe. His detailed instructions laid out exactly who would command and crew each boat, and what their tasks would be. Some men would carry axes, to cut the bow and stern anchor cables, while others – topmen – would race aloft to unfurl the sails. The rest of the boarding party would secure the ship.

First (Starboard) Division

Boat	Launch	Pinnace	Jollyboat
In Charge	First Lieutenant	Captain	Carpenter
Crew	25 men	20 men	10 men

Second (Larboard) Division

Boat	Gig	Black Cutter	Red Cutter
In Charge	Surgeon	Second Lieutenant	Boatswain
Crew	16 men	16 men	16 men

Also on board Hamilton's pinnace was the gunner, John Maxwell, and a midshipman. They would board the frigate at her starboard gangway, and most of the boarders would make for the quarterdeck, to secure the ship's wheel. Four topmen, though, would climb aloft to loosen the main topsail. The jollyboat was to board on the starboard quarter, where three men with axes would cut the stern anchor cables. Two topmen would then loosen the mizzen topsail. Lieutenant Wilson also had a midshipman in his launch, which was modified to hold a small platform at the boat's stern – the three axemen would use this to cut the bow cables. Most of the rest would clamber on board over the starboard bow, and secure the quarterdeck. On each boat the axemen and two or four others would remain behind, so the boats could be used to tow the frigate's head round once the cables were cut.

In the Second Division, the surgeon, John McMullen, had volunteered to take part, as he knew that after the death of the first lieutenant, Hamilton was short of officers. Now he found himself in charge of the ship's gig, and 16 men. They would board over the larboard bow, and four topmen would loosen the fore topsail, four more would crew the boat, while the remainder would secure the frigate's forecastle. The second lieutenant, Robert Hamilton, would be accompanied by the French émigré lieutenant of marines, Louis de la Tour du Pin. Their black cutter would board amidships, over the larboard gangway. Her crew included a file of 11 Royal Marines, and were charged with reinforcing Hamilton on the quarterdeck. Finally, the red cutter, commanded by the boatswain, would board over the larboard quarter, and then help secure the main deck.

Hamilton realised that all the planning in the world wouldn't be enough. With the odds stacked so heavily against him, the key to success was surprise. If his boats could reach the *Santa Cecilia* undetected, then their chances of success would be greatly increased. Fortunately, his crew were old hands at cutting out expeditions. Having captured over 80 prizes since they came to the Caribbean and carried out dozens of cutting out ventures, he knew that as long as they held the element of surprise, he could rely on the professionalism of his crew. There was one more major element, though, and that was completely imponderable. All it took was a loud noise as the boats approached the harbour, or an extra vigilant guard on the shore or a patrol boat, and the game was up. So, Hamilton also needed luck – and plenty of it.

Having briefed his officers, he ordered all hands to assemble in front of the break of the quarterdeck. As Hamilton put it later: 'I had the hands up to acquaint the officers and ship's company of my intentions to lead them to the attack.' He added that if they left the area, they would have to go home empty-handed, and some other frigate would have the glory of recapturing the *Hermione*. So, he added: 'Our only prospect of success is by cutting her out this night.' His speech was rewarded with three rousing cheers. Then Hamilton issued his orders. Some of the crew would be disappointed as they would be left behind. Others were probably equally disappointed they had been chosen for such a dangerous mission. Hamilton, though, was happy with the way his men had reacted. He said later that their cheers had 'greatly increased my hopes' for the success of what would be a desperate venture.

The decision made, all that was left was to prepare for the expedition, and to wait. That day – Thursday 24 October 1799 – the sky was cloudy, and there was a light breeze blowing from the south-west. At noon, when the master plotted their position, Puerto Cabello lay 20 miles away to the south-west. They would run in towards the port after dusk. Having checked the tides with the master, Hamilton planned to carry out his attack at 2am. Then, he hoped, apart from a handful of sentries, everyone on board the frigate would be asleep. It also meant that the ebbing tide would help the frigate out of the harbour. So, now, there was nothing left but to make all the little preparations that could spell the difference between success and failure. The boat's oars were muffled with sacking, the oarlocks greased, cutlasses, boarding pikes and axes sharpened, and firearms oiled and cleaned.

Then, as dusk approached, and the *Surprise* began her run in towards the coast, Hamilton issued his final instructions. All of the men in the boats were to wear dark clothing – nobody would wear white of any kind, as it would show up too easily in the dark. The password, called out to tell friend from foe in the darkness was 'Britannia!', while the counter was 'Ireland!'. Finally, Hamilton stressed the importance of the boats reaching the *Hermione* as quickly as possible once they had entered the harbour. If anything unexpected happened once they had boarded, then the men would rendezvous on the frigate's quarterdeck, where Hamilton would be stationed. The main thing, though, was to get the frigate out of the harbour as quickly as possible, before the enemy could stop them. The scene was set for what would be one of the most daring raids in the history of naval warfare.

13

The Cutting Out

Now the die was cast. Captain Hamilton and his men were fully committed to the enterprise. That evening, as the frigate ran in towards the coast, tacking in the face of the light airs which were coming from the south, many would have wondered exactly what they'd let themselves in for. However, it was too late for second thoughts. At 7.30pm, when the *Surprise* was 7 miles out from the port, they brought the way off the frigate and quietly hoisted out the boats. The boarding parties clambered aboard and settled in place. Then, with the captain's pinnace in the lead, they began the long row towards their objective.

Before they left, Hamilton had taken the precaution of linking each division of boats together using 4-fathom lengths of rope. That way, in line astern, none of them would go astray in the dark. In the pinnace, Hamilton used a compass to keep his coxswain on the right course. In all the boats, the men who would actually board the *Santa Cecilia* took the first turn at the oars. Then, halfway to the harbour, the men would switch around, so they would have a chance to rest before the attack. At that point, Hamilton had briefed his boat captains to remind their crews that silence was essential. A single dropped musket or scrape of a cutlass scabbard might give the whole game away by alerting the Spaniards. The men, though, given their experience, were well aware of the importance of stealth in a cutting out attack, especially one as desperate as this.

Puerto Cabello lay on the eastern side of a small, shallow semi-circular bay, roughly two-and-a-half miles across. Most of the coast was fringed by sandy beaches or low-lying fetid mangroves. A couple of low sandy islands marked the outer edges of the bay. In the middle of the bay's eastern side was the entrance to a narrow channel, which led to a small inland lagoon, fringed by more mangroves, as well as scrub and salt pans. The town itself lay on a dog-legged spit of land on the south side of the entrance to the lagoon. To the north, across the 200-yard-wide channel, lay another curving spit of land, and the small headland of Punta Brava, at the end of which sat the squat stone walls of the Castillo San Felipe. The main anchorage lay at the eastern end of the channel, but the *Hermione* was moored 200 yards off its western end, beneath the guns of the fortress, with her head pointing south.

A little after midnight they were crossing the mouth of the bay, and the light offshore breeze had now veered round to blow from the south. They could still smell the mangroves, though, and the smells of the land. Shortly before midnight they saw the dark outline of Punta Brava off their larboard beam. Ahead of them lay the *Santa Cecilia* – and the fortress. Hamilton knew that she was a large hexagonal stone fort built in the early

1700s, mounting 18-pounder guns. Another stone-faced gun battery lay beside it, a little further to the north, at the edge of the shoreline. Other guns protected the fortress from attack on her landward side, but they didn't concern him. It was the seaward batteries which could sink his boats, or disable the *Santa Cecilia* before she made it out of the harbour.

Another worry was that, according to Vice-Admiral Parker, the Spanish were using a couple of the frigate's boats as guard boats. Hamilton would expect them to be patrolling to seaward of the frigate, either to the north or the west – or both. There was also a good chance that the Spanish would protect the *Santa Cecilia* by a boom – a floating barrier – designed to snag any approaching boats. Parker's intelligence had suggested it might be there. So Hamilton and his men were ready for them. Then they saw the darker silhouette of the frigate ahead of them, and beyond her they could make out the town. A little closer and they saw the fortress, and to the right of it the entrance to the harbour, with the masts of several vessels at the end of it. The big question now was where were those guard boats – and that boom?

Moments later they had their answer. There was a bright flash in the darkness ahead of them, followed by a bang. It was one of the guard boats. She carried a single huge 24-pounder gun in her bow, and this was now fired to sound the alarm. They saw her now, to the left of the frigate, guarding her northern side. They saw a second guard boat too, to their right, off the frigate's starboard beam. Both had been out patrolling in their assigned areas, and someone on board the northern boat had keen eyes. Less than a minute later Hamilton heard a drum beating on the *Santa Cecilia*. They were beating to quarters! That was it – all chance of surprise had gone. Their only hope now was a mad dash towards the frigate, before the men in the fortress could bring their guns into action. By his estimate the *Santa Cecilia* was still about 1,600 yards away – five minutes of fast rowing.

Hamilton gave the order to cast off their ropes, and row like their lives depended on it. His men gave three cheers and put their backs into it. It was now all about speed, and muscle power. The Spanish guard boats were firing muskets at them now, but Hamilton ignored them. They didn't pose any threat – it was all about reaching the frigate as quickly as possible. Every second could make the difference between triumph or disaster. Then, glancing astern, he saw musket flashes erupt from one of his boats, followed by another. Two of them were firing back at the guard boats. In the excitement they had forgotten Hamilton's orders – if detected, then they had to ignore everything else and head towards the frigate. He couldn't be sure, but he thought the two boats were the launch and the red cutter. Still, he didn't have time to worry – the *Santa Cecilia* was looming ahead of them.

As they came within the last 100 yards they saw the starboard side of the frigate erupt in flame. She was firing a full broadside. The roundshot roared past well over their heads. If they had been trying to hit the approaching boats then they were firing over the top of them. However, it did encourage the oarsmen to pull even harder. The smoke from the guns was blanketing them now, so when Hamilton heard the discharge of muskets overhead he didn't worry about it – they were hidden from the defenders. Hamilton ordered the coxswain to steer close to the stern of the frigate, beneath her captain's windows, which were illuminated by the glow of lanterns. Somewhere ahead of him, he heard gunfire from the fort, too. Hamilton ordered the pinnace to aim for the foot of the starboard gangway but, seconds before they bumped alongside, the boat was stopped dead in the water.

The lurch took them by surprise. At first the coxswain thought they had run aground, but that was impossible – the frigate was in 60 feet of water. It turned out that the pinnace's rudder had become entangled in a rope – probably one securing the anchor buoy to the ship. The quickest way to free themselves was to unship the rudder – the work of moments – and then, using oars as fenders, they bumped their way along towards the bow. Above them the frigate's guns fired another deafening broadside. Ignoring them, Hamilton saw the cathead above them, with the frigate's starboard anchor hanging from it. So, the *Santa Cecilia* was at single anchor. That would help when it came to cutting her loose. A moment later Hamilton leaped out of the boat, and almost lost his footing. Instead, though, he grabbed the foremast shrouds and hauled himself to safety. He was now on board the frigate!

The time was now 12.30am. Captain Hamilton pulled himself over the bulwark onto the forecastle. John Maxwell, the gunner, and the rest were right behind him. There, standing in front of them, were two bewildered Spanish sentries. They had been so busy peering in the direction of the firing that they hadn't bothered to look over the side. Moments later they were cut down, before they had a chance to react. Hamilton looked aft, along the upper deck. Like most frigates, the *Santa Cecilia*'s waist was really a big open space, spanned by beams which supported the ship's boats. Four-foot-wide gangways ran down each side of this space, leading to the quarterdeck. The whole upper deck looked deserted. Then Hamilton realised why. Looking down, he saw that the gun deck was fully manned. Amazingly, the gunners seemed oblivious to the fact that the enemy had now boarded their ship.

Hamilton ordered Maxwell and his men to follow him, and then jumped down from the forecastle, and onto the starboard gangway. He was heading for his objective – the quarterdeck. With the ship's wheel in his hands, he could control the ship – or at least he would until the Spaniards cut thorough the tiller ropes which linked it to the rudder. Below him the Spanish gunners kept on firing their guns into the night. Afterwards, he learned that the Spanish thought that two British frigates had entered the bay, and they were firing at imaginary targets. For the moment, though, he was just glad they hadn't spotted him. Moments later, as he approached the quarterdeck, he spotted a group of armed Spaniards clustered around the wheel. The two parties saw each other at the same instant, and they rushed at each other and set to with cutlasses, axes and boarding pikes.

The fight had only just started when the surgeon's boarding party arrived. The gig came on board at the larboard bow, less than a minute behind the captain. McMullen was surprised to find the forecastle empty, apart from the two dead Spaniards. Then he saw the fight at the far end of the starboard gangway. He ordered his topmen aloft to loosen the fore topsail, and then led the rest down the empty larboard gangway. When he reached the quarterdeck, he found it deserted. Moments later Hamilton appeared. Having seen the surgeon clamber on board, he left the gunner to continue the fight, then ran back to the forecastle and down the larboard gangway behind McMullen. Before the captain could stop him, though, the surgeon led his men towards the starboard gangway, to attack the Spaniards in the rear. As a result, Captain Hamilton found himself standing alone on the enemy's quarterdeck.

So far his whole scheme hadn't been going to plan. Only two of the six boats had arrived, which meant that only 34 of his 100 men had boarded the frigate. They were outnumbered about ten to one. The only saving grace was that, at least until now, most of the Spanish crew still seemed oblivious to the fact that their ship had been boarded. Looking forward, Hamilton saw that Maxwell's men were being driven back towards the forecastle, but McMullen's boarders were pushing the enemy back too, so the fight was gradually moving away from him. Then, four Spaniards appeared, emerging from the ladder leading to the gun deck. They set upon him, one man slashing his left leg with his cutlass, while another stabbed his right leg with a boarding pike. Hamilton fell to the deck, just as a third man smashed him over the head with the butt of a musket.

Next, three British seamen appeared – men from McMullen's group. They had seen the Spaniards and raced back to the quarterdeck, arriving just in time to save their captain's life. The Spaniards were driven off, fleeing down the companionway ladder leading down into the lower deck. They were just helping Hamilton to his feet when another larger group of Spanish seamen emerged from the same companionway ladder. It was clear the Spaniards on the gun deck were now aware that there was fighting going on above them, on the upper deck. For a few seconds it looked like Hamilton and his rescuers would be overwhelmed. Then, a cheering cut through the din of battle. British reinforcements had arrived, in the very nick of time. It was the crew of the black cutter, led by Lieutenant Robert Hamilton. Now, at last, the crack men of the Royal Marines had joined the fight.

They might have appeared two minutes sooner, were it not for a lone and very brave Spanish seaman. When the cutter approached the frigate's larboard gangway, Lieutenant Hamilton led the way, but just as he reached the frigate's deck a Spanish sailor appeared and chopped at him with his cutlass. He struck the young officer a glancing blow, causing him to fall back into the boat. Thinking the upper deck was held by the enemy the cutter pushed off, then circled around to the frigate's starboard side. There, though, they saw the melee raging above them, and Spanish marksmen leaning out of gunports to fire at them with muskets. They circled back to the larboard side again, and this time they found it completely empty. The lone Spaniard had rejoined his companions fighting Maxwell and McMullen. So, another 16 British seamen and marines boarded by the larboard gangway.

For Captain Edward Hamilton, it wasn't a moment too soon. His small group of men had been trying to defend the ship's wheel from the growing number of Spaniards emerging up the companionway in front of them. Now, the second lieutenant's men drove the Spaniards back, while Lieutenant du Pin's marines formed themselves up into a small firing line. On Hamilton's orders they fired three volleys down the companionway, which seemed to deter the Spanish – at least for the moment. That meant that the quarterdeck was now completely in British hands. The trouble was, while they had control of the wheel, and some of the foresails had now been unfurled, the frigate wasn't going anywhere, as she was still secured by her anchor cables. Worse, none of the axemen had arrived to chop them free.

Back on the starboard gangway, the Spaniards who had been fighting Maxwell and McMullen's men were now either dead, badly wounded or had surrendered. They had put up a real struggle though, and Maxwell had been badly wounded by a cutlass slash to the forehead. However, this meant that the entire upper deck was now clear of Spaniards. Down below, on the gun deck, the frigate's 12-pounders had stopped firing. They had finally realised the upper deck had been taken. However, any attempt to clamber up by way of ladders or hatches was thwarted by the musketry of the marines. So for the moment there was an impasse, as the Spanish fired at anyone they could see on the upper deck, and the marines did the same to the Spaniards down below. Just 53 British officers, sailors and marines, led by a wounded captain, were holding off seven times their number of Spaniards.

———

The situation was still extremely volatile. All it would take would be a determined Spanish assault and the boarders could lose control of the ship. So Captain Hamilton decided that the only way he could break the impasse was to drive the Spaniards from the gun deck and hoard them in the lower deck below. That way they wouldn't present such a danger to him as he tried to steer the frigate out of the harbour. However, common sense told him that, despite the priceless addition of the marines, he didn't have the men or the numbers he needed to pull it off. So far, his small group of boarders had managed to gain control of the upper deck thanks to the lack of Spaniards stationed there, and the confined spaces of the gangways and ladders, which meant the Spaniards couldn't overwhelm his men. Furthermore, he realised that he didn't have the luxury of waiting for reinforcements.

So, after gathering his men on the quarterdeck, he made sure everyone was armed and ready. As muskets and pistols were reloaded, Hamilton outlined his plan. With all other hatches and skylights secured, he had blocked off all access from the gun deck to the upper deck, save for the main companionway ladder leading onto the quarterdeck, which was his way down. He ordered Lieutenant du Pin to form up his marines again and deliver a volley into the crush of Spaniards who appeared below them. Several men fell, and the rest recoiled out of sight. At that moment Hamilton ordered his boarders to charge down the ladder and into the gun deck. At his word, 50 British seamen and marines poured down through the hatch and began cutting and slashing at the press of heavily armed Spaniards in the dimly lit gun deck with their cutlasses, axes, pikes and bayonets.

The attack was, of course, the height of folly, but by this stage Captain Hamilton had run out of more sensible options. With half his boats and men still missing, and the Spanish batteries now firing at the frigate, the chances of him successfully cutting out the *Santa Cecilia* were fading by the minute. Only aggression could win the day. The fight now was in an even more confined space than before. The gun deck of the frigate was divided in two by a line of masts, pumps, the lower capstan, open hatchways and even the huge galley stove. On each side stood a row of 12-pounder guns and carriages, together with all their equipment. Therefore, as a fighting place it was every bit as cramped as the gangways of the upper deck. Further aft, the captain's quarters formed another barrier. The aggressive British assault had also divided the Spanish defenders in two.

In that confined and dimly lit deck, where there was barely room to stand upright, let alone wield a cutlass, the Spaniards were fighting at a slight disadvantage. Many of them had been working the guns and hadn't armed themselves with hand-to-hand weapons. Only a few men could fight the British at any one time, and many of them lacked the skill and training of the British sailors and marines in this kind of fighting. After all, after numerous cutting out expeditions and the capture of dozens of ships, the attackers knew how to wield a cutlass, and about the importance of sheer aggression. Gradually, step by step, the British began widening their foothold.

Aft of the companionway ladder, about 60 Spanish seamen were being penned in by a dozen British sailors. As many of the defenders hadn't managed to arm themselves properly, they were fighting back with whatever lay to hand – belaying pins, trailspikes from nearby guns or even knives. Eventually they were forced back to the door leading to the captain's quarters – the same door the mutineers had poured through when they attacked Captain Pigot two years before. Now, finding themselves trapped there, the remaining Spaniards laid down their weapons and surrendered. After taking their weapons, the British seamen locked them in, and Hamilton placed marine sentries outside the door to make sure they stayed there. That allowed the remainder of the boarders to move forwards, to reinforce their shipmates.

Here the fighting was harder and more bloody. Every gun acted like a barrier, and progress was slow and vicious. Three British seamen in the front of the fight fell wounded – all petty officers – but it was clear the defenders were gradually being pushed back, first past the chain pump and then to the level of the mainmast. Each step increased the crowding amid the mass of Spaniards, and wounded men weren't able to escape. So, many ended up being cut down. By then it was almost 1am. Just as the attackers began to flag, a new boatload of reinforcements arrived. The jollyboat had reached the frigate, and after leaving his axemen to cut the stern cables, the carpenter led everyone else onto the quarterdeck. Captain Hamilton met him there and sent two men aloft to loosen the mizzen topsail, while the rest were sent below to take over from some of the men in the melee.

With the stern cables cut, the *Santa Celicia* was only being held fast by her larboard anchor cable. Cutting it had been the task of the first lieutenant, William Wilson, in the launch, the *Surprise*'s largest boat. However, he had been drawn into a fight with one of the Spanish guard boats, and so the heavy anchor cable was still intact. Finally, just after 1am, Wilson arrived, and his boat pulled alongside the starboard bow. There, using their specially built chopping platform, the axemen set to work, while Wilson led his men up onto the forecastle. That meant that, of all the *Surprise*'s six boats, only one of them – the red cutter – was still out there somewhere in the harbour. A few minutes later she too appeared off the frigate's larboard quarter. Now, with all his men in play, Hamilton could finally get the captured frigate under way.

Once the bow anchor cable had been cut, the *Santa Cecilia* was cast loose. The light wind blowing from the south began pushing her slowly backwards, and Hamilton yelled down to the boat crews, ordering them to pull her head round to starboard. Slowly the frigate began to turn, and the movement wasn't missed by the gunners in the fortress. They had taken some time preparing their guns, and then they had been joining the frigate's gunners in randomly shooting at imaginary targets. Once the *Santa Cecilia* began to turn, though, even a hapless landsman could work out what was happening. So the guns on the shore began firing at the frigate. With the range just over 200 yards, it would be hard to miss. An 18-pounder roundshot could easily punch its way through the side of the frigate. So far, however, most of the gunners had held their fire. After all, the *Santa Cecilia* was a Spanish ship.

Gradually, the frigate began to move faster, and as he stood on the quarterdeck Captain Hamilton could feel it heel slightly as the topsails began to draw. Some of the boarding party were already standing by to haul home the sheets and braces, so the sails could catch the wind. On the wheel, the wounded gunner and two able seamen reported they could feel the rudder starting to bite. The frigate was under way. Her bows had now been turned towards the south-west. Their job done, the six ships boats clustered around the frigate's stern and their crews secured their towing lines. That meant that if the *Santa Cecilia* escaped from the harbour she would tow her boats out behind her. Over his right shoulder, Hamilton had noticed the floating boom to the north of the anchorage, so he planned to keep well clear of it as he turned the frigate towards the open sea.

As the ship got under way, she heeled over as her topsails filled. She was turning faster, too, but the combination of the turn and the heel briefly exposed a few planks of her larboard hull below the waterline. At that moment an 18-pounder ball fired from the Castillo San Felipe struck her a foot below the waterline and smashed a jagged 6-inch hole in her lower planking. Then, once the frigate steadied again on an even keel, the water began pouring in. Realising what had happened, Hamilton sent a runner below, ordering some of the men fighting in the gun deck to break off and man the pumps. Soon a steady gush of water was being squirted over the side. Looking behind him, Hamilton saw the fortress drop further astern. He was still well within range of her guns, which could pierce the frigate's hull at 1,000 yards, or worse, bring down a mast. Still, they were now slowly heading out of danger.

Down on the gun deck the brutal fight was still raging. The Spanish, though, soon discovered the frigate was getting under way. Many would also have guessed she was taking in water, as they heard the clanking of the chain pump. The British fighting in the confines of the gun deck sensed this too, and noticed that the Spaniards seemed noticeably less aggressive. It felt as if the fight was draining out of them. At that point the Spanish captain, de Eschales, tried to rally his men and encourage them to fight harder – to make one last push to retake the ship. Instead he was wounded, albeit not seriously, and his men dragged him back through the press of men to safety. Next, it seems several of the Spanish crewmen began clambering out of the open gunports and jumping over the side. Better a short swim to the shore or a guard boat than risk becoming a prisoner of war.

However, the fight wasn't quite over yet. Hamilton's coxswain, while clambering up from the launch, had overheard the Spanish in the great cabin talk about blowing up the ship.

As he was Portuguese, he understood them reasonably well. He warned Hamilton, who ordered du Pin to have his men fire through the quarterdeck skylight, down into the captain's great cabin, to discourage any such move. But, even so, they weren't quite out of danger yet; the guns on shore were still firing, and a Spanish roundshot cut through the main stay, which held up the mainmast. Several spring stays had also been cut, so there was a risk that the mast might topple over the side when they reached rougher water. For the moment, though, Hamilton needed every man he had to fight the Spanish and sail the ship. The frigate was making around 4 knots now, and he ordered Maxwell at the wheel to steer towards the north-west, and the *Surprise*.

Down on the gun deck, the Spaniards had been pushed forwards as far as the hatchway to the lower deck. The deck was slippery with blood, and behind the thin British line it was littered with the dead, wounded and dying. Many of the defenders had already escaped down through the hatchway, and so escaped from the fight. Those who stayed behind soon knew that they were trapped and that further resistance was futile. They began dropping their weapons and edging away from the equally weary British boarders. Within minutes the whole press of Spanish crewmen on the upper deck had surrendered. That meant that the ship was now securely in British hands. With the fighting over, all that remained now was to secure the prisoners, collect the weapons, repair the ship and escape to the open sea.

In the end, it was all relatively simple. First, Hamilton sent some of his men aloft to secure the mainmast by repairing the stays. This needed to be done before they cleared the entrance to the bay. He also sent the carpenter and his men below to plug the shot hole which was causing the flooding, and any other shot holes they could find. They had to tend to the wounded and arrange proper guards for the Spanish prisoners, while other sailors gathered up their dropped weapons. First, though, Captain Hamilton had a very symbolic gesture to make. The huge red and gold Spanish ensign had been hauled down at sunset, but now, as the frigate slipped out of the bay, Hamilton ordered it hoisted again. Above it flew an equally large British red ensign, brought along especially for the occasion by the captain's coxswain.

A mile off their port beam, the mangrove-covered islet of Guayguasa marked the western end of the bay. They were a mile and a half from the Castillo San Felipe, and beyond the reach of the Spanish guns. It was now a little after 2.30am. Four miles to the north-west, the *Surprise* lay waiting for them. Given the light wind, which had now dropped to a whisper, it took the best part of three hours to reach her. As the frigate's master recorded laconically in the ship's log: 'Half past five, the boats returned with the *Hermione.*' It didn't really do justice to what had just happened. For the rest of the morning the two frigates lay beside each other, as the *Surprises* dealt with the wounded, continued the repairs, and the men guarding the prisoners were relieved. Hamilton still had the problem, though, of what to do with all his prisoners. Fortunately, a solution soon presented itself.

At 7am a sail was spotted to the east. As both frigates were busy Hamilton sent one of his cutters off to intercept her. The vessel turned out to be an American schooner, sailing from La Guaira to Puerto Bello. Despite their protestations, the boarding party made her crew head towards the two frigates. There, Hamilton asked the American master to take the Spanish prisoners with him. He agreed and the transfer began. This took time, as many of the Spaniards were wounded, but it gave Hamilton the chance to invite his counterpart Don Ramón de Eschales over to the *Surprise* to breakfast with him. The two wounded captains, now suitably bandaged, discussed the night's battle and compared the extent of their casualties.

By then, both men had a shrewd idea of the butcher's bill. For Hamilton, it turned out to be surprisingly light. Of the 100 men who formed *Surprise*'s boarding party, 12 had been wounded. Of these, only four were in a serious condition. One of these was the gunner, John Maxwell. Amazingly, none of the *Surprises* had been killed in the fight. The Spanish toll, though, was shocking. According to de Eschales, a total of 385 officers and men were on board the frigate that evening. A further 20 men were manning the two guard boats, and seven married officers had leave to spend the night ashore in Puerto Cabello. An incredible total of 29 of the *Santa Ceclilia*'s crew had been killed during the battle, and a further 231 taken prisoner. Another 15 escaped capture by jumping over the side. Of the prisoners, 97 were wounded, many of them quite badly. Now, though, they would soon be in the port hospital.

These figures speak volumes about the slaughter that took place on the gun deck. The Spanish there had been hemmed in by the boarders, and many of this press of men didn't have proper weapons. Instead they fought with whatever they could find, or hung at the back, leaving the fighting to those with weapons. Most of the crew were also raw, either freshly raised seamen or men drafted in from merchant ships. A few were seconded from the local garrisons, but even they had little or no combat experience. By contrast the British boarding party were all hand-picked men, and the veterans of numerous cutting out expeditions and boarding actions. The *Surprise* was a crack frigate, with an extremely well-disciplined and well-trained crew. This training included hand-to-hand fighting. So, while the *Surprises* lacked the numbers, in terms of quality they had a marked edge over their opponents.

Eventually, all but three of the prisoners were transferred onto the now seriously overcrowded schooner. The exceptions were Don Ramón de Eschales and his two most senior officers. They would be taken back to Jamaica, to be exchanged at some point for British prisoners of war. With the prisoners on their way home, Hamilton was free to hoist in the boats, and prepare for the voyage home. By now the *Santa Cecilia*'s shot-through rigging had been repaired, she was no longer taking in water, and the detritus of battle had been cleared away. The sailmaker was busy preparing the Spanish for their burial at sea, and the blood had been swabbed off the decks. A little after noon, as the last of the boats was stowed away, the two frigates turned towards the north-west, and set a course for Port Royal. Ahead of them lay a hero's welcome, and the fleeting celebrity that came with it.

14

Retribution

On 1 November, the *Surprise* slipped past Gallows Point and dropped anchor off Port Royal. Behind her the captured *Santa Cecilia* did the same, with the red ensign flying proudly from her mizzen topgallant brace, and the Spanish naval ensign fluttering below it. The warships in the harbour were lined with cheering men, while more cheers erupted from the shore. Captain Hamilton, looking suitably martial with his bandaged head, might have been slightly nervous as he entered port. After all, he had disregarded Vice-Admiral Parker's instructions. If the cutting out had failed, he would have been facing a court martial. Now, though, with the operation a resounding success and the *Hermione* back in the naval fold, this little problem would be swept aside. Hamilton and his men were the heroes of the hour, and as the admiral who sent them to the Spanish Main, Parker could share some of the glory.

Before the *Surprise* reached Jamaica, Captain Hamilton penned his report. This was important – not only would it give his excuses to the admiral, but he knew perfectly well his report would be passed on to the Admiralty and then the British press. First, he had to explain why he had taken the gamble. 'The honour of my country and the glory of the British Navy were strong inducements', he wrote. He went on to describe the battle, and then, rather than hog the glory, he modestly heaped praise on his men instead. 'Every officer and man on this expedition behaved with an uncommon degree of valour and exertion.' He went on to praise two of the men whose actions had made all the difference that night – the surgeon, John McMullen, and the gunner, John Maxwell. He made no mention of his acting first lieutenant, William Wilson, whose actions had come close to derailing the whole venture.

Vice-Admiral Parker, of course, was more than happy to ignore Hamilton's disobedience of orders, as his gamble had paid off so handsomely. Three days later he wrote a full report to Evan Nepean, secretary to the Board of the Admiralty. He took great delight in breaking the news: 'I have a particular satisfaction in communicating to you ... that His Majesty's late ship *Hermione* is again restored to his Navy.' He fulsomely described the cutting out as 'as daring and gallant an enterprise as to be found in our naval annals'. He heaped praise on Hamilton, writing that the action 'adds infinite honour to Captain Hamilton as an officer'. After describing the attack, he called it 'a bold and daring undertaking, which must have rank among the foremost of the many gallant actions executed by our Navy in this war'. Parker knew that the Admiralty, and the British public, would be overjoyed at the news.

In his report, Parker included a little snippet about the *Hermione*, as for the moment the *Santa Cecilia* had reverted to her old British name. He said: 'I find the *Hermione* has had a thorough repair, and is in complete order. I have therefore ordered her to be surveyed and valued, and shall commission her as soon as the reports are made to me from the officers of the yard.' Then he suggested a change of name, because he knew that the name *Hermione* would always be associated with the bloody mutiny. So he finished his letter to Nepean by saying that once the frigate had been thoroughly repaired and re-commissioned into the service, she would bear the name *Retaliation*. It seemed appropriate, given the circumstances. By remaining on the Jamaica Station she would be used against the Spanish – an excellent form of retaliation for their tacit acceptance of the frigate, and their protection of the mutineers.

The Admiralty, though, had other ideas. After reading Parker's report, and seeing his chosen name, the board ordered Nepean to reply to the admiral, telling him that: 'Under the present circumstances their Lordships will not disapprove of his having purchased the ship without first receiving their Lordship's authority for doing so.' It was a gentle reminder that while Parker had the authority to commission ships into naval service, and to appoint their captains, the final say rested with the Admiralty. This done, they then stamped their mark on the frigate in another way. The letter concluded that rather than naming her the *Retaliation*, the name Parker had chosen, the Admiralty had decided to call her the *Retribution* instead. For them, Parker's choice hadn't been extreme enough; this wasn't about retaliation against the Spanish – it was about exacting retribution on the mutineers.

Another problem was the valuation of the *Santa Cecilia*. This was important for Captain Hamilton and his crew as it was directly linked to the amount of prize money the *Surprises* would get. As captain, Hamilton would get two-eighths of the total value of the prize. Parker would get another eighth, as the *Surprise* was sailing under his orders. An eighth went to the officers, another to the warrant officers and yet another to the petty officers and midshipmen. The remaining two-eights was divided out among the rest of the *Surprise*'s crew. The Jamaican shipyard valued the *Santa Cecilia* and her fittings as being worth almost £16,096. However, the Navy Board refused to pay out, and instead, after much delay, they came up their own much smaller value of £12,132. Essentially, the quill-pushers at the Admiralty cheated the sailors who had risked their lives of a quarter of their prize money.

For Captain Hamilton, though, there were other honours in store. The Jamaican House of Assembly held a banquet for the captain and his officers, and presented him with an ornamental sword worth 300 guineas. Hamilton spent several weeks in Jamaica, recovering from his wounds, and while he was there, the honours kept on coming. First, he was presented with a Naval Gold Medal, a prestigious mark of gratitude by the Admiralty, and in February 1800 he was given a knighthood in absentia by King George III. The following month, while he was still in Jamaica, Sir Edward Hamilton was given the freedom of the City of London, as well as a gold box valued at 50 guineas, bearing the city's crest. When he finally left for home in May 1800, he must have felt confident that a rosy future and a plum command lay ahead of him.

Unfortunately for him, his return wasn't that straightforward. He sailed home on a packet bound from Kingston to Falmouth, but she was captured by the French in the western approaches to the English Channel. Hamilton became a prisoner of war, but because of his new-found fame he wasn't sent to one of the usual prisons where British officers were housed. Instead he was taken to Paris, where, apparently, 'he was taken notice of by Bonaparte'. After six weeks there, he was exchanged for four French midshipmen held in Britain. He was back in London by mid-August, where he was received by the Lords of the Admiralty. After a few more audiences and banquets, he was finally given his plum ship, the 36-gun frigate *Trent*. However, his future turned out to be less rosy than he had imagined.

On taking command of the *Trent* in October, Hamilton was ordered to join the Channel Fleet. He spent most of 1801 on blockade off Le Havre, Cherbourg or St Malo – dull, monotonous duty where he never had a chance to shine. Slowly, though, it appeared that his nature had changed for the worse. In the *Surprise*, Hamilton rarely flogged. But now flogging and other punishments became commonplace. Finally, in late 1801, he went too far when he tied his gunner and his mates into the rigging for failing to meet his exacting standards. This led to a court martial, and in February 1802 he was dismissed from the service. However, he was soon rehabilitated and ended his career as the captain of the royal yacht. It was suggested that his new-found irascibility stemmed from the injuries he had received in Puerto Cabello. Hamilton finally died in 1846 as a baronet and a full admiral.

Meanwhile, the search for the *Hermione* mutineers continued. As far as the navy was concerned there would be no forgiveness, and no end to the manhunt. Still, after the execution of Thomas Nash in Port Royal in August 1799, there was a short pause in the round of trials and executions. But it wasn't for a lack of trying. The Admiralty had ordered that the mutineers who had turned King's evidence, along with those who had already testified in earlier trials, should be kept ready at hand, in case their evidence was needed again. Therefore, from 1800 onwards, the trials of any newly caught mutineers tended to be held in Portsmouth, where reliable ex-*Hermiones* were available to testify against their shipmates. In fact some of them – men like John Jones and James Perrett – were ordered to spend their days walking around the dockyard looking for familiar faces among the crowds of seamen.

The first mutineer to be captured was James Duncan, a young topman. He was one of those who had travelled to Cumaná to find a ship. He joined the same Danish vessel as John Williams – the man who had given himself up to the authorities in Liverpool. However, when the craft was captured by a British privateer, he was identified as a former *Hermione*. When the Danish crew were repatriated to St Thomas, Duncan went with them, where he was arrested and placed on board a homeward-bound Danish frigate. After a spell of incarceration in Elsinore – the same castle that formed the setting for Shakespeare's *Hamlet* – he was transferred to the British sloop *Kite*, and so on to Portsmouth. He stood trial there on board the *Gladiator* on 3 July 1800. Southcott, Plaice, Jones, Perrett and Williams all gave evidence against him, and Duncan was hanged on board the 74-gun *Puissant* a week later.

He was small fry – one of those who went along with the mutiny, but took no major part in it. So too was the next mutineer to fall into the navy's net. John Watson, an able seaman who had supposedly been near blind with scurvy when the mutiny erupted, was captured during a search of a neutral American ship in the West Indies. He was taken to Martinique, where he was identified as a mutineer by Corporal Nicholas Doran, the one remaining ex-*Hermione* to be serving in the West Indies Station. More importantly, accompanying Watson was another young mutineer, James Allen, the bloodthirsty teenage servant of Lieutenant Douglas. As he lacked other *Hermiones* to act as witnesses, Rear-Admiral Henry Harvey had the pair transported to Portsmouth, which by then had become the epicentre of justice and retribution for the *Hermione* mutineers.

They were tried on board Rear-Admiral John Holloway's flagship *Gladiator* in late July, three weeks to the day after the court martial of their shipmate James Duncan. Lieutenant Southcott identified both men and testified that, after the mutiny, Watson had confessed he had only been shamming blindness. The steward John Jones said he saw Watson dancing and drinking with the ringleaders after the mutiny. In the eyes of the court, that alone was enough to condemn him. The same two witnesses also identified James Allen, as did Sergeant Plaice and James Perrett. This time, though, their testimonies were damning. First, Southcott told the court that young Allen had joined in the hunt for Lieutenant Douglas, and on finding him hiding under a cot he yelled out to the mob 'Here he is! Here he is!' The evidence of the next witness, though, produced groans of horror from the court.

The ship's butcher, Perrett, told how, amid the frenzy surrounding Douglas being dragged through the wardroom, several men took swings at him with their swords and axes. Allen was one of them, shouting: 'Let me have a chop at him!' He then struck the officer with an axe as he was being dragged up the hatchway ladder. As if this weren't enough, Sergeant Plaice next told how Allen had had a part in dragging Lieutenant Douglas out from under the cot of the dying marine officer, when he was hacked and stabbed up to 20 times. Jones's only defence was his youth – he had only been 14 at the time. But this didn't impress the court, especially as the boy was later seen wearing his dead master's clothes. Both men were duly found guilty, and were hanged from the flagship's yardarm on 7 August 1800.

In September 1800, a curious instance of Anglo-American cooperation yielded up another mutineer. Technically the Dutch were French allies, but on the island of Curaçao, support for the French was lukewarm. So that summer, a French force invaded the island and laid siege to the forts protecting the main town of Willemstad. The Dutch governor asked the British and Americans for assistance, and on 10 September the British frigate *Néréide* arrived, and with their help the French were driven off. The British took temporary control of the island, and on 15 September a former *Hermione*, William Johnson gave himself up. He was the youngster who had once served as Captain Pigot's writer, before a more experienced clerk appeared. Since arriving in

Curaçao two years before, he had worked as a clerk for the American consul. He was duly sent home to Portsmouth, to stand trial.

The occupation of Curaçao netted another bigger fish. The Danish-born able seaman Hadrian Poulson had taken part in the murder of Pigot. He was handed to the *Néréide* by the Dutch as a suspected *Hermione*, having served for a year on board the Dutch frigate *Syren*. So he too was shipped back to Portsmouth. The two men were tried together on board the *Gladiator* the following June. At the court martial both men were identified by Southcott, but while he didn't recall Johnson taking part in the mutiny, he confirmed that Poulson had been in the very thick of it. He had even boasted of killing his captain and heaving him overboard. In the end, both men were sentenced to death, but the court pleaded clemency in the case of Johnson. He was eventually pardoned. There would be no mercy for Poulson though, and on 3 July 1801 he was hanged from the yardarm of the *Puissant*.

The following month, the marine John Pearce was tried by the same court, having been caught in Malta, then shipped back to Portsmouth. Here the main witness was his superior, Sergeant Plaice. He recalled seeing Pearce among the mob of mutineers in the gunroom who dragged out the dying Lieutenant McIntosh. He also recalled seeing him in La Guaira, wearing the uniform of a Spanish artilleryman So, not only had Pearce been active in the mutiny, but he had also sided with the enemy. The steward, John Jones, added that Pearce had been consorting with the mutineers after the murders, and he had seen him heave his uniform over the side before they reached the Spanish Main.

The outcome, then, was never in doubt. On 31 August 1801, seven weeks after Poulson, the former marine was also strung up from the yardarm of the *Puissant* as she swung at anchor in Portsmouth harbour.

Another mutineer who fell foul of the navy in Malta was William Bower, who had changed his surname to Miller before signing on to an American merchantman. All went well for two years, until November 1801, when his brig put in to Valetta. There he was pressed by a boarding party from the frigate *Minerva*, and so was back in the Royal Navy. The frigate then returned to Portsmouth, and on 14 January 1802, as one of the captain's bargemen, Able Seaman Miller was forced to go ashore during a visit to the dockyard. There he was spotted by James Perrett, and arrested. This time the court martial was under the jurisdiction of Vice-Admiral Sir Andrew Mitchell. The trial was held in February, and both Southcott and Plaice were able to identify him, and confirmed he had actively participated in the mutiny. Bower was sentenced to death, and hanged three days later, on 18 February.

Shortly afterwards, in March 1802, Britain and France signed the Treaty of Amiens. That brought a temporary end to the war. It would last a mere 14 months, but it gave the Royal Navy a much-needed breathing space. So, many warships which had spent years overseas were ordered home to be paid off, or to undergo refit. One of these was the 18-gun three-masted sloop *Bittern*, which had spent the past three years in the West Indies Station. Her master and commander was

Lieutenant Edward Kittoe, who had enjoyed a number of successes on the station, including the capture of a 12-gun French privateer. Now that his sloop had returned to Portsmouth and was about to be placed in reserve, Kittoe was kept busy, and so used his ship's barge regularly. He had no idea, though, that one of his bargemen was one of the most notorious mutineers of them all.

On Monday 22 March, Lieutenant Kittoe went ashore to pay some official visits in the dockyard. His bargemen had time to kill, so most headed for one of the many alehouses or brothels which were clustered around the Point – the area known today as Old Portsmouth. A line of fortifications separated it from Portsmouth proper, and from the nearby dockyard. It was at King James's Gate (or Point Gate), one of the entrances to the Point, that one of the *Bittern*'s bargemen, Thomas Williams, felt someone tap his shoulder. It was his old shipmate John Jones, the captain's steward. Jones seized the seaman and called for help from the guards. Minutes later Williams was being frog-marched to the naval dockyard, where he was thrown into the guardhouse. It turned out that the young bargeman Lieutenant Kittoe knew as Able Seaman Thomas Williams was actually David Forester, formerly of the *Hermione*.

By now, Rear-Admiral John Holloway was something of an expert in the *Hermione* mutiny. He had presided over several court martial boards, and his flagship the *Gladiator* had been the scene of almost as many executions. So it was apt that he went to question the prisoner. A witness describes what happened: 'Admiral Holloway and several other officers went to interrogate him concerning the mutiny, when he confessed himself to have been the person who killed, and afterwards threw Captain Pigot overboard.' So, there it was – a full confession. Given this confession, the court martial that followed just over a week later on Tuesday 30 March was something of an anticlimax. Still, it was a necessity, as was the detailed re-visiting of the whole murderous incident.

At the court martial, Thomas Williams was formally identified as David Forester, a native of Sheerness, who at the time of the mutiny was 16 years old and a maintopman on the *Hermione*. The three witnesses who identified him were Lieutenant Southcott, John Jones, the man who had recognised him in the Point, and James Perrett, the mutineer who had turned King's evidence. Southcott began by saying of Forester that 'he was as active in the mutiny as any in the ship'. He added that when he saw the ringleaders in the captain's cabin 'They were boasting of what horrid deeds they had done in murdering the officers, and the prisoner said that he had assisted in murdering Captain Pigot.' According to Southcott's testimony, Forester was heard boasting that 'He had cut him three or four times, that he had assisted in throwing him out of the stern window.' This was utterly damning.

As if this wasn't evidence enough, Southcott testified that Forester had been instrumental in handing the *Hermione* over to the Spanish in La Guaira. Then, John Jones spoke. He told how, after killing Captain Pigot, Forester had passed him in the doorway when leaving the captain's quarters, and said: 'I have just launched your bloody master overboard.' He also told him: 'The bugger – I gave him his death wound I think, before he went out of the window.' So, Forester was one of the principal murderers of Captain Pigot. But this wasn't the end of it. Jones also told how Forester had struck at Lieutenant Douglas, when he was being dragged from the gunroom to the upper deck. He added that 'when the prisoner could not chop at him he stabbed him'. There was no doubt the navy had finally caught one of the most bloodthirsty of all the *Hermione* mutineers.

David Forester was hanged from the main yardarm of the *Gladiator* on Thursday 1 April 1802, as she swung at anchor within sight of Portsmouth Point, and within a few hundred yards of Forester's old ship, the *Bittern*. On the evening before his execution, Forester dictated a full confession. In it he said that he 'went into the cabin and forced Captain Pigot overboard through the port, while he was still alive.' Later, on the quarterdeck he found 'the First Lieutenant begging for his life... and assisted in heaving him overboard'. During the hunt for the second lieutenant, Archibald Douglas, he 'found the lieutenant under the Marine lieutenant's cabin ... he then called the rest of the people, when they dragged him on deck, and threw him overboard'.

This wasn't even the end of his part in the killings. Forester then described how he 'caught hold of Mr Smith, midshipman ... he struck him with a tomahawk, and threw him overboard'. Finally, he confessed to killing the captain's clerk, John Manning. All told, according to this confession, David Forester, just 16 years old at the time of the mutiny, was guilty of the murder of four men, including his captain and two lieutenants. In fact, other evidence suggested he was also involved in the murder of the purser, Stephen Pacey, and the ship's surgeon, Hugh Sansom. Together with Archibald Douglas, Samuel Reed,

Thomas Smith and of course Hugh Pigot, that meant that on the night of 21 September 1797, Forester took part in the murder of seven people. He was like a manic serial killer, getting all of his grisly butchery done at the one time.

The hanging of David Forester wasn't the last of the *Hermione* executions. There would be one more before the navy's taste for retribution had run its course. It wasn't for want of looking – the navy never gave up the search – but the renewal of the war, this time against Napoleon, meant that the Royal Navy had other priorities. James Hayes, the 14-year-old doctor's servant on board the *Hermione*, must have thought himself safe. However, in October 1806 – a year after the battle of Trafalgar – he was taken, and stood trial in Plymouth on board the 112-gun First Rate *Salvador del Mundo*, which had been captured at the battle of Cape St Vincent seven months before the *Hermione* mutiny. The sole witness at the court martial was Lieutenant Southcott, who told how the boy had boasted of having put his master to death, 'to be revenged' on him. It was damning stuff.

Hayes tried to plead his youth at the time, but the court martial board were stone-hearted. Hayes was found guilty, and on Friday 17 October 1806, he was hanged from the flagship's yardarm. This young man was the last of the *Hermione* mutineers to be hanged for their crimes. That meant that, since the mutiny, a total of 33 *Hermione* mutineers had been brought to trial. Of these, 24 had been hanged, and one transported into penal servitude. Several of these – John Elliott, David Forester, Thomas Nash and Richard Redman – had been ringleaders as well as mutineers. Others, such as

Hadrian Poulson and James Allen, had been cold-blooded killers. However, most of the other hanged men were neither leaders nor murderers, but were still guilty, as they not only took part in the mutiny, but were also complicit in handing their ship over to the enemy.

For the navy, all of the condemned men deserved their fate. Given the bloody circumstances, the court martial boards were also surprisingly lenient. It was a testimony to the relative fairness of the naval judicial system that eight of the men brought to trial had either been judged not guilty of mutiny, or in two cases they had been convicted, but the boards had pleaded for clemency for them from the Crown. However, these men still represented a fraction of those who had taken part in the mutiny. Several ringleaders, such as Lawrence Cronin, John Farrel, Thomas Jay and William Turner, were never caught. They, presumably, evaded justice by blending into the background, and made new lives for themselves in the United States or on the Spanish Main. Today, their descendants are probably oblivious to the part their ancestors played in the bloodiest mutiny in British naval history.

As for the main character in this story, the once powerful frigate that began life as the *Hermione* would not be allowed a happy ending. In the age of sail there was no retirement home for unwanted wooden-hulled warships. In September 1800, almost ten months after her recapture, the 32-gun frigate *Retribution*, formerly the *Hermione*, *Santa Cecilia* and *Retaliation*, was re-commissioned into naval service. Captain Samuel Forster became her new commander. For the best part of a year she served in the Jamaica Station, then, in December 1801, after more than eight years in the Caribbean, she returned home to Britain. The *Retribution* arrived in Portsmouth on 20 January 1802. There, Captain Forster was told to sail her round to Chatham, where she would be paid off. With peace in the offing, this 20-year-old frigate had become surplus to requirements.

On reaching Chatham that February her crew were paid off, her guns, stores, upper masts and rigging were removed, and her naval ensign was lowered for the last time. Effectively she was placed in mothballs, while the navy decided whether to scrap her or not. Two decades before, when the *Hermione* had left Bristol, the frigate had been a state-of-the-art warship. Now, though, most modern frigates carried 18-pounder guns, and more of them. So she was seen as old and obsolete. But then it appeared that fortune smiled on her once more. The *Retribution* was saved from the breaker's yard – at least for a while – by Trinity House. They ran the lighthouses and lightships which surrounded the British coast, and maintained the marker buoys. They bought the *Retribution* and towed her up the Thames to Woolwich, where she was refitted. From now on, she would be a lighthouse tender.

Unfortunately for the old *Hermione*, this was to be an all-too-brief reprieve. She sailed on her first and only voyage for Trinity House on 16 October 1803. She performed well enough, but it seemed the old former frigate wasn't really up to the job. When she returned to the Thames in early June 1804, she was taken to Deptford, and in August her copper sheathing was removed. It looked like her eight years in the Caribbean had taken their toll, and rot had taken hold. Trinity House inspected her and decided the damage was just too expensive to repair. She was finally broken up in Deptford in June 1805 – four months before the battle of Trafalgar. She wasn't the last *Hermione* or *Retribution* to serve the Royal Navy. After her passing there would be three more of each. However, the chances are their crews were never told the full story of what had happened on board their infamous namesake back in 1797.

Gradually, over the years, the story of the *Hermione* mutiny has largely been forgotten. So too has her daring recapture. Only the *Surprise* lived on, through the marvellous historical fiction of the late Patrick O'Brian. The real frigate was broken up in 1802, but in O'Brian's Aubrey and Maturin books she was spared and lived on as a privateer. The Admiralty took some heed of the mutiny, though, and those at Spithead and the Nore. Conditions for British sailors were improved a little, and the authority of naval captains was placed under slightly greater scrutiny by flag officers and the Admiralty. However, 'flogging captains' still remained, and the use of the cat-o'-nine-tails was only finally abolished in 1879. The navy remained a harsh and unforgiving service throughout the Napoleonic Wars, and for much of the 19th century. Things only really began to improve under the reign of Queen Victoria.

Surprisingly the main impact of the *Hermione* mutiny was felt in the United States. The extradition of the mutineer Thomas Nash fed a political whirlwind that swept President John Adams from office in 1800, and marked the end for his Federalist party. Thanks to his forged American citizenship, Nash, under his alias of Jonathan Robbins, became an all-American martyr. The widespread resentment of British 'heavy-handedness' in the American press led to a growing rift between the two countries. Ultimately, in 1812, this led to war. All of this might easily have been avoided if Captain Hugh Pigot had been a less mercurial character, and less prone to acts of favouritism and petty brutality. Above all, though, the mutiny lifted the rock which exposed the brutality that underlay the navy during the 'Age of Nelson'. In the cutting out of the *Hermione*, though, it also showed the navy at its very best.

Notes

CHAPTER I THE *HERMIONE*

Page 17: 'She was a Hermione-class frigate...' Rif Winfield, *British Warships in the Age of Sail, 1714–1792* (Barnsley, 2007), pp.208–09. Also see J. J. Colledge and Ben Warlow, *Ships of the Royal Navy* (Newbury, 2010), p.183.

Page 18: '"Frigates! Were I to die at this moment..."' Quoted in James Henderson, *Frigates, Sloops & Brigs* (Barnsley, 2011), p.15.

Page 19: 'In 1793, when *Hermione* left Britain...' Otto von Pivka, *Navies of the Napoleonic Era* (1980), pp.160–69.

Page 19: 'By 1780, however, the year the keel of *Hermione* was laid...' William Falconer, *Falconer's Marine Dictionary* (Newton Abbot, 1970), pp.134–35.

Page 20: 'To a navy man, the other defining characteristic of a frigate...' Brian Lavery, *Nelson's Navy* (London, 1989), pp.49–52.

Page 20: 'In the navy, all warships carrying 20 guns or more...' Lavery, p.40.

Page 21: 'At the start of the French Revolutionary Wars...' C. A. Sapherson and J. R. Lenton, *Navy Lists* (Leigh-on-Sea, 1996), pp.1–5.

Page 23: 'During the ten years of the French Revolutionary Wars...' Von Pivka, pp.217–21.

Page 23: 'Like many new warships...' Robert Gardiner, *Frigates of the Napoleonic Wars* (London, 2000), pp.87–89; Robert Gardiner, *Warships of the Napoleonic Era* (Barnsley, 2011) pp.43–49.

Page 25: 'The *Hermione* was actually the first of a class...' Winfield, p.219.

Page 27: 'On 9 September 1782, the frigate was launched...' Ibid, p.219.
Page 29: 'At the apex of this hierarchical pyramid...' Henderson, p.20; Lavery, pp.98–99.
Page 30: 'Next in the hierarchy were the officers.' Lavery, pp.96–97.
Page 31: 'The other principal warrant officers...' Ibid, pp.100–04.
Page 31: 'All of these warrant officers...' Ibid, pp.135–37.
Page 32: 'The rest of the ship's company...' Ibid, pp.129–34.
Page 34: 'The ship's company were divided...' Ibid, pp.194–203.

CHAPTER 2   CRISIS IN THE CARIBBEAN

Page 36: 'At 10am on 25 January 1793...' This account of King Louis XVI's execution is drawn from J. M. Thompson, *English Witnesses of the French Revolution* (Oxford, 1938) and Henry Essex Edgeworth de Firmont, *Memoirs of the Abbé Edgeworth* (London, 1815).
Page 37: 'In fact the first shots had already been fired...' Rif Winfield, *British Warships in the Age of Sail, 1793–1817* (Barnsley, 2008), p.275; Nicholas Tracy, *The Naval Chronicle* Vol. 1 (London, 1998), p.117.
Page 38: 'When the war began...' Winfield, p.219.
Page 41: 'The strategic situation was fluid...' Martin R. Howard, *Death Before Glory!* (Barnsley, 2015), pp.29–44 provides a detailed account of the political and military situation in the region during this period.
Page 42: 'Of all of France's colonies...' Michael Duffy, *Soldiers, Sugar and Seapower* (Oxford, 1987), pp.5–27.
Page 42: 'In August 1791, amid a raging thunderstorm...' Ibid, p.29.
Page 43: 'One of the first acts of its new Republican commissioner...' Ibid, pp.29–30.
Page 44: 'His 50-gun flagship *Europa*...' Ibid, pp.35–36. Also see Robert Gardiner (ed.), *Fleet Battle and Blockade* (London, 1996), p.63.
Page 46: 'In the end the operation went without a hitch.' Duffy, p.35. Also see James M. Perry, *Arrogant Armies* (New York, NY, 1996), p.72.

Page 47: 'Meanwhile, news of the capture...' Howard, pp.45–48; Duffy, pp.41–58. Also see Rev. C. Willyams, *An Account of the Campaign* (London, 1796), pp.8–10.

Page 48: 'In October Whitelocke led a 50-man detachment...' Howard, p.36.

Page 48: 'Back in Britain a force of 7,000 soldiers...' Ibid, pp.45–46; Duffy, pp.41–58. Also see J. W. Fortescue, *A History of the British Army* Vol. IV (London, 1915), pp.351–52.

Page 49: 'These troops were commanded...' Howard, p.40.

Page 50: '*Hermione* played her part.' Winfield, p.209. Her involvement was also described in *The London Gazette*, 17 July 1794.

Page 50: 'During the surrender...' Duffy, pp.101–04. For a detailed account of the capture of Port-au-Prince, see Fortescue, pp.339–41; Howard, pp.41–42.

Page 51: 'The defection of L'Ouverture...' Howard, p.42–44.

Page 52: 'Of Grey's garrison in Port-au-Prince...' Ibid, p.87.

Page 53: 'Captain Hills himself fell ill...' Winfield, p.209.

CHAPTER 3 THE SEEDS OF MUTINY

Page 54: 'It probably began on 5 September 1794...' *Hermione* Captain's log 1794–95, NA, ADM. 51/1104; Vice-Admiral Parker's Journal 1794, NA, ADM. 50/65. Also see Dudley Pope, *The Black Ship* (Barnsley 2009), p.43.

Page 55: 'His father, Thomas Wilkinson...' Pope, p.43. Also see C. S. Forester (ed.), *The Adventures of John Wetherell* (London, 1954), pp.172–75.

Page 56: 'Captain Patrick Sinclair...' Rif Winfield, *British Warships in the Age of Sail, 1793–1817* (Barnsley, 2008), p.336; J. W. Norie, *The Naval Gazeteer, Biographer and Chronologist* (London, 1843), p.406.

Page 56: 'Consequently, when Captain Hills of the *Hermione* died...' Winfield, p.209.

Page 57: 'One of her crew, John Wetherell...' Forester, pp.186–87.

Page 58: 'He was given command of the floating battery *Gorgon*...' Winfield, p.130.

Page 59: 'During the last months of 1794...' ADM 51/1104.

Page 59: 'The *Hermione* reached Port Royal…' Ibid. Also see Pope, pp.45–46.

Page 60: 'Then, in April, there were two major incidents.' ADM. 51/1104; Pope, p.46. Pope, p.334, also provides a full listing of the floggings administered on board *Hermione* between January and October 1795.

Page 60: 'A ship's captain had immense latitude…' Admiralty (1806), *Regulations and Instructions*. Also see Brian Lavery, *Nelson's Navy* (London, 1989), p.218. Pope, pp.59–69 also contains a detailed account of the procedures and effects of naval flogging.

Page 64: 'The *Hermione* was employed escorting convoys…' ADM. 51/1104.

Page 64: 'A change in the routine came in early July…' Ibid; *Jersey Chronicle*, 22 August 1795. Also see A. Roger Ekirch, *American Sanctuary* (New York, NY, 2019), p.9; Paul A. Gilje; *Liberty on the Waterfront* (Philadelphia, 2004), p.157.

Page 65: 'At the same time Walter St John…' ADM 51/1104; Pope, p.334.

Page 66: 'The new commander was Vice-Admiral Sir Hyde Parker…' ODNB; ADM 50/65.

Page 67: 'The only respite from the tedium…' Howard, pp.87–88.

Page 67: 'In a letter to a friend…' Ibid, p.88; Duffy, pp.250–52; ADM 50/65.

Page 69: 'That spring the yellow fever…' Howard, pp.86–87.

Page 69: 'However, the operation turned out to be…' ADM 50/65; Pope, p.47.

CHAPTER 4   THE FORTUNATE SON

Page 71: 'It had all started on the night of 30 June…' ADM 1/533; ADM 50/65; Dudley Pope, *The Black Ship* (Barnsley, 2009), pp.17–35. This account also draws on ADM 1/2/939 Admiralty to Commanders-in-Chief; FO 5/14/90 Sir Robert Liston to Secretary of State.

Page 75: 'By the end of the month…' FO 5/14 Sir Robert Liston to Lord Grenville gives examples of the outrage; press reaction is also described in A. Roger Ekirch, *American Sanctuary* (New York, NY, 2019), pp.14–15.

Page 75: 'After reading an account...' Robert B. Hanson, *The Diary of Dr. Nathaniel Ames* (Camden, ME, 1998), p.606.

Page 75: 'Acting on instructions from the Board of the Admiralty...' ADM 50/65; FO 5/14.

Page 77: 'It was held in Pigot's great cabin.' A full account of the court martial can be found in ADM 1/5338, 23 January 1797.

Page 78: 'Pigot stated...' Ibid.

Page 79: 'Hill reckoned that the American...' Ibid.

Page 80: 'The only black mark...' Ibid.

Page 82: 'The exchange took place...' ADM 50/65; ADM 1/248 Letters, Admiral's Dispatches.

Page 82: 'He had taken command of the *Success*...' ADM 51/1102; ADM 9254–9255 commission and warrant books. For Pigot's early career, see ODNB entry. Also see Pope, pp.49–58.

Page 85: 'The *Swan*, however, was just a stepping stone.' ADM 51/1102. The same source, together with ADM 36/13192 muster books, provide this basis of Pigot's command of the *Success*. Also see Rif Winfield, *British Warships in the Age of Sail, 1793–1817* (Barnsley, 2008), pp.194–95; Pope, pp.64–70.

Page 87: 'A clear pattern emerged.' Pope, p.68.

CHAPTER 5   THE CARIBBEAN HONEYMOON

Page 90: 'Their captain then stood up and greeted them.' ADM 36/14745 and ADM 36/12011 muster books for *Success* and *Hermione*. Redman's description of the event from ADM 1/5348 Court Martial of Richard Redman, 13–15 March 1799. Also see Dudley Pope, *The Black Ship* (Barnsley, 2009), pp.73–76.

Page 92: 'A few days later Pigot and his crew...' ADM 51/1179; ADM 1/248; ADM 50/65. Also see Pope, pp.84–94.

Page 93: 'Tucked among them...' Pope, pp.80–81.

Page 94: 'David Casey, a 19-year-old...' ADL Q/54 David Casey, *Memorandum of Service* fol. 5r–7r, ODNB. Also see A. Roger Ekirch, *American Sanctuary* (New York, NY, 2019), p.30; Pope, pp.81–82.

Page 94: 'Pigot was still short of a few warrant officers...' ADM 36/12011.

Page 95: 'The previous day, Parker had sent Captain Otway...'
ADM 50/65.

Page 96: 'On Wednesday 22 March...' ADM 1/248; ADM 50/65.

Page 97: 'On Pigot's orders they were well armed...' ADM 50/65;
Pope, pp.86–88.

Page 99: 'While this didn't necessarily antagonise...' Pope, p.90.

Page 100: 'So it was with particular delight...' ADM 50/65.

Page 100: 'By the evening of Wednesday...'ADM 1/248; ADM
50/65; Pope, pp.95–99; Ekirch, p.26.

Page 102: 'The total haul...' Pope, p.90 provides a listing of the
vessels captured during the operation.

Page 103: 'As the admiral was unwilling...' ADM 50/65.

Page 104: 'The frigate was making 5 knots...' ADM 1/5339 Court
Martial of Lieutenant John Harris.

Page 106: 'More pumps were rigged...' Ibid. Also see ADL Q/54.

CHAPTER 6 THE FLOATING POWDERKEG

Page 109: 'When Pigot reported to Vice-Admiral Parker...' ADM
1/248.

Page 110: 'According to the Admiralty's rules...' Admiralty
Regulations and Instructions (1806).

Page 110: 'On that Friday morning...' ADM 1/5339; ADM 50/65;
ADL Q/54; Dudley Pope, *The Black Ship* (Barnsley, 2009),
pp.114–21.

Page 112: 'Meanwhile, on the *Hermione*...' ADM 36/12011; ADM
9254–9255.

Page 112: 'As one of the *Successes* put it...' ADM 1/5348.

Page 113: 'The following day, the same court...' ADM 1/5339.

Page 113: 'Strangely, in front of Bligh's court...' Ibid. Also see ADM
36/14745.

Page 114: 'In fact the dispatches, dated 3 May 1797...' ADM
1/2/939; ADM 50/65. Veronica Coates and Philip MacDougall
(eds), *The Naval Mutinies of 1797* (Woodbridge, 2011) provide
a useful look at the 1797 mutinies, as do B. Dobree and G. E.
Manwaring, *The Floating Republic* (London, 1937) and James
Dugan, *The Great Mutiny* (New York, NY, 1965).

Page 115: 'Fed up with their young Irish officer's brutal regime...'
Pope, p.123; ADM 1/2/939; ADM 50/65.

Page 117: 'After her return to Môle Saint-Nicolas...' ADM
36/12011; ADM 1/5348 where it pertains to the court martial
of Jacob Fulga; Pope, pp.126–28.

Page 117: 'Finally, on Saturday 12 August...' ADM 1/248.

Page 118: 'Early on Thursday 31 August...' ADM 51/1215 Captain's
Log, *Diligence*, 1797.

Page 120: 'So it was that on the evening of Thursday
14 September...' ADL Q/54; A. Roger Ekirch, *American
Sanctuary* (New York, NY, 2019), pp.30–31; Pope, pp.130–34.
The account that follows is based on Casey's own recollections
of what happened.

Page 120: 'The 19-year-old David O'Brien Casey...' ONDB. Also
see ADL Q/54.

Page 124: 'Later, during the evening watch...' ADL Q/54.

Page 125: 'The unfortunate Midshipman Casey...' Ibid.

Page 126: 'The flogging of Midshipman Casey...' The repercussions
of the incident are described in Pope, pp.137–38.

CHAPTER 7   MURDER IN THE NIGHT

Page 128: 'In his cabin off the wardroom...' Sergeant Plaice's
description of Lt. McIntosh's situation was provided in a court
martial, ADM 1/5360, 30 March 1802. Also see Dudley Pope,
pp.139–40.

Page 128: 'By noon the *Diligence* was well ahead...' ADM 51/1215;
ADM 52/2935, Master's Log, HMS *Diligence*. Also, *Captain
Mends's Narrative* describes the operational situation that evening.

Page 129: 'He began yelling and cursing...' This account is based on
Casey's description of events, in ADL Q/54.

Page 130: 'Captain Pigot then yelled out another horrific order...'
Ibid.

Page 132: 'At dawn on Thursday 21 September...' ADM 51/1215;
ADM 52/2935.

Page 132: 'In all, 13 mizzen topmen...' ADL Q/54.

Page 134: 'Later, he described it as...' Ibid.

Page 134: 'A signal from *Diligence...*' ADM 51/1215; ADM 52/2935. Also, *Captain Mends's Narrative* describes the operational situation that afternoon and evening.

Page 136: 'Waiting for Pigot was his steward...' This account is drawn largely from the testimony of Steward John Jones, together with that of the other *Hermiones* who described the events of that night in ADM 1/5346. It also draws on the court martial evidence of various mutineers. Also see Dudley Pope, *The Black Ship* (Barnsley, 2009), p.152 et seq.

Page 137: 'At 9pm – two bells...' Brian Lavery, *Nelson's Navy* (London, 1989), pp.200–02.

Page 137: 'Some time after "Lights Out"...' ADM 1/5353.

Page 138: 'According to witnesses...' John Brown and William Herd, whose accounts are contained in ADM 1/5344, Pope, pp.154–55.

Page 139: 'A knot of men rushed forward...' These events are reconstructed from ADM 1/5343; ADM 1/5348; ADM 1/5344; ADM 1/5347; and ADM 1/5360. Also see Nicholas Tracy, *The Naval Chronicle*, Vol. 4, p.156 and Vol. 7, p.350. The account and Depositon of John Mason appended to *Captain Mends's Narrative*. Also see Pope, pp.155–59.

Page 140: 'He yelled out "Where are my bargemen" ...' ADM/1/5347; ADM 1/5360.

Page 140: 'It was David Forester who struck the first blow...' Confession of Joseph Mansell, appended to *Captain Mends's Narrative*.

Page 140: 'Pigot's shouts had indeed reached the ears...' Testimony of John Brown, in ADM 1/5344.

Page 142: 'The newcomers, led by Nash and Farrel...' Ibid. Also, testimony of John Jones in trials of several of those involved in the killing of Lieutenant Foreshaw.

Page 143: 'He was leaning against his couch...' This account is primarily compiled from the court martial of Thomas Nash, ADM 1/5350, as well as the confession of other mutineers present in the great cabin during Pigot's murder, ADM 1/5343, ADM 1/5348 and ADM 1/5357.

Page 144: 'Now the mutineers had to get rid of the body.' Pope, p.159. The principal witness during this final act in the great cabin was the Steward John Jones.

Page 144: 'One of the first to react...' Southcott gave a full description of these events, which are found in ADM 1/5346.

Page 145: 'The 24-year-old cockney...' ADM 1/5348; ADM 36/12011.

Page 145: 'Later, he recalled what happened...' ADM 1/5346; ADL Q/54.

Page 146: 'A few moments earlier, after he was attacked...' ADM 1/5346.

CHAPTER 8 THE EVIL THAT MEN DO

Page 148: 'Up in the maintop...' ADM 1/5344.

Page 149: 'Later, Brown claimed he had to take it...' Ibid. Also, his testimony as given in Kingston is appended in *Captain Mends's Narrative*.

Page 150: 'When the mob had first appeared...' Evidence supplied by Sergeant Plaice in ADM 1/5353.

Page 150: 'Seconds later 20 or more mutineers...' ADM 1/5343. Confession of Joseph Montell also appended in *Captain Mends's Narrative*.

Page 151: 'Others were doing the same, and it was another youngster...' ADM 1/5353.

Page 151: 'He headed forwards, to the midshipmen's berth...' ADM 1/5346; ADL Q/54.

Page 152: 'As Casey put it...' ADL Q/54.

Page 153: 'It was Henry Foreshaw...' John Brown's testimony, appended in *Captain Mends's Narrative*. Also see Pope, p.165.

Page 154: 'They included four of the captain's murderers...' ADM 1/5343; ADM 1/5344.

Page 155: 'The lights of Commander Mends's brig...' ADM 51/1215; ADM 52/2935.

Page 155: 'Following the mutineers' order...' Pope, p.167.

Page 156: 'By all accounts there were 20 of them...' These ringleaders were first identified in the confession of John Mason, carpenter's mate, appended to *Captain Mends's Narrative*. Other witnesses then corroborated this list.

Page 156: 'according to John Jones...' While John Jones was never tried, as he willingly became a prisoner of war, he issued a full statement to the same board that tried the *Hermione*'s surviving officers for the loss of their ship in August 1798.

Page 157: 'The Ringleaders'. This list is the result of a cross-reference of the muster books of both the *Success* (ADM 36/14745) and *Hermione* (ADM 36/12011) with the list of ringleaders compiled by Mason, appended to *Captain Mends's Narrative*, and those of the surviving officers, as well as John Holford the elder.

Page 158: 'As he put it later...' Confession of John Mason, carpenter's mate, appended to *Captain Mends's Narrative*.

Page 159: 'Nash then went down to the gunroom...' ADM 1/5346; ADL Q/54.

Page 160: 'On the *Hermione*, the surgeon's mate...' ADM 36/12011.

Page 161: 'In their cabins, Reed, Southcott, Casey and the others...' ADM 1/5346; ADL Q/54.

Page 161: 'As Casey later put it...' Ibid.

Page 162: 'Beside him, his 14-year-old servant...' Ibid.

Page 163: 'The door of his cabin was yanked open...' Testimony of Sergeant John Plaice, given on 9 August 1798, and appended to ADM 1/5346.

Page 164: 'After gathering together a few half-drunk men...' Described in Richard Redman's confession, appended to ADM 1/5348. Also appears in the testimony of Steward John Jones, given on 9 August 1798, and appended to ADM 1/5346.

Page 165: 'This time, the "snatch squad"...' Ibid.

Page 165: 'Earlier that evening...' ADL Q/54.

CHAPTER 9 THE SPANISH MAIN

Page 167: 'Later, David Casey recalled what he went through...' ADM 1/5346; ADL Q/54.

Page 168: 'Edward Southcott had a similar time...' ADM 1/5346; Dudley Pope, *The Black Ship* (Barnsley, 2009), pp.179–82.

Page 168: 'Both the *Hermione* and the *Diligence*...' ADM 51/1215; ADM 52/2935.

Page 169: 'Watching all this was John Jones...' ADM 1/5346.

Page 170: 'This time, they brushed Elliot's guards aside...' Ibid; Pope, pp.181–82.

Page 171: 'They probably included Thomas Nash...' ADM 1/5348.

Page 171: 'Then came the vote.' Ibid; ADM 51/1797. Also see Pope, pp.185–86.

Page 173: 'Cronin worded it...' ADM 51/1797.

Page 173: 'That done, the ringleaders set about distributing the plunder...' Ibid. Also see Pope, pp.193–94.

Page 174: 'During their brief exercise periods...' ADM 1/5346; ADL Q/54.

Page 175: 'So, William Turner, who knew the rudiments of navigation...' ADM 1/5346.

Page 176: 'One of them, the ship's butcher...' Ibid. Also, ADM 1/5348 contains the testimony given by Perrett during his court martial on 13–15 March 1799.

Page 177: 'On board the *Hermione*...' ADM 1/5346; ADL Q/54. Also see Pope, pp.197–98.

Page 178: 'As they approached the port under a white flag...' This account is drawn from several sources, including the confession of John Mason, appended to *Captain Mends's Narrative*, the frigate's muster book ADM 36/12011, and the court martial records of several mutineers, contained in ADM 1/5343, ADM 1/5344, ADM 1/5350, July 1799, and ADM 1/5357, as well as the testimony of the surviving officers in ADM 1/5346.

Page 179: 'Don José Vásquez may have been easily duped...' An appreciation of the Spanish reaction to the arrival of the *Hermione* is contained in Parker's correspondence and papers, ADM 1/248, ADM 50/65. Also see the AGM Bazán 9 Collection of Don Álvaro de Bazán.

Page 179: 'So, Don José sent the mutineers' petition...' Bazán 9. Also see Pope, pp.198–200.

Page 180: 'Edward Southcott, who overheard all this...' ADM 1/5346.

Page 180: 'Meanwhile, the captain-general's junta met...' Bazán 9.

Page 181: 'Part of the captain-general's agreement...' Ibid.

Page 182: 'Master and Commander Robert Mends...' ADM 51/1215; ADM 52/2935; *Captain Mends's Narrative*. Also, a copy of Mends's report is included in the first court martial of mutineers in March 1798, ADM 1/5343.

Page 182: 'In fact, some of his crew...' *Captain Mends's Narrative.*

Page 183: 'On Monday 16 October he captured...' ADM 51/1215; ADM 52/2935

Page 183: '"It is with inexpressible pain..."' *Captain Mends's Narrative.*

Page 185: 'Shortly before 2am on 31 October...' ADM 51/1797; ADM 1/248; ADM 50/65.

Page 185: 'Vice-Admiral Parker's journal...' ADM 50/65.

Page 186: 'He also wrote to the British naval commander...' ADM 1/248; ADM 50/65.

CHAPTER 10 THE MANHUNT

Page 188: 'The news finally reached the Admiralty...' ADM 3/118, Board of the Admiralty minutes. Also see Dudley Pope, *The Black Ship* (Barnsley, 2009), pp.215–16.

Page 189: 'A few, though, were luckier than their shipmates.' See John Jones's testimony, attached to the court martial records of August 1798, ADM 1/5346.

Page 189: 'When the *Hermione* officially became the *Santa Cecilia*...' Bazán 9.

Page 190: 'These draftees included John Holford...' ADM 1/5344.

Page 190: 'On 5 December the *Magicienne* and *Diligence*...' ADM 51/1215; ADM 52/2935.

Page 190: 'In his report to the Admiralty...' ADM 1/248.

Page 191: 'These included John Mason...' Mason's confession and testimony, in *Captain Mends's Narrative*, and ADM 1/5344. Also see Pope, pp.226–27.

Page 191: 'However, Joe Montell, who had had a hand in killing five officers...' ADM 1/5343.

Page 193: 'The first catch was the German-born sailmaker...' ADM 1/5348. Also see A. Roger Ekirch, *American Sanctuary* (New York, NY, 2019), p.55.

Page 194: 'On 1 March, six weeks after Slushing's capture...' Mason's confession and testimony, in *Captain Mends's Narrative*; ADM 1/5343; ADM 1/5344. Also see Pope, pp.226–27; Ekirch, pp.55–56.

Page 195: 'On Saturday 17 March...' ADM 1/5343; ADM 50/65.

Page 196: 'Interestingly, shortly before his death...' ADM 1/5343.

Page 196: 'Parker immediately dictated a letter...' ADM 1/248; ADM 50/65.

Page 197: 'When they were interviewed by the admiral...' ADM 1/5346; *London Gazette*, 24 May 1798.

Page 197: 'So, on Monday 1 May...' ADM 1/5344. Also see Mason's confession and testimony, in *Captain Mends's Narrative*; Pope, pp.238–42.

Page 198: 'Three former *Hermiones*...' ADM 1/5344; ADM 50/65.

Page 199: 'His written statement made interesting reading...' Mason's confession and testimony, in *Captain Mends's Narrative*.

Page 199: 'The court martial was held on Friday 5 May...' ADM 1/5344.

Page 200: 'It was held on board the 64-gun *Director*...' ADM 1/534; ADM 2/1118.

Page 201: 'In April, off Puerto Rico...' ADM 1/5344.

Page 202: 'The court martial was convened...' Ibid.

Page 202: 'Vice-Admiral Parker was incensed.' ADM 1/248; ADM 50/65.

Page 203: 'In his letter to the Admiralty...' ADM 1/248.

Page 203: 'Parker's next prisoner was John Coe...' ADM 50/65; ADM 1/5347.

Page 204: 'The frigate's commander, Captain Boys...' ADM 1/248; ADM 1/5347.

Page 204: 'All three of them were taken...' ADM 1/5348; ADM 1/248.

Page 205: 'However, their guilt was clear...' ADM 1/5348.

Page 206: 'In fact, just two months after the last court martial...' ADM 1/5348.

Page 207: 'In Liverpool, he met the father...' Ibid. Also see Pope, pp.265–66.

Page 207: 'In late July 1798...' ADM 1/5348.

Page 208: 'The court martial was finally convened...' Ibid.

CHAPTER 11 AN INTERNATIONAL INCIDENT

Page 212: By 1799, according to the testimony of Joe Montell... ADM 1/5343.

Page 213: 'The British stop-and-search policy...' For details, see
Brian Lavery, *Nelson's Navy* (London, 1989), pp.120–27;
A. Roger Ekirch, *American Sanctuary* (New York, NY, 2019),
pp.18–23.

Page 214: 'The muster books of the *Hermione*...' ADM 36/12011.

Page 214: 'In 1812, this same stop-and-search policy...' Otto von
Pivka, *Navies of the Napoleonic Era* (Newton Abbot, 1980),
p.132; Ekirch, p.210.

Page 215: 'In early June 1799...' ADM 1/5350.

Page 215: 'The court martial of James Barnett...' Ibid.

Page 216: 'The brainchild of John Jay...' Ekirch, pp.75–80.

Page 217: 'More relevant was Article 27...' Ibid, p.77. Also see
Christopher Pyle, *Extradition, Politics and Human Rights*
(Philadelphia, PA, 2010), pp.10–26.

Page 218: 'A copy of the widow's deposition...' FO 5/14/90; Ekirch,
p.74.

Page 218: 'On 19 February he wrote to US Secretary of State
Thomas Pickering...' *British Notes*; Ekirch, p.76.

Page 218: 'In early February, the American brigantine *Relief of New
York*...' Ekirch, pp.78–79.

Page 219: 'He filed it on 29 March.' *British Notes*; FO 5/14/90.

Page 219: 'The United States was therefore under no legal
obligation...' Ekirch, pp.79–80.

Page 220: 'When the proceedings began...' *New York Gazette*,
14 April 1798; *British Notes*.

Page 221: 'Liston blamed the decision...' FO 5/14/90.

Page 221: 'On 1 June, Liston received a bombshell...' ADM 1/248;
FO 5/14/90.

Page 222: 'Therefore, on 8 June...' *British Notes*. Also see Ekirch,
p.86.

Page 222: 'A month after the Brigstock case collapsed...' Ekirch,
pp.87–89.

Page 223: 'Therefore, Sir Robert began a campaign...' *British Notes*;
FO 5/14/90.

Page 224: 'That morning a young American seaman...' FO 5/14/90;
ADM 1/5350; ADM 1/248. Also see Ekirch, pp.90–91.

Page 225: 'So, Moodie needed help.' *British Notes*; FO 5/14/90.

Page 225: 'Liston sent it to Pickering...' *British Notes*.

Page 227: 'From Quincy, Massachusetts, John Adams replied...'
Ibid, pp.96–97.

Page 227: 'On 3 June, Pickering wrote to Judge Bee...' Ekirch, p.94.

Page 227: 'It was at this point that fate intervened...' Ibid, p.100.

Page 228: 'It was dated 20 May 1795...' FO 5/14/90; *British Notes*;
ADM 1/5350.

Page 229: 'However, on the morning of the hearing...' Ekirch,
pp.103–04.

Page 231: 'Three days later, on Saturday 27 July...' FO 5/14/90;
ADM 1/5350.

Page 231: 'The court martial was convened on board...' ADM
1/5350; ADM 50/65.

Page 233: 'While some newspapers presented the facts...' Ekirch,
pp.111–39. Ekirch devotes a whole chapter to the aftermath of
the Nash court martial in the United States, and its impact on
Anglo-American relations.

CHAPTER 12 THE *SURPRISE*

Page 235: 'In the late afternoon of Thursday 17 September...'
ADM 50/65; ADM 52/3469, Master's Log, HMS *Surprise*. For
details of the *Surprise*, see Rif Winfield and S. Stephen; *French
Warships in the Age of Sail* (Barnsley, 2015), p.168.

Page 236: 'The *Surprise* was smaller and less well armed...' Winfield
and Stephen, p.168; Brian Lavery and Geoff Hunt, *The Frigate
Surprise* (London, 2008), pp.11–15.

Page 237: 'Parker's intelligence sources...' ADM 50/65. Also see
Dudley Pope, *The Black Ship* (Barnsley, 2009), p.304.

Page 238: 'They made landfall off Bahia Honda...' ADM 52/3469.

Page 238: 'So he lingered off the mouth of the Gulf of Venezuela...'
Ibid.

Page 239: 'Lieutenant Busey led the attack...' Ibid. Also see ADM
1/249, Vice-Admiral Parker's Dispatches, 1799; ADM 50/65;
The London Gazette, 21 January 1800.

Page 240: 'On Sunday 20th they caught a Spanish schooner...'
ADM 52/3469; *The London Gazette*, 21 January 1800.

Page 240: 'So, that night, Hamilton ordered the master...' ADM
52/3469.

Page 241: 'Hamilton gave the order for the ship's boats to be lowered...' Hamilton's report of his patrol, forwarded to the Admiralty by Parker, ADM 1/249.

Page 242: 'A boarding party was sent over...' Pope, p.308.

Page 242: 'When the *Hermione* had arrived in La Guaira...' Bazán 9.

Page 244: 'In early 1798...' Bazán 11.

Page 245: 'By the time she was re-armed...' Rif Winfield, *British Warships in the Age of Sail, 1793–1817* (Barnsley, 2008), p.209.

Page 245: 'By September, Captain de Eschales...' Bazán 21. Also see Pope, pp.308–09.

Page 246: 'That evening, as the frigate ghosted along...' ADM 36/14942–14943, muster books, HMS *Surprise*. Also see Pope, p.310.

Page 246: 'Once they had gathered, he outlined his plan.' ADM 1/249; *The London Gazette*, 21 January 1800. Also see Pope, pp.311–14.

Page 249: 'As Hamilton put it later...' *The London Gazette*, 21 January 1800.

Page 249: 'That day – Thursday 24 October 1799...' ADM 52/3469.

Page 250: 'The password, called out to tell friend from foe...' Pope, p.312 provides a possible explanation for the choice.

CHAPTER 13 THE CUTTING OUT

Page 251: 'At 7.30pm, when the *Surprise* was 7 miles out...' ADM 52/3469.

Page 251: 'Before they left...' This account of the approach is drawn primarily from Nicholas Tracy, *The Naval Chronicle*, Vol. 5 (London, 2003); James S. Clarke, *The Naval Chronicle*, Vol. 7 (London, 2018); and William James, *Naval History of Great Britain* (London, 1824, reprinted New York, NY, 2018), as well as ADM 1/249. Also see Dudley Pope, *The Black Ship* (Barnsley, 2009), pp.315–18.

Page 252: 'Shortly before 1am...' Clarke, p.165.

Page 253: 'Moments later they had their answer.' Tracy, p.5.

Page 254: 'As they came within the last 100 yards ...' *The London Gazette*, 21 January 1800; Pope, p.317.

Page 255: 'The lurch took them by surprise.' Pope, pp.317–18.

Page 255: 'Captain Hamilton pulled himself over the bulwark...' ADM 1/249. Also Pope, p.318.

Page 256: 'The fight had only just started...' ADM 1/249; *The London Gazette*, 21 January 1800. Also see Pope, pp.319–21.

Page 257: 'They had seen the Spaniards...' Pope, pp.319–20.

Page 258: 'So, another 16 British seamen and marines...' ADM 1/249.

Page 259: 'Down below, on the gun deck...' Ibid.

Page 260: 'With all other hatches and skylights secured...' Ibid. Also see Tracy, p.5.

Page 260: 'The gun deck of the frigate...' Plans of this class of 12-pounder frigate form part of the collection of the National Maritime Museum. Also see David White, *The Frigate Diana* (London, 1987).

Page 261: 'Aft of the companionway ladder...' ADM 1/249; *The London Gazette*, 21 January 1800. Also see Pope, p.322.

Page 262: 'Three British seamen in the front of the fight...' *The London Gazette*, 21 January 1800; ADM 36/14942–14943; ADM 1/249.

Page 262: 'Finally, just after 1am...' ADM 1/249.

Page 264: 'At that moment an 18-pounder ball...' Ibid. Also see Pope, p.323.

Page 264: 'Hamilton's coxswain, while clambering up from the launch...' Tracy, p.5.

Page 266: 'They had to tend to the wounded...' ADM 1/249; *The London Gazette*, 21 January 1800; ADM 36/14942–14943.

Page 266: 'As the frigate's master recorded...' ADM 52/3469.

Page 266: 'The vessel turned out to be an American schooner...' ADM 1/249. Also see Pope, p.325.

Page 267: 'By then, both men had a shrewd idea...' ADM 1/249; *The London Gazette*, 21 January 1800. Also see Pope, p.325.

Page 268: 'They would be taken back to Jamaica...' ADM 1/249.

CHAPTER 14 *RETRIBUTION*

Page 269: 'On 1 November, the *Surprise* slipped past Gallows Point...' ADM 52/3469.

Page 270: '"The honour of my country..."' *The London Gazette*, 21 January 1800.

Page 270: 'Three days later he wrote a full report...' ADM 1/249. Extracts are reprinted in *The London Gazette*, 21 January 1800.

Page 271: '"I find the *Hermione* has had a thorough repair..."' Ibid.

Page 271: 'After reading Parker's report...' ADM 50/65. Also, ADM 2/294, Letters to Navy Board, 1800 contains a copy of the Jamaican survey of the *Retaliation*, and notes on the Admiralty's own evaluation of her worth.

Page 272: 'For Captain Hamilton, though...' Dudley Pope, *The Black Ship* (Barnsley, 2009), pp.326–28.

Page 272: 'Unfortunately for him...' This account of Hamilton's career after 1799 is based on the ONDB, and James S. Clarke, *The Naval Chronicle* Vol. 7 (London, 2018), p.179.

Page 274: 'The first mutineer to be captured...' ADM 1/5353.

Page 274: 'He stood trial there on board the *Gladiator*...' Ibid.

Page 275: 'John Watson, an able seaman...' Ibid.

Page 276: 'He was the youngster...' ADM 1/5357.

Page 277: 'He was handed to the *Néréide*...' Ibid.

Page 277: 'The following month, the marine John Pearce...' ADM 1/5357.

Page 278: 'The frigate then returned to Portsmouth...' ADM 1/5360.

Page 279: 'Now that his sloop had returned to Portsmouth...' Ibid.

Page 279: 'On Monday 22 March...' Ibid. Also see Pope, pp.294–95.

Page 281: 'David Forester was hanged from the main yardarm...' ADM 1/5360.

Page 282: 'James Hayes, the 14-year-old doctor's servant...' Ibid.

Page 283: 'In September 1800...' Rif Winfield, *British Warships in the Age of Sail, 1714–1792* (Barnsley, 2007), p.209.

Page 284: 'The *Retribution* was saved from the breaker's yard...' Ibid.

Bibliography

PRIMARY SOURCES

NAL   National Archives, London
NAW   National Archives, Washington DC
LOC   Library of Congress, Washington DC
AGM   Archivo General de Marina, Madrid
NMM   National Maritime Museum, Greenwich

UNPUBLISHED SOURCES

NA

ADM 1/2/939 Admiralty correspondence to Commanders-in-Chief, 1797
ADM 1/248 Letters, Admiral's Dispatches, Jamaica, 1795–97
ADM 1/249 Letters, Admiral's Dispatches, Jamaica, 1798–1800
ADM 1/5339 Record of Admiralty Court Martial, 16 June 1797
ADM 1/5343 Record of Admiralty Court Martial, 17 March 1798
ADM 1/5344 Record of Admiralty Court Martial, 1 May 1798
ADM 1/5346 Record of Admiralty Court Martial, 9 August 1798
ADM 1/5347 Record of Admiralty Court Martial, 8 December 1798
ADM 1/5348 Record of Admiralty Court Martial, 13–15 March 1799
ADM 1/5350 Record of Admiralty Court Martial, 17 August 1799
ADM 1/5353 Record of Admiralty Court Martial, 31 July 1800
ADM 1/5357 Record of Admiralty Court Martial, 2 July 1801
ADM 1/5360 Record of Admiralty Court Martial, 30 March 1802
ADM 2/294 Letters to the Navy Board, 1800
ADM 2/1118 Board of the Admiralty, Correspondence, 1798–99

ADM 3/118 Board of the Admiralty, Minutes
ADM 36/14745 Muster Book, HMS *Success*, 1796–97
ADM 36/12011 Muster Book, HMS *Hermione*, 1796–97
ADM 36/14942–14943 Muster Book, HMS *Surprise*, 1799
ADM 50/65 Vice-Admiral Hyde Parker's Journal, 1794–1800
ADM 51/1102 Captain's Log, HMS *Success*, 4 September
    1794–30 September 1795
ADM 51/1104 Captain's Log, HMS *Hermione*, 5 September
    1794–9 September 1795
ADM 51/1179 Captain's Log, HMS *Hermione*, 10 September
    1795–10 February 1797
ADM 51/1215 Captain's Log, HMS *Diligence*, 1 May–31 October
    1797
ADM 52/2935 Master's Log, HMS *Diligence*, 1 May–31 October
    1797
ADM 52/3469 Master's Log, HMS *Surprise*, 1799–1800
ADM 9254–9255 Board of the Admiralty, Commission and
    Warrant Books, 1793–1802
FO 5/14/90 Foreign Office Correspondence, Sir Robert Liston to
    Secretary of State

NMM
ADL Q/54 Casey, David, *Memorandum of Service*

NAW
British Notes from the British Legations in the United States to the
    Department of State, 1791–1906 M50 microfilm, roll 3

AGM
Bazán 9 Collection of Don Álvaro de Bazán, Corso y Presas (Caracas
    Junta Records, 1796–97)
Bazán 11 Collection of Don Álvaro de Bazán, Corso y Presas
    (Caracas Junta Records, 1797–98)
Bazán 13 Collection of Don Álvaro de Bazán, Corso y Presas
    (Caracas Junta Records, 1799–1800)
Bazán 26 Collection of Don Álvaro de Bazán, Corso y Presas (Naval
    Records, 1793–1802)

BIBLIOGRAPHY

PUBLISHED SOURCES

Admiralty *Regulations and Instructions Relating to His Majesty's Service at Sea* (London, 1806)

LOC   *Jersey Chronicle*
LOC   *New York Gazette*
LOC   *Captain Mends's Narrative of the mutiny, murder and piracy comitted on board His Majesty's Ship Hermione*, Reproduced by Library of Congress by Gale Ecco Print Editions, 2019.
NA   *The London Gazette*

The Naval Chronicle, 1793–1802
Oxford Dictionary of National Biography (ODNB)
Willyams, Rev. C., *An Account of the Campaign in the West Indies in the Year 1794* (London, 1796)

SECONDARY SOURCES

Clarke, James S., *The Naval Chronicle* Vol. 7 (reprinted London, Forgotten Books, 2018)

Coates, Veronica and MacDougall, Philip (eds), *The Naval Mutinies of 1797: Unity & Perseverance* (Woodbridge, Boydell Press, 2011)

Colledge, J. J. and Warlow, Ben, *Ships of the Royal Navy: The Complete Record of all the Fighting Ships of the Royal Navy from the 15th Century to the Present* (Newbury, Casemate Publishing, 2010)

Dobree, B. and Manwaring, G. E., *The Floating Republic: The 1797 Naval Mutiny at the Nore and Spithead* (London, Pelican, 1937)

Duffy, Michael, *Soldiers, Sugar and Seapower: The British Expeditions to the West Indies and the War against Revolutionary France* (Oxford, Clarendon Press, 1987)

Dugan, James, *The Great Mutiny* (New York, NY, G. P. Putnam's, 1965)

Edgeworth de Firmont, Henry Essex; *Memoirs of the Abbé Edgeworth, Containing his Narrative of the Last Hours of Louis XVI* (first published London, 1815: reprinted Leopold Classic Library, 2016)

Ekirch, A. Roger, *American Sanctuary: Mutiny, Martyrdom and National Identity in the Age of Revolution* (Pantheon Books, New York, 2017)

Falconer, William, *Falconer's Marine Dictionary* (first published London, 1780: reprinted Newton Abbot, David & Charles Ltd, 1970)

Forester, C. S. (ed.), *The Adventures of John Wetherell* (London, Michael Joseph, 1954)

Fortescue, J. W., *A History of the British Army* Vol. IV (London, Macmillan & Co., 1915)

Gardiner, Robert (ed.), *Fleet Battle and Blockade: The French Revolutionary War, 1793–1797* (London, Chatham Publishing, 1996)

Gardiner, Robert, *Frigates of the Napoleonic Wars* (London, Chatham Publishing, 2000)

Gardiner, Robert, *Warships of the Napoleonic Era: Design, Development and Deployment* (Barnsley, Seaforth Publishing, 2011)

Gilje, Paul A., *Liberty on the Waterfront: American Maritime Culture in the Age of Revolution* (Philadelphia, University of Pennsylvania Press, 2004)

Hanson, Robert B. (ed.), *The Diary of Dr. Nathaniel Ames of Dedham, Massachusetts* (Camden ME, Picton Press, 1998)

Henderson, James, *Frigates, Sloops & Brigs* (Barnsley, Pen & Sword, 2011)

Howard, Martin R., *Death Before Glory! The British Soldier in the West Indies in the French Revolutionary & Napoleonic Wars* (Barnsley, Pen & Sword, 2015)

James, William, *The Naval History of Great Britain: From the Declaration of War by France in 1793 to the Accession of George IV.* (first published London, 1824: reprinted New York, NY, Hard Press, 2018)

Lavery, Brian, *Nelson's Navy: The Ships, Men and Organisation, 1793–1815* (London, Conway Maritime Press, 1989)

Lavery, Brian and Hunt, Geoff, *The Frigate Surprise: The Complete Story of the Ship Made Famous in the Novels of Patrick O'Brian* (London, Conway Maritime Press, 2008)

Norie, J. W., *The Naval Gazeteer, Biographer and Chronologist* (London, C. Wilson, 1843)

Perry, James M., *Arrogant Armies: Great Military Disasters and the Generals behind Them* (New York, NY, John Wiley & Sons, 1996)

Pivka, Otto von, *Navies of the Napoleonic Era* (Newton Abbot, David & Charles Ltd, 1980)

Pope, Dudley, *The Black Ship* (Barnsley, Pen & Sword Maritime, 2009)

Pyle, Christopher, *Extradition, Politics and Human Rights* (Philadelphia, PA, Temple University Press, 2010)

Sapherson, C. A. and Lenton, J. R., *Navy Lists from the Age of Sail Vol. 1 1793–1801: Fleets of the Revolution* (Leigh-on-Sea, Partizan Press, 1996)

Thompson, J. M., *English Witnesses of the French Revolution* (Oxford, Basil Blackwell, 1938)

Tracy, Nicholas, *The Naval Chronicle* Vol. 1 (London, Chatham Publishing, 1998)

Tracy, Nicholas, *The Naval Chronicle* Vol. 5 (London, Chatham Publishing, 2003)

White, David, *The Frigate Diana* (London, Conway Maritime Press – Anatomy of the Ship Series, 1987)

Winfield, Rif, *British Warships in the Age of Sail, 1714–1792: Design, Construction, Careers and Fates* (Barnsley, Seaforth Publishing, 2007)

Winfield, Rif, *British Warships in the Age of Sail, 1793–1817: Design, Construction, Careers and Fates* (Barnsley, Seaforth Publishing, 2008)

Winfield, Rif and Stephen, S., *French Warships in the Age of Sail, 1786–1871: Design, Construction, Careers and Fates* (Barnsley, Seaforth Publishing, 2015)

HMS *Hermione* – Ship's Specifications

A Sixth Rate frigate of the Hermione class.

Ordered: March 1780

Laid down: June 1780

Launched: 9 September 1782

Completed: January 1783

Builder: Sydenham Teast's Yard, Bristol

Displacement: 715 tons

Official complement: 215 officers, men and boys

Hull length: 129 feet

Length at waterline: 106 feet 10½ inches

Beam: 35 feet 5½ inches

Draught at stern: 15 feet 3 inches
(fully laden)

Armament: twenty-six 12-pounders,
six 6-pounders, six 18-pounder carronades

Sail plan

1	Jib	6	Main topsail
2	Foresail	7	Mainsail
3	Fore topsail	8	Mizzen topsail
4	Fore topgallant	9	Mizzen sail
5	Main topgallant	10	Mizzen staysail

A frigate, heaving-to in calm seas. Engraving from
D. & J. T. Serres, *Liber Nauticus* (London, 1805).

Index